Charles Hodge 1797–1878
Thomas Chalmers 1780–1847
Mary Winslow 1774–1854
Archibald Alexander 1772–1851
1810
1820
1830
1840
1850
1860
1870
1880
1890
1900

Evangelical HEROES

Evangelical HEROES

Volume 1

by Joel R. Beeke and Douglas Bond

Reformation Heritage Books
Grand Rapids, Michigan

Reformation Heritage Books
3070 29th St. SE
Grand Rapids, MI 49512
616-977-0889
orders@heritagebooks.org
www.heritagebooks.org

Scripture taken from the King James Version. In the public domain.

Printed in the United States of America
23 24 25 26 27 28/10 9 8 7 6 5 4 3 2 1

Library of Congress Cataloging-in-Publication Data

Names: Beeke, Joel R., 1952- author.
Title: Evangelical heroes / by Joel R. Beeke and Douglas Bond.
Description: Grand Rapids, Michigan : Reformation Heritage Books, [2023]- | Includes bibliographical references.
Identifiers: LCCN 2023025009 (print) | LCCN 2023025010 (ebook) | ISBN 9798886860559 (hardback) | ISBN 9798886860566 (epub)
Subjects: LCSH: Evangelists—Biography.
Classification: LCC BV3780 .B44 2023 (print) | LCC BV3780 (ebook) | DDC 269/.20922—dc23/eng/20230821
LC record available at https://lccn.loc.gov/2023025009
LC ebook record available at https://lccn.loc.gov/2023025010

Cover artwork by Caffy Whitney. For additional artwork by Caffy Whitney, see pages 3, 72, 111, 122, 136, 162.

For additional Reformed literature, request a free book list from Reformation Heritage Books at the above regular or e-mail address.

With much love
for our precious grandchildren,

**Emma, Edalette, Tyler, Selah, Hendrick, Hannah,
Abraham, Liberty, Ezra, and Sophia,**

with the prayer that you may grow up with evangelical Reformed heroes,
and follow them as far as they followed Christ.

— Grandpa & Grandma Beeke

With warmth and gratitude to all
our grandchildren,

**Gwenna, Amelia, Ailyn, Margot, Nova, Asa, Theo,
Otis, Calum, Thatcher, and Reuben.**

Remember those who "have spoken unto you the word of God:
whose faith follow, considering the end of their conversation."

— Douglas Bond

Table of Contents

Foreword

Heroes are not in style in contemporary Western culture. Ours has become a culture of cynicism and shaming, one in which heroes have no place. Even the traditional comic book heroes like Batman and Captain America have become troubled, deeply flawed individuals.

What shall we make of this from a biblical standpoint? How do we evaluate such a trend from the point of the Scriptures? Are there no heroes in the Bible? How does God's Holy Word deal with this subject?

Well, first of all, there is a gritty realism with which the Bible approaches this whole matter. Great men of God like Abraham and David and Peter and Timothy are shown to be what we all are: flawed and bent people, wounded and ever prone to wounding others—in a word, sinners. Abraham got entangled with his wife's maidservant at her sinful behest and later lied to the Egyptian pharaoh about his wife, Sarah. David committed adultery and then murdered to cover it up. Peter was a coward and lied to save his skin and later yielded to peer pressure when he refused to eat with Gentiles. Timothy let his fears control his actions.

But that is not the end of the story by any means. Hebrews 11 has a long list of people of faith whom the author clearly wants his readers then (and now) to emulate. In fact, in Hebrews 13:7, we read these words: "Remember them which have the rule over you, who have spoken unto you the word of God: whose faith follow, considering the end of their conversation." In a word, this is a call to emulate the lives and faith of those who had preached the Word of God in the first century.

And then we have the huge amounts of biography in the historical portions of God's Word: the life of Joseph, for instance, in Genesis; the large amount of space given to the life of David in the historical books of the Old Testament; and the two-thirds of Acts devoted to telling the story of Paul's life. The Holy Spirit, who inspired these passages and indeed all of God's Word, must deem it important for us to know something about the lives and faith of those who have gone before. Their flaws are important for us to know, but so are their triumphs, that we might take heart and be courageous for God.

It is a joy, then, to introduce this two-volume set of evangelical heroes by Joel Beeke and Douglas Bond. Like the biblical heroes, these are flawed men and women. But like the men and women in Scripture, their lives are on record for us to see what is possible in the walk of faith and, like them, (to paraphrase the words of one of my heroes, William Carey) to "expect great things from God and to attempt great things for Him."

One final, vital word is needed about this subject of heroes. There is a great hero in the history of the world that God points us to. One who has no flaws, not even a speck. And that is Jesus of Nazareth, the Lord Christ. In every story in the Bible, where God's heroes do great things, they ultimately reflect the Lord Jesus: His perfect faith in God,

His courage and zeal, His kindness and humility. And the same is true in this book: the great hero of the history of the Christian faith is Jesus. He is the One the men and women in this book point toward, and it is His beautiful character that they reflect.

Do you know Him? Do you love Him? Is He the One you ultimately wish to serve and follow? It is the prayer of this writer and those who have written this book that this series of small biographies would help you to know Jesus Christ as your Savior and Lord and help you faithfully serve Him all the days of your life.

—Michael A. G. Haykin

Preface

It has often been said, "Any nation that does not honor its heroes will not long endure." In an age when debunking heroes has become as American as apple pie and hot dogs, an age of flag-burning ingratitude, of pompous disdain for the past, these words should cause us great concern. Maybe we've come too close. Maybe we're there already. Maybe we are a people who mock at real heroes and, in their place, are now bowing down before the real villains.

All Men Honor Heroes

Nineteenth-century Scottish historian Thomas Carlyle wrote that "hero-worship cannot cease till man himself ceases." In the fifth century, Augustine referred to men as *homo adorans*, man made to adore, to worship, to venerate heroes. Thus, kings and generals are followed by their adoring armies even into the jaws of death. "Once more unto the breach, dear friends," cried Shakespeare's Henry V as he rallied his men before the battered walls of Harfleur, "or close the wall up with our English dead!" In the first century BC, Julius Caesar was so adored by his legions that they were prepared to cross the Rubicon and march in defiance against Rome and Pompey. The young Alexander the Great motivated thousands to fight and die so that he might spread Greek culture and language and rule the world.

The literature of Western civilization is the fascinating saga of great achievement, an enduring celebration of heroes. Great poetry praises the deeds of heroes, real or imagined, from the three hundred Spartans at Thermopylae, to the bloody triumphs of Beowulf, to the dragon-slaying Red Cross Knight of Edmund Spenser's epic allegory, to the six hundred courageous men of Tennyson's Light Brigade, even to the humble heroics of Tolkien's mythical Frodo the Hobbit—it all fires the blood and fascinates the imagination.

One thing is overwhelmingly clear: we were made to admire heroes. We pay attention with all our being to great men and women.

Beware of False Heroes

This ingrained tendency to honor heroes, however, poses particular challenges for young men and women growing up in a culture inundated by glitzy, muscle-bound icons of popular culture and the sports arena. Pop culture particularly plays on our love of heroes. It could not survive without it. The icons of entertainment demand our worship. They live and die for it.

Many historians argue that the history of the world is the history of men following heroes. It would be just as accurate to say that the history of the world is the history of young men and women blindly following the wrong heroes, unworthy examples whose vices are tragically compounded in their fawning worshipers.

So, who are your heroes? Paul urges the Philippian Christians to join with others in following his example (Phil. 3:17–21)—that is to say, follow the right men and women;

set up real heroes who follow Christ alone, the only perfect hero, for yourself and be like them. Speak as they speak; do as they do. The Bible often speaks this way. Twenty-eight times we are told to imitate others, often to follow Christ, the captain of our salvation, but fully seventeen of those times we are commanded to follow other men, like Paul, insofar as they heroically follow Christ.

Paul is in earnest. This is no casual advice, take it or leave it. He reminds us, "I have told you often, and now tell you even weeping." Why with tears? Why so earnest? Because many live as "enemies of the cross of Christ" (v. 18). Because an earthly hero has his mind on "earthly things" (v. 19). And the young man or woman who chooses to follow worldly heroes, to applaud their entertainments, to listen to their music, to cheer their achievement, to spend his or her money on their products, to paper the walls of his or her bedroom with their posters—that young man or woman should not be surprised if he or she follows those heroes right into the jaws of hell. From this, you and I are duty bound to draw the line in the sand. This is no trivial matter. Don't follow the enemies of the cross of Christ. Their destiny, Paul declares without equivocation, is destruction (v. 19). And so will be yours if you follow them.

Moreover, the more impressed you are by the status and achievement of unbelievers—by their sophisticated good looks, by their clothes, their shoes, their posture, their swagger, their prowess in sports, their associations, their way of speaking, their money and fancy cars, lavish houses, planes, and yachts—the less you will be able to separate out their vices. Soon they won't seem like vices at all. At the last their vices will be yours. Know that their end will be yours as well. Fully expect to become like those you adore.

"We are all creatures of imitation," wrote nineteenth-century Anglican bishop J. C. Ryle. "Precept may teach us, but it is example that draws us."[1] And since those examples can draw us from both directions, you must beware of the tendency to go easy and tolerate sin on the parts of your sports or music heroes' lives that you know are sinful.

Do you honestly think that you will be unaffected by the foul language, the unfaithful living, the hostility to truth, or the swaggering arrogance of your worldly heroes? We doubt it. And the more impressed you are with their achievement, the more likely you are to embrace other elements of their lifestyle.

Don't expect to see it coming like a tidal wave. It all happens gradually. Rarely does a young man or woman who is growing up in a Christian home plunge headlong into sin with back defiantly turned against all he or she has been taught. Generally, it happens little by little, one what's-the-big-deal step at a time. "The safest road to hell," C. S. Lewis portrayed one tempter advising another, "is the gradual one."[2]

The best way to avoid the gradual road to hell is to cultivate honor for and imitation of truly worthy heroes, and above all to worship Jesus Christ alone. *Evangelical Heroes* is a two-volume set of short biographies of Christ-grounded heroes from the end of the Puritan age until today—nearly three centuries. Immerse yourself in the lives of these men and women and, by the grace of God alone, you will have models to imitate throughout your life—ones who will not

---

1. J. C. Ryle, "Twelve Hints to Young Men," in *The Priest, the Puritan, and the Preacher* (New York: Robert Carter and Brothers, 1856), 289.

2. C. S. Lewis, *The Screwtape Letters* (New York: HarperCollins, 2001), 61.

disappoint. Ultimately, the reason these men and women are heroes is because they lived for something larger than themselves, for *Someone* larger than themselves. Celebrities spend their lives and energies trying to get everyone else to extol them for their greatness.

True heroes spend their lives and energies pointing away from themselves to the only perfect hero, the only one who had no flaws, no foibles, no spot or wrinkle, no sin whatsoever—the Lord Jesus Himself. The heroes included in this volume point away from themselves to Christ. Imitate them as they imitated our Lord and Savior.

—Douglas Bond and Joel R. Beeke

Acknowledgments

We are grateful to be able to offer you two more illustrated "Heroes" volumes published by Reformation Heritage Books for children and young people (though adults can profit too!). I had the privilege of working on the first volume, *Reformation Heroes* (2007), with Diana Kleyn, and the second volume, *Puritan Heroes* (2018), with Glenda Mathes. And I am looking forward to coauthoring a fifth volume in the near future, *Ancient and Medieval Heroes*, with Michael Haykin.

It should be noted that the first section of several chapters take factual events or convictions in the life of the biography being addressed and adds a realistic but fictional conversation to stir up interest in the "hero" being studied. This same approach was used in *Puritan Heroes*. The rest of each chapter aims to be strictly non-fictional.

It has been a true pleasure to work on this present two-volume work, *Evangelical Heroes*,[1] with my friend, Douglas Bond, a well-known, able, and engaging writer of Christian books for young people that often contain a mix of fictional and nonfictional material. (When I told my son—now a father of four children—that I was coauthoring this book with Douglas, he excitedly responded, "Douglas Bond, really? He was my favorite author in my midteens!") Our working agreement was simple: we both wrote up a list of evangelical Christian heroes who lived from the eighteenth century until today, then whittled that list down slowly and painfully (there are hundreds to pick from!) to about thirty men and women. We evenly divided the task of writing the chapters and then edited each other's work. I wish to thank Douglas immensely for laboring and persevering on these volumes with me and can only hope that the reader will not immediately recognize his chapters because they are written considerably better than mine!

Later on in the process, I asked Michael Haykin, a church historian at Southern Baptist Theological Seminary and a very good friend, to write the chapter on Andrew Fuller because he is the world's leading scholar on this forefather. He not only did so willingly but also edited our entire volume and wrote the foreword as well. Many thanks to you, dear brother Michael, for your valuable contributions to this volume. I also express our gratitude to Bruce Baugus, now professor at Puritan Reformed Theological Seminary (PRTS), for writing the chapter on the Chinese evangelical Wang Mingdao (see volume 2). Bruce is very involved with the Chinese evangelical movement around the world and has written extensively on the subject.[2] And a hearty thanks to PRTS student Devon Rossman for writing the first draft of the chapter on Lemuel Haynes.

---

1. See Joel R. Beeke, *What Is Evangelicalism?* (Darlington, England: Evangelical Press, 2012), for a definition of *evangelical* and *evangelicalism* and how Christians experience the biblical, evangelical faith.

2. See especially Bruce Baugus, ed., *China's Reforming Churches: Mission, Polity, and Ministry in the Next Christendom* (Grand Rapids: Reformation Heritage Books, 2014).

I owe a big thanks also to Dr. Ian Turner, a PhD graduate from Puritan Reformed Theological Seminary and now a Reformed Baptist pastor in Carlisle, Pennsylvania, for his valuable writing and research assistance on a number of my entries when he served me on a part-time basis as a teacher's assistant in 2021. This book would not be what it is without him.

Heartfelt gratitude is again expressed to Caffy Whitney for doing the amazing cover artwork of George Whitefield preaching to a group of coal miners (vol. 1) and a formal portrait of Dr. Martyn Lloyd-Jones (vol. 2) as well as about a dozen portraits scattered throughout these volumes of the heroes presented. She has done such a great job on each of these volumes and has been so great to work with. Thanks much, Caffy! And thanks to PRTS student Joshua Ng for hunting down and supplying the additional artwork and illustrations throughout this book drawn from other sources. Your hard work and great job on this is deeply appreciated.

Thanks, too, to the Reformation Heritage Books team: our quality typesetter, Linda den Hollander; our excellent cover designer, Amy Zevenbergen; and our faithful editors and proofreaders for their quality work on this volume. You are all appreciated more than you know.

Finally, allow me to say that I am very grateful to God that these volumes on heroes have sold far more copies than I originally envisioned and have proved useful for teens and adults who want to become better acquainted with the heroes of church history as well as for Christian homeschooling families and Christian schools throughout America and beyond.

May God bless both volumes of *Evangelical Heroes* to the glory of His name and to the spiritual well-being of readers of all ages. May it especially serve to give young people real heroes rather than the mostly fake heroes that the world seeks to promote and press into their lives.

—Joel R. Beeke

~ 1 ~

Anne Dutton

1692–1765

Anne Dutton stepped inside John Hart's London printing office as she closed the door against the flurries of snow rushing in. Brushing off the thin coat of snow that dusted the stack of papers she carried, Anne handed her new manuscript to the printer's assistant. "Mr. Hart is expecting this manuscript. It is to be sold by Mr. Lewis," she said.

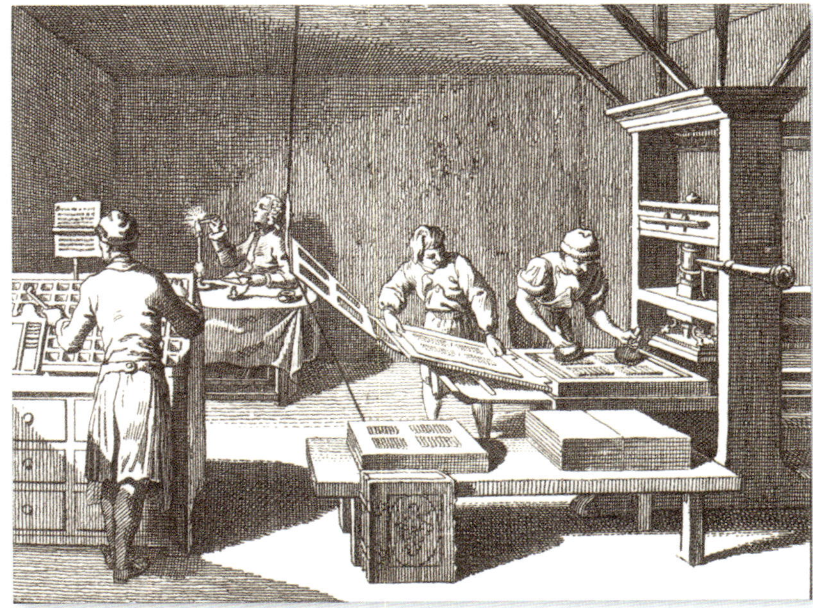

The printer's assistant recognized her. "Thank you, Mrs. Dutton," he said. "I see you're one day ahead of the deadline."

"Better early than never," she said as she adjusted her hat and turned toward the door.

"If it's no inconvenience, may I trouble you with a question?" the assistant asked.

"Of course," Anne said, facing the assistant.

"I admire your writings," the assistant said. "In fact, I benefited much from your book on the Lord's Supper. It helped me see that by faith Christ is lovingly present during the Supper by the Holy Spirit and that He is present to strengthen my faith. I am privileged to partake of such a solemn ordinance."

"It is indeed solemn," Anne said. "The Lord's Supper is the nearest approach to Christ's glorious self that we can make on this side of heaven in an ordinance way."

"It's just that"—Benson hesitated—"A few of my friends did not approve of me reading a theological book written by…well…"

"By a woman?" Anne asked.

"Well, yes," the assistant said. "They said that by writing these books, you were disobeying 1 Timothy 2:12 and 1 Corinthians 14:34–35, and that by reading them, I was too. I was not persuaded when they said that doctrinal writing is something for which women are unfit or unworthy or that publishing books makes women arrogant and self-affirming. That is proved wrong by your writings themselves. But I am struggling with the notion that a woman instructing men in theological writings—and my reading of them—is disobedience to Scripture."

Anne took a deep breath. She had given much thought to her role as a female writer of theological books and had just published a tract about this issue.[1] "I appreciate your asking," Anne said. "Permit me to offer a few reflections with which the Lord has helped me think this through."

"I would be much obliged," the assistant said.

"The first thing to get right," Anne said, "is the sense and context of the Scriptures you mentioned. Paul was not forbidding women from writing but from public, authoritative teaching in the church. Your reading my books is much like what we are doing now—having a private conversation—much like when Priscilla, with her husband Aquilla in Acts 18:26, taught Apollos in private."

"That makes perfect sense," the assistant said.

"Moreover," Anne continued, "my writing for the sake of building up those who are new in Christ or weak in the faith, as I have seen my calling, is obedience to Scripture. Romans 14:19 directs all believers, men and women, to 'follow after the things which make for peace, and things wherewith one may edify another.' If a woman is gifted and inclined to write and publish truths about Christ, she is not only free to do so but commanded, it seems, to do so."

"So, when I open your books in my home and read them alone or with my family," the assistant said, "it is as if you are simply paying us a visit and sharing in profitable Christian conversation."

"I couldn't have said it better myself," Anne said. "There are women today using their writing skills for trifles. So, shall no others of the female sex be suffered to appear on Christ's side, to tell of the wonders of His love, to seek the good of souls and the advancement of the Redeemer's interest? If I can further fellowship within the church by writing for the glory of God and the good of souls, then I am the happiest of creatures in my Lord's service."

"Well said, Mrs. Dutton," the assistant said. "Thank you for entertaining my question. Your response clarified much for me. Good day."

"Good day," Anne said, as she opened the door and stepped out into the wintery air.

---

1. See Anne Dutton, *A Letter to Such of the Servants of Christ, Who May Have Any Scruples about the Lawfulness of Printing Any Thing Written by a Woman* (1743).

Anne Dutton

Early Life and Conversion

Anne Williams Dutton was born in 1692 to godly parents in Northampton, England. At about thirteen years of age, "after a serious illness,"[2] she experienced deep conviction of sin and conversion under the ministry of John Hunt at the Castle Hill Independent Church in Northampton. The way she later wrote of these experiences showed her sensitivity to sin as an offense to God and reminds us that she was influenced early on by reading the Puritans.

Anne became a communicant member there two years later, in 1707. Around this time, she matured in her understanding of true faith. She realized that experiences or emotions, or even our estimate of how strong faith is, are never a sure foundation for living in Christ; our faith must be in Christ alone—"in the Lord, not in your frames. In the Lord, not in what you enjoy from him, but in what you are in him." When Anne made Christ alone the object of her faith, she wrote, "The Lord sealed my instruction, and filled my heart brim-full of joy, in the faith of my eternal interest, and unchangeable standing in him; and of his being an infinite fountain of blessedness, for me to rejoice in always; even when the streams of sensible enjoyments failed…. And then I began to rejoice in my dear Lord Jesus, as always the same, even when my frames altered."[3]

After John Hunt died in 1709, Anne was dissatisfied with his successor, Thomas Tingey, and left to join College Lane

---

2. Michael A. G. Haykin, "English Calvinistic Baptists and Vocation in the Long Eighteenth Century, with Particular Reference to Anne Dutton's Calling as an Author," *Southern Baptist Journal of Theology* 22, no. 1 (2018): 76.

3. JoAnn Ford Watson, ed., *Selected Spiritual Writings of Anne Dutton: Autobiography* (Macon, Ga.: Mercer University Press, 2006), 3:63.

Baptist Church in Northampton, pastored by John Moore, under whose preaching she matured spiritually. Moore's ministry provided the biblical doctrine Anne's new faith craved, and under it Anne received training in Bible, religion, music, and hymnody.[4] She described Moore as "a great doctrinal preacher" and one who settled her understanding and acceptance of the doctrines of the gospel.[5]

Marriage and Loss

In 1714 Anne was married to Thomas Cattell, of whom little is known. The couple moved to London and attended a Baptist church in Curriers Hall, Cripplegate, pastored by the hyper-Calvinist John Skepp (1675–1721). Under Skepp's ministry, the church grew. Anne was much edified by Skepp's preaching and his manner of delivery, although, quite remarkably, she did not follow his hyper-Calvinism nor did she appear to be influenced by the imbalances of other hyper-Calvinists she was fond of reading, such as Joseph Hussey.[6] She herself

might better be classified as a high Calvinist in the mold of Thomas Goodwin, who greatly shaped her views on the Trinity and the covenant of redemption.

Early in 1719, Anne's husband died. She wrote, "It pleased the Lord to take away my Yokefellow by Death. And some Circumstances attended, which made it very trying. But my kind Lord comforted me" and "I was in some measure quieted under the Hand of God."[7] Anne's loss made it necessary for her to return to her family in Northampton. She was "full of heaviness, …but my sweet Lord Jesus drew me to Himself, as my everlasting all!"[8]

During this time, Anne experienced many emotional ups and downs, from joy and relief to gloom and back again. This was a time of spiritual struggle, depression, and searching. Whenever she was overcome with grief under the clouds of dark providence or inner turmoil, she searched the Scriptures for God's promises. Anne's autobiography is full of examples where God helped her through seasons of despair by enabling her to hold on to verses of Scripture. Anne wrote that during this time, she looked for God "in his ordinances, in one place and another; but alas! I found him not."[9] She wrote, "I found grief, love, desire, humility and holy resignation, variously working in me. I saw that there

---

4. JoAnn Ford Watson, "Anne Dutton: An Eighteenth Century British Evangelical Woman Writer," *Ashland Theological Journal* 30 (1998): 51.

5. Haykin, "English Calvinistic Baptists and Vocation," 77.

6. Hyper-Calvinism: Traced to Joseph Hussey (1659–1726), this theological error has many variations and perspectives, but in general it reasons that since men do not have the ability to repent and believe the gospel, then there is no reason we should offer the gospel freely to impenitent sinners and command them to repent.

7. Watson, *Selected Spiritual Writings*, 3:63.

8. Watson, *Selected Spiritual Writings*, 3:64.

9. Haykin, "English Calvinistic Baptists and Vocation," 78.

was not only a fullness of life in [Christ], suited to quicken me at *first*, when I was dead in sin; but a fullness also, that was sufficient to revive me *under*, and recover me *from* all my backslidings."[10] Anne kept returning to one particular verse, "Commit thy way unto the LORD; trust also in him; and he shall bring it to pass" (Ps. 37:5). She said, "This precious promise being cast into my heart, became a living seed, and taking root there, it sprang up into desires, expectations, and earnest prayers to the Lord, for the longed-for mercy."[11]

Loneliness and the loss of her husband do not seem to have been the only reasons for Anne's struggles. Rather, like many believers, she knew the psalmist's experience of finding resolution in God's character after much soul-struggle: "Why art thou cast down, O my soul? and why art thou disquieted within me? hope in God" (Ps. 43:5). Often God sovereignly orders seasons of struggle so that we will learn to trust in Him and be ready for future situations that call for spiritual resilience.

A New Gospel Work with a New Yokefellow

Anne had been at Northampton for about a year when, as she wrote, "I was again married."[12] Benjamin Dutton (ca. 1691–1747), a draper, or dealer in fabric or cloth, who had entered the Baptist ministry, became her husband. Anne and Benjamin involved themselves in ministry opportunities around Cambridgeshire. This led to Benjamin's call as a pastor to a congregation in Great Gransden, Huntingdonshire. By this time Anne had already begun writing letters,

tracts, and books. In 1734 she published a fifteen-hundred-line poem in heroic couplets, "Narration of the Wonders of Grace." It tells the story of God's redemptive acts in history and has many Scripture references in the margins. In 1735 Anne published one of her most popular books, *A Discourse upon Walking with God*. John Wesley, who read this book, developed much respect for Dutton.[13] George Whitefield also spoke of how this book influenced many who read it.[14]

Anne's Writing Ministry

Dutton was a prolific writer of letters, tracts, and books. She corresponded with Howell Harris, John Wesley, George Whitefield, and William Seward. Seward, an early Methodist helper of Whitefield and later coworker of Howell Harris, received a letter from Dutton in May 1739 and found it full of helpful wisdom. Through her writings, Dutton became renowned for her simple, biblical piety among evangelicals in England and America. George Whitefield, who helped promote and publish Dutton's writings, once said after a meeting with her, "Her conversation is as weighty as her letters."[15]

In her letter writing, Dutton was not merely building up a social network; she wrote in order to "contend for the faith which was once delivered unto the saints" (Jude v. 3). The occasion for many of her letters was to correct theological error and make a biblical case for the truth. Yet she did

13. Watson, "Anne Dutton," 52.

14. Watson, "Anne Dutton," 52.

15. George Whitefield, "Letter to Mr. [Jonathan] B[ryan], July 24, 1741," in *Letters of George Whitefield for the Period 1734–1742* (1771; repr., Edinburgh: Banner of Truth, 1976), 280.

10. Watson, *Selected Spiritual Writings*, 3:67–68.

11. Watson, *Selected Spiritual Writings*, 3:69.

12. Watson, *Selected Spiritual Writings*, 3:65.

so respectfully. It was in this spirit that Dutton maintained a correspondence with John Wesley and others in response to some of their peculiar theological views. Dutton wrote letters to Wesley and published booklets correcting his teachings. She defended Calvinism against Wesley's Arminianism in *A Letter to the Reverend Mr. Wesley, in Vindication of the Doctrine of Absolute, Unconditional Election, Particular Redemption, Special Vocation, and Final Perseverance* (1742). She also wrote against Wesley's teaching that a Christian's growth in holiness could be perfected in this life by a "second blessing" that made a Christian unable to sin. In the early 1740s, John Wesley preached this doctrine of sinless perfection and believed that God bestowed this second blessing on some of his hearers (though he himself did not claim sinless perfection). In response, Dutton wrote a biblically reasoned booklet refuting the doctrine. It was published in 1743 as *Letters to the Reverend Mr. John Wesley against Perfection as Not Attainable in This Life.* Around the same time, George Whitefield wrote a letter to Dutton and received a reply that helped him think through a biblical response to Wesley's doctrine of Christian perfection. Whitefield published this response in America in *The Pennsylvania Journal.* Here are some excerpts from her letter:

> I can look upon it to be no other than a delusion of the enemy of souls, and a deceit of the heart, for any to think, that there is such a thing attainable in this life, as an entire, sinless perfection.… Strange it is, that any should think, or affirm, that they have not sinned in thought, word or deed for months!… Do your utmost, my dear brother, to disentangle the ensnared in Bristol. For the delusion which prevails, will have most pernicious consequences. And that it is a delusion, the Word of God most clearly manifests.… For "if we say that we have no sin," (says the Apostle John) "we deceive ourselves, and the truth is not in us," 1 John 1:8. And says the Holy Ghost by Solomon, "there is not a just man upon the earth that doeth good, and sinneth not," Ecclesiastes 7:20. The great work of the Grace of God, which bringeth salvation to the saved ones is teaching them, that denying "ungodliness and worldly lusts, they should live soberly, righteously, and godly in this present world," Titus 2:11–12. The word *teaching*, being in the present tense, denotes the constant work of divine grace upon the subjects thereof, while they are in this world. The word *denying*, denotes the constant duty, and business of Christians, so long as they are in this present world.… Therefore, no man can be perfect in holiness in this life.[16]

By 1740 Anne had written seven books; between 1741 and 1743, fourteen more followed. By 1750 she had published thirty-five books.[17] Her writings are characterized

____

16. Michael A. G. Haykin, "Writing to George Whitefield: A Letter from Anne Dutton on Sinless Perfection," *The Southern Baptist Journal of Theology* 18, no. 2 (2014): 84–86.

17. Michael A. G. Haykin, "Anne Dutton and Her Theological Works," in *Eight Women of Faith* (Wheaton, Ill.: Crossway, 2016), 58.

by both Calvinistic theology and spiritual experience that are deep and profound and yet accessible to typical church members who have some knowledge of the doctrines of grace. These qualities made her writings to be treasured by many of God's people despite the fact that she often inter-mixed notes of exhortation and corrections, acting at times as a systematic theologian and a biblical apologist. That led her to often engage in controversy, particularly writing against Arminianism, perfectionism, antinomianism, and erroneous views of the Trinity.

Ministry in Great Gransden and Beyond

Meanwhile, the church of which Benjamin Dutton was pastor prospered under his preaching. Regular attendance ranged between 250 and 350 people each week. A new chapel and a church parsonage, which the Duttons had to finance, had to be built in 1743 because of the growth. In August 1743, Benjamin traveled to America to raise funds for his ministry, no doubt to pay off the costs of the new chapel, and to promote his wife's published works. On his way back from America in 1747, the ship carrying Benjamin sank off

Shipwreck off a Rocky Coast
ABRAHAM HULK

the coast of Britain, and he was lost at sea at age fifty-six. The money he raised had arrived in England on another ship, so at least the funds for the new chapel and building projects ensured that Anne—now widowed a second time—would not be crushed by debt along with the grief of losing her second husband.[18] Anne remained a widow for the rest of her life.

Anne Dutton did not have any children, but she considered her books to be something like her children. After Benjamin's death, Dutton stayed in the Great Gransden congregation and published a steady stream of tracts, hymns, treatises, collections of letters, and poems.[19] One of her best pieces, published anonymously in 1748, is a devotional study of the Lord's Table: *Thoughts on the Lord's Supper, Relating to the Nature, Subjects, and Right Partaking of This Solemn Ordinance.*

Dutton died in 1765, possibly from throat cancer. A friend describes her near the time of her death as

a woman of seventy-four laden with the fruits of the Spirit.… Not shriveled, wrinkled, nor spotted with doubts, fears, deadness, etc.… I had heard, that precious in the sight of the Lord was the *death* of his saints, and now I saw he [i.e., God] was true to his word, for he was present by his Spirit in the sickness and death of Mrs. Dutton. Her illness was a sore throat, and one of her expressions was, "My dear Sir, I am rejoiced to think that there is but a hair's breadth betwixt me and my father's house. 'Tis but for God to

----

18. Haykin, "English Calvinistic Baptists and Vocation," 78.
19. Haykin, "English Calvinistic Baptists and Vocation," 79.

stop my breath and I am with him. And so shall I ever be with the Lord."[20]

Her memorial stone, erected in Great Gransden, sums up her life this way: she "spent her life in the cause of God [and] was the author of 25 vols of choice letters & 38 smaller works."

Anne Dutton's Significance

Anne Dutton is an important figure in the eighteenth-century English revival, not only because she wrote theological works at a time when very few other women were doing so but because her work was marked by biblical depth and experiential piety and was noticed by well-known revivalists of the time as being of great value. Mrs. Dutton has been well described as "perhaps the most theologically capable and influential Baptist woman of her day."[21] Her importance has recently been recognized in a six-volume set of her selected works.[22]

Dutton can and should be an encouragement to anyone in God's kingdom, male or female, who has received a gift and an inclination to write for the edification of fellow believers, the unfolding of biblical doctrine, and the defense of the truth.

Study Questions

1. What are some reasons Anne gives for the appropriateness of women writing theological works?

2. What are some of the positive ways in which Anne demonstrated growth as a young Christian?

3. Think about the losses in Anne's life. What was her way of dealing with the spiritual depression that often afflicted her?

4. Think about how Anne needed to be theologically informed enough to know the errors of her day and concerned enough to correct those errors in public letters and books. How does her letter-writing ministry demonstrate key aspects of mature Christian character?

5. Anne used her gifts in the service of the Lord and His church despite the many contrary opinions in her time about women authors. What gifts has God given you, and how might you need to use them faithfully to stand boldly against the opinions and culture of our day?

---

20. Haykin, "Anne Dutton and Her Theological Works," 65.

21. Karen O'Dell Bullock, "Dutton [*née* Williams], Anne," in *Oxford Dictionary of National Biography* (Oxford: Oxford University Press, 2004; online ed., January 2009), in Haykin, "Writing to George Whitefield," 83.

22. Anne Dutton, *Selected Spiritual Writings of Anne Dutton*, ed. JoAnn Ford Watson (Macon, Ga.: Mercer University Press, 2003–2009).

~ 2 ~

Charles Wesley

1707–1788

Charles Wesley was born December 18, 1707. Little did his mother, Susanna Wesley, know on that day that she had just given birth to a son who would grow up to be a Great Awakening preacher and one of the greatest English hymn writers of all time. As a point of reference, that same year, 1707, Isaac Watts began to publish his own collection of *Hymns and Spiritual Songs*.

Charles Wesley was the eighteenth of nineteen children whom his mother would deliver into this world. Susanna Wesley herself was already accustomed to large families, being the twenty-fifth of twenty-five children. Her gifted son Charles would grow up to be, along with his elder brother John, one of the most influential men of the eighteenth century. His most enduring influence, however, comes from the sixty-five hundred hymns that he wrote, several of which rank among the very finest poetry in the English language.

A Godly Mother

Susanna Annesley Wesley (1669–1742) is often called the "Mother of Methodism." By any measure she was an extraordinary woman: strong in faith, rich in character, able in mind, disciplined in life, and both wise and firm as a parent. She was the youngest daughter of prominent Puritan preacher Dr. Samuel Annesley, one of the many faithful ministers of the Word ejected from the Church of England in 1662. He continued to preach to congregations of Dissenters until his death in 1696.

Susanna Wesley

Though blessed with a methodical and godly mother, Charles was not equally blessed in his father, Samuel Wesley, rector of the Anglican parish church in Epworth, Lincolnshire. Despite being highly educated, Samuel was negligent in providing for his family. He racked up considerable debt and was eventually thrown into debtors' prison. Charles's father was also impulsive and made rash decisions,

The rescue of John Wesley from the Epworth Rectory Fire
HENRY PERLEE PARKER

seemingly without considering the adverse effects those decisions had on his wife and children. On a whim, he once left his post as a vicar and joined the navy as a chaplain, leaving Susanna to fend for herself and the children. Two months later he left the navy because he didn't like the food on board ship. Once, over a political disagreement with Susanna, he packed his things, walked out the door, and abandoned his wife and children for over a year.

Friendless in her marriage, Susanna turned to the Friend of sinners. "Enable me to live so as to deserve a friend," she prayed, "and if I never have one on earth, be thou my friend, for in having thee I shall have all that is dear and valuable in friendship."[1] In spite of her many marital disappointments, Susanna remained faithful to her husband and to her duties, finding grace and strength to raise her children in the nurture and admonition of the Lord.

Along with a difficult marriage, Susanna endured many other tragedies. Twice the Wesley house caught fire and burned to the ground, all their meager possessions consumed in the flames. Nine of her nineteen children died as infants, including a newborn whom her husband took to a neighbor to nurse while Susanna recovered from giving birth. But in the night, the nurse accidentally rolled onto the baby, who suffocated and died.

Meticulous and methodical (the source of the name Methodist), however busy the day was, Susanna always found time for daily prayer and Bible reading, and she taught her children to do the same. Sometimes pulling her apron over her face for a bit of needed privacy from her ten children, Susanna would pray, "Help me, O Lord, to make true use of all disappointments and calamities in this life, in such a way that they may unite my heart more closely with thee."[2] It was her intimate closeness with Christ that she so warmly conveyed to her son Charles.

Early Life and Education

Early in life Charles showed an unusual concern for the downtrodden, a characteristic seen in his later ministry and evident in many of his hymns. Nine-year-old Charles, sent off to Westminster School adjoining the great abbey in London, soon noticed a small Scottish boy named Murray regularly getting kicked around by the school bully. One day Charles had had enough. He rolled up his sleeves, took his stand between poor Murray and the school bully, and, fists flying, gave the bully a trouncing.

After Charles distinguished himself as the King's Scholar at the "School of the Muses," as Westminster School was called, his father received a letter from a wealthy Anglo-Irish relative, Garret Wesley, who wanted to make Charles his heir. Though the financial stability Garrett Wesley would have provided was attractive, Charles chose not to go to Ireland. Another cousin, Richard Colley, went in Charles's stead and became Richard Colley Wesley—the grandfather of Marquis Wellesley, who colonized India, and of the Duke of Wellington, who defeated Napoleon at Waterloo. How much history hung on a small boy's decision! Yet Charles Wesley also left a heritage, one more permanent than any empire and larger than any army.

---

1. Eric Metaxas, *Seven Women, and the Secret of Their Greatness* (Nashville, Tenn.: Nelson Books, 2015), 46.

2. Metaxas, *Seven Women*, 46.

Christ College

Due to his brilliant mind and poetic gift, Charles followed his older brother John to Oxford and was accepted as an undergraduate in Christ College. There the Wesleys organized a regular meeting for Bible reading and prayer. George Whitefield, who became a celebrated preacher of the Great Awakening, joined the group. "Enlightened" students, however, derisively dubbed the student prayer meeting the "Holy Club." Because of their stress on living by a strict schedule or "method," they were called "Methodists." By their own account both brothers were still unconverted, strangers to the gospel of salvation by grace alone through faith. Their "Methodism" was only another system of salvation by devotion to good works and upright living.

Charles completed his degree in 1729. Shortly after, he was ordained into the ministry of the Church of England. By his own testimony, however, he would attempt to fulfill his ministerial duties without a true saving knowledge of Christ.

Singing in the Storm

An opportunity arose in 1736 for John and Charles to join General James Oglethorpe in the American colony of Georgia. Oglethorpe had established a colony made up mostly of prisoners, and he needed a chaplain (John) and a private secretary (Charles) to help further establish the colony.

In the eighteenth century, sailing from England to America over treacherous seas took many weeks. On board ship, Charles met a group of Moravian Christians from Germany. He marveled at their genuine love for Christ, and he found himself moved deeply by their singing. He learned that the Moravian Church traces its beginnings to the ministry of proto-Reformer Jan Hus of Bohemia. His followers fled from persecution in their native land and reestablished themselves as the community of Herrnhut in Germany. They sent missionaries to other lands; the ones aboard ship with the Wesleys were going out to serve German settlers in Georgia. The Moravians were famous for their robustly evangelical hymns and the tunes they composed for them. The Anglican Church in which Charles had been raised sang only versifications from the Psalms, but Moravians had a tradition of singing hymns on various biblical themes and passages throughout the Bible. They traced this tradition back more than two hundred years to Martin Luther and the Protestant Reformation.

One day, while the Moravians were singing a hymn below deck, a violent storm arose. Waves broke over the ship, the mainsail split into shreds, and the sea poured in between decks. While the crewmen and the other passengers

Ship in a Storm
IVAN AIVAZOVSKY

screamed in terror, the fearless Moravian Christians kept on singing, their voices rising above the violence of the wind and the pounding of the waves against the vessel. And they never stopped singing through the entire storm. Charles would never forget their singing, and it would no doubt have a profound effect on his future as a hymn writer.

But once they settled in their new positions in Georgia, things did not go so well for Charles and his brother John. After only a brief time in Georgia, Charles, private secretary to Oglethorpe, fell out of favor with his employer, as did John. Sick and humiliated, the Wesley brothers returned to England, Charles in 1736 and John in 1738.

A Heart Strangely Warmed

Both Wesley brothers had been profoundly impressed by the Moravian Christians they had met on board their ship to Georgia. God was at work, using the witness of these Moravian believers. Newly returned from the American colonies, Charles fell seriously ill, and he feared he might be dying. In his journal dated May 21, 1738, Charles wrote that while in prayer he felt "a strange palpitation of heart" and suddenly cried out loud, "I believe, I believe!" He concluded, "I now found myself at peace with God, and rejoiced in hope of loving Christ." He sent for his brother and told him all about it.

A few days later, on May 24, 1738, John Wesley found himself in a building only a few yards from where the London Museum stands today. This is John's account of what happened next:

> In the evening I went very unwillingly to a society in Aldersgate Street, where one was reading Luther's preface to the epistle to the Romans. About a quarter before nine, while the leader was describing the change which God works in the heart through faith in Christ, I felt my heart strangely warmed. I felt I did trust in Christ alone for salvation; and an assurance was given me that he had taken away my sins, even mine, and saved me from the law of sin and death.[3]

Soon after trusting "in Christ alone for salvation," John Wesley translated and versified (in 1740) a marvelous hymn written originally in German by a Moravian, Count Nikolaus Ludwig von Zinzendorf, "Jesus, Thy Blood and Righteousness":

> Jesus, Thy blood and righteousness
> My beauty are, my glorious dress;
> 'Midst flaming worlds, in these arrayed,
> With joy shall I lift up my head.
>
> Bold shall I stand in Thy great day;
> For who ought to my charge shall lay?
> Fully absolved through these I am
> From sin and fear, from guilt and shame.
>
> When from the dust of death I rise
> To claim my mansion in the skies,
> E'en then this shall be all my plea,
> Jesus hath lived, hath died, for me.
>
> Jesus, be endless praise to Thee,
> Whose boundless mercy hath for me—
> For me a full atonement made,
> An everlasting ransom paid.
>
> O let the dead now hear Thy voice;
> Now bid thy banished ones rejoice;
> Their beauty this, their glorious dress,
> Jesus, Thy blood and righteousness.[4]

Though later in life John would align himself with Arminian theology and become an outspoken opponent of Calvinism, the doctrines of grace, and the doctrine of imputed righteousness, in this hymn John beautifully wrote

---

3. G. R. Balleine, *A History of the Evangelical Party in the Church of England* (London: Longmans, Green, 1933), 24.

4. John Wesley, "Jesus, Thy Blood and Righteousness," in *Trinity Hymnal* (Suwanee, Ga.: Great Commission Publications, 1991), 520.

a poetic summary of the Reformed doctrine of the passive and active obedience of Christ. Christ fully obeyed His Father's will and imputed that perfect righteousness to the account of all those His Father had chosen before the foundation of the world (Eph. 1:3–11). And Christ actively took on Himself the curse and penalty of all the sins of all the elect. Hence, John could write that on the resurrection day, when standing before the glory of God in heaven, "E'en then this shall be all my plea, Jesus hath lived, hath died, for me."

As an Anglican, John Wesley was a faithful adherent to the established Church of England in which he had been steeped from childhood, yet his Arminianism differed substantively from that of the "high churchmen" whose rituals had flourished in the church since the days of Archbishop William Laud. For example, Wesley embraced the doctrine of total depravity whereas an archbishop like Laud would at minimum downplay such a doctrine. Nevertheless, Wesley's Arminian theology was so important to him that he was willing to split the ranks of Methodism by initiating a public dispute with his junior colleague, George Whitefield, and others who stood firmly in the faith of the Reformers and the Puritans. In sum, though John Wesley continued expressing his conversion in terms of "the change which God works in the heart" and declaring that he "did trust in Christ *alone* for salvation," his rejection of predestination and his embrace of Arminianism inevitably led him into controversy with various Reformed preachers.

The Dungeon Flamed with Light

Following his brother's example, Charles also sought out the Moravian society in Aldersgate Street, London, and came under the influence of godly Peter Boehler. The Spirit

John Wesley, the brother of Charles
PORTRAIT BY GEORGE ROMNEY

of God had already been at work in Charles's proud heart, and he came to see that all his outward religious deeds did nothing to wash away his sins. Charles opened his Bible and read Psalm 40:3: "He hath put a new song in my mouth, even praise unto our God: many shall see it, and fear, and shall trust in the LORD."

The following year Charles wrote out his "new song" autobiographically in a beautiful hymn describing what happens to a sinner when God's Spirit frees him from the bondage of sin and applies the saving work of Christ to his account. In this moving hymn, Charles expressed his astonishment at the death of Christ on his behalf in a series of rhetorical questions:

And can it be that I should gain
An interest in the Savior's blood?
Died He for me, who caused His pain?
For me who Him to death pursued?
Amazing love! how can it be
That Thou, my God, shouldst die for me?

Overwhelmed with Christ's love, in a stanza influenced by Acts 12:6–9, employing a prison metaphor, Charles wrote one of the finest summaries ever penned of what happens to a sinner when God's Spirit pours His quickening grace on a human soul.

Long my imprisoned spirit lay
Fast bound in sin and nature's night;
Thine eye diffused a quickening ray,
I woke, the dungeon flamed with light;
My chains fell off, my heart was free;
I rose, went forth, and followed Thee.

Ironically, Charles, who claimed to be an Arminian like his brother, penned thoroughly Calvinistic stanzas on the doctrine of irresistible grace and the effectual calling of the Spirit of God regenerating the heart of a dead sinner. The act of worshiping God in song often serves as a corrective to otherwise bad theology. Charles simply could not write a hymn to be sung to God that extolled his own free will, choosing on its own to awake and believe the message of the gospel. No, Charles described *God's* eye diffusing a life-giving ray, thereby awakening the sinner; the prison flaming with the light of God's grace; the dead sinner's bondage to sin broken by the sovereign will and activity of God; the sinner's heart set free; and, in the inevitable response to the new birth, the sinner, now regenerated, rising and following the Lord. Charles concluded this marvelous hymn drawing from Paul in Romans 8:1: "There is therefore now no condemnation to them which are in Christ Jesus":

No condemnation now I dread,
Jesus, and all in Him is mine;
Alive in Him, my living Head,
And clothed in righteousness divine.
Bold I approach the eternal throne,
And claim the crown through Christ my own.[5]

Some years later, Charles wrote another hymn on the anniversary of his conversion to Christ; it originally had nineteen verses, about fifteen more than most people have patience for today. It begins with "O for a thousand tongues to sing," a phrase inspired by Charles's Moravian friend, Peter Boehler, who once, in an ecstasy of devotion, declared, "Had I a thousand tongues, I would praise him with all of them." This hymn was Charles's way of giving Peter Boehler a thousand tongues—and many more. Imagine the countless number of Christians over the centuries who have praised God with Boehler's words immortalized in Charles's poetry.

---

5. Charles Wesley, "And Can It Be," in *Trinity Hymnal*, 455.

O for a thousand tongues to sing
My great Redeemer's praise,
The glories of my God and King,
The triumphs of His grace.

My gracious Master and my God,
Assist me to proclaim,
To spread through all the earth abroad,
The honors of Thy Name.

Jesus, the Name that charms our fears,
That bids our sorrows cease;
'Tis music in the sinner's ears,
'Tis life and health and peace.

He breaks the power of reigning sin,
He sets the pris'ner free;
His blood can make the foulest clean,
His blood availed for me.

He speaks and, listening to His voice,
New life the dead receive;
The mournful, broken hearts rejoice;
The humble poor believe.[6]

Charles expressed his deep compassion for sinners behind bars in the line, "He sets the prisoners free," a poetic description of the very ministry that would occupy a great deal of Charles's time in the years ahead.

Prison Ministry

As in the final line of his first hymn, Charles "rose, went

____

6. Charles Wesley, "O for a Thousand Tongues to Sing," in *Trinity Hymnal*, 164.

forth, and followed" the Lord by immediately looking for ways he could minister to the poor and needy in England. He didn't have far to look. Examples of injustice and misery stood on every street corner.

Between 1700 and 1760 a widespread addiction to gin took hold of Great Britain, especially in the squalid streets of London. Sometimes called "the mothers' ruin," gin—a cheap hard liquor distilled from juniper berries—flowed throughout the country. The distillation process was simple and juniper berries were everywhere. Some people distilled gin in their bathtubs. Since the water in London was unfit to drink, nearly everyone consumed excessive quantities of gin, cluttering the streets with drunkenness, poverty, and crime.

Meanwhile, the British judicial system was in serious need of reform. In Charles's day, wigged and robed judges delivered the sentence of hanging—women and children included—for 160 different offenses. If a poor boy stole more than a shilling from the pocket of a gentleman or snared a rabbit on a gentleman's estate, the boy would be hanged.

Charles, convinced that social or political reform could not solve the problem, wisely sought a spiritual solution rather than a temporal one. Saddened by the deplorable condition of inmates in England's prisons, Charles did what he could. He took the gospel to the condemned at notorious Newgate Prison, a horrible place where many died from disease before they could face their sentence of death by hanging. Certainly, some deserved to be there, and some deserved execution, but many did not.

Charles, burdened for souls, spent his days telling prisoners how Jesus had been condemned to die in the place of sinners. He prayed and sang hymns with many—even children as young as ten years old. Executions in eighteenth-century Britain were public events, even popular entertainment spectacles. Every six weeks at Tyburn Hill, London, thousands gathered to watch prisoners die by slow-drop hanging.

Newgate prisoners in the exercise yard
ILLUSTRATION BY GUSTAVE DORÉ

When one African prisoner accused of stealing from his master heard Charles tell of the suffering of the Son of God for the salvation of sinners such as he, he wept in amazement that God would stoop down and save him. Others listened with mounting attention as the day of their execution approached. Charles described going with heavy heart to minister to the condemned men for the last time. Guards shoved prisoners onto an ox cart and drove them through the street to the gallows. Charles followed close behind on foot. When the cart halted below a row of suspended nooses, he climbed up into the cart to pray with the condemned men. As the nooses were fitted around the prisoners' necks, Charles led the men in singing a lesser-known Isaac Watts hymn of faith in Christ:

> A guilty, weak and helpless worm,
> On Thy kind arms I fall:
> Be Thou my life, my righteousness,
> My Jesus, and my all.[7]

At a nod from the chief justice, the executioner drove the ox cart from under the believing prisoners, leaving them hanging by the neck until dead but safe in the arms of Jesus.

Open-Air Evangelism

Charles spent much of his time at the prisons, in part because churches were closed to him. Many Anglican ministers were hirelings, timeservers who cared little for the salvation of their flock; many were not true Christians themselves.

---

7. Isaac Watts, "How Sad Our State by Nature Is [Salvation through Christ]," in *Hymns & Sacred Songs*, 1707. See also John Julian, *Dictionary of Hymnology* (1907).

Anglican curate John Newton estimated that of the ten thousand parishes in England in his day, nine thousand of them had unbelieving pastors. Unwelcome in many of those parish churches, John and Charles, under the influence of George Whitefield, began preaching in village squares, in markets, and on street corners. This open-air preaching was considered improper and undignified by most Anglican clergymen.

Charles moved to Bristol in 1739, and for the next fifteen years he visited prisoners in the city prison and traveled thousands of miles, mostly on horseback, preaching to poor miners in Wales, mill workers in England, and farmers across the sea in Ireland. Meanwhile, in his travels, he wrote down many of his hymns in a notebook while riding his horse.

Jealous of his success, some Anglican churchmen stirred up violence against Charles. One day a frenzied mob surrounded his house in Bristol, breaking windows and yelling threats. They finally drove his horse into a nearby pond. Charles, self-controlled and concerned more for their souls than for his property, forgave them. On a similar occasion, he invited the angry mob into his home and preached the gospel to them for two hours.

In 1749 Charles fell in love with and married Miss Sarah Gwynne. His wife became a great support to her husband's calling and often accompanied him on evangelistic tours. God blessed them with two musically inclined sons and a daughter who inherited some of her father's poetic genius.

Charles Wesley
PORTRAIT BY JOHN RUSSELL

Final Years of Ministry

Charles left Bristol in 1771 and brought his family with him to live in London. Once back in the metropolis, he returned to his regular visits to Newgate Prison, preaching to debtors, petty thieves, and murderers, to the condemned awaiting the noose and execution at Tyburn Hill. In his London home he had a small upright organ on which he likely tried out many of the musical settings needed for the thousands of hymn lyrics he had written.

Meanwhile, the preaching of the Wesleys and their colleagues had sparked a widespread revival that brought many more people to church. Charles never broke fellowship with the Church of England, and he wanted to bring new converts to faithful Anglican churches where the gospel was still preached. His brother John, however, had more ambitious plans. He organized his followers into small groups known as classes and societies and put them under the leadership of lay preachers.

John acquired for the headquarters of his ministry an old unused cannon factory off City Road in London called the Foundry. After renovating it, John began holding services in his new church building in 1778, during the height of the American War for Independence, and made it his headquarters for the network of societies he had founded. Charles, always faithful to the Anglican Church, did not approve of his brother setting up his own chapel and even ordaining ministers without the authority of the Anglican bishop. John lived and died in the communion of the

Church of England; his societies separated from the national church only after his death and became the vanguard of the worldwide Methodist Church.

Despite their differences, many of Charles's hymns were first sung by the crowds of people cramming into the Wesley Chapel in London, today the worldwide headquarters for Methodists. John's house is positioned to the right and in front of the chapel. So many filled the regular pews in the sanctuary that John had a carpenter modify the seating so that both ends of each pew had a clever overflow sliding seat for latecomers to pull out and sit on.

John often said that the world was his parish, and certainly thousands of the poor of London sat on the pews in the old cannon factory where they heard his preaching and sang Charles's Christ-centered hymns. Today, in a tiny chapel next to the main sanctuary, Charles's little organ is tucked into a space no larger than a coat closet. John contributed to Christian hymnody by publishing hundreds of his brother's hymns, translating German ones, and writing a few of his own. *A Collection of Hymns for the Use of the People Called Methodists* was published by John in 1780.

A statue commemorating John Wesley, leader of the Methodist Revival, stands in the courtyard in front of his chapel. John died on March 2, 1791, and rather than be buried in the consecrated ground of an Anglican churchyard, he chose to be laid to rest in a little plot behind the chapel he had founded.

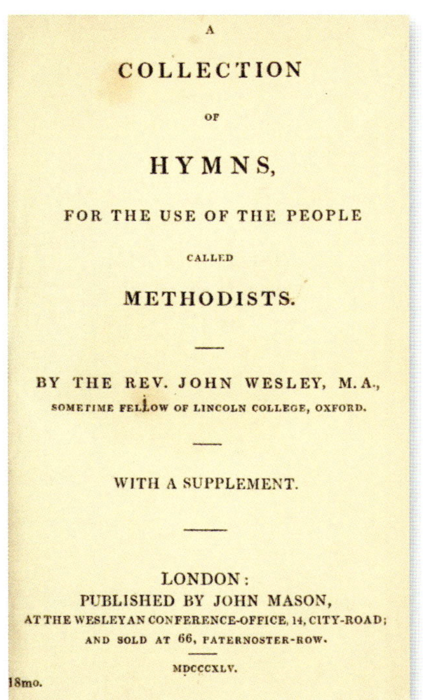

1845 edition of the Wesley hymnbook

Across City Road from the Wesley Chapel is the Nonconformist cemetery called Bunhill Fields. Many of the great men and women of English church history are buried there: Puritans John Owen, Thomas Goodwin, Joseph Caryl, and John Bunyan; hymn writers Isaac Watts and Joseph Hart; Daniel Defoe; and Charles's dear mother, Susanna Wesley, who died July 23, 1742, at the age of seventy-three.

No More to Die

One of Charles's best-loved hymns, "Hark! the Herald Angels Sing," is based on Luke 2:10–14, where the angel hosts appeared to the shepherds and announced the glorious news of the newborn Savior and King. Charles's exhilarating lyrics are usually reserved for singing near the time that Christ's birth is commemorated, but it is appropriate for any season.

Hark! the herald angels sing,
"Glory to the newborn King;
Peace on earth, and mercy mild,
God and sinners reconciled!"
Joyful, all ye nations, rise,
Join the triumph of the skies;
With th'angelic host proclaim,
"Christ is born in Bethlehem!"
    Hark! the herald angels sing,
    "Glory to the newborn King."

Christ, by highest heav'n adored,
Christ, the everlasting Lord!

Late in time behold Him come,
Offspring of the Virgin's womb.
Veiled in flesh the Godhead see;
Hail th'incarnate Deity,
Pleased as man with men to dwell,
Jesus, our Emmanuel.
   Hark! the herald angels sing,
   "Glory to the newborn King."

Hail, the heav'n-born Prince of Peace!
Hail the Sun of Righteousness!
Light and life to all He brings,
Ris'n with healing in His wings.
Mild He lays His glory by,
Born that man no more may die,
Born to raise the sons of earth,
Born to give them second birth.
   Hark! the herald angels sing,
   "Glory to the newborn King."[8]

The Lord Jesus was "born that man no more may die." Charles Wesley died on March 28, 1788, and is buried in Marylebone churchyard, London. The church is gone, and all there is to see is a gravestone next to a busy London sidewalk. Imagine Charles's joy in the presence of the "Sun of Righteousness," in the glorious presence of the Prince of Peace, singing the praises of Jesus for endless days—no more to die!

---

8. Charles Wesley, "Hark! the Herald Angels Sing," in *Trinity Hymnal*, 203.

Study Questions

1. What role did Wesley's mother play in his preparation for ministry and for his prodigious hymn writing? What challenges was she forced to bear and how did she overcome them? What lessons can we as believers learn from her? What lessons might a believer who is married to an unsupportive and unbelieving spouse learn from her?

2. What particular concern did Wesley have that became obvious in his childhood? Is it ever right to roll up one's sleeves in the defense of the defenseless? What biblical boundaries regulate such an action?

3. Describe the experience John and Charles Wesley had on the voyage to the American colony in Georgia. How did this experience shape Charles's future priorities?

4. What is ironic about the theological content of the hymn versification written by John Wesley?

5. In one of Charles Wesley's hymns included in this chapter, he uses a prison metaphor. How is this consistent or inconsistent with his declared soteriology (doctrine of salvation)? What might this tell us about doxology and singing our praises before the face of God in worship?

6. Besides hymn writing, what other ministries did Charles immerse himself in throughout his life? How did his ministry grow out of the particular concerns for people that he displayed even in his childhood and at school?

~ 3 ~

Selina Hastings

1707–1791

Countess of Huntingdon

The Duchess of Richmond's Ball
ROBERT ALEXANDER HILLINGFORD

"Selina, may I have a word with you?" asked Lady Betty, Selina's sister-in-law. Betty took Selina's extended hand and led her from the middle of the exquisitely decorated dance hall lit with dozens of sparkling chandeliers to a side room. They passed by finely dressed gentlemen, some in red or blue military uniforms, dancing with noble ladies dressed in the sparkling embroidery of the mid-eighteenth century's latest fashions.

"What is it, sister?" asked Selina, half out of breath.

Lady Betty, first checking to see no one could overhear them, said, "I want to speak with you about your new friends. I do not have a good feeling about these Methodist preachers stirring up the common folk and preaching the most unimaginable things. The way you've been letting them carry on at your mansions is not reflecting well on you and I am not the only one who holds this opinion." Lady Betty was distressed that Selina seemed to be following in the footsteps of her sister, Lady Margaret Hastings, who had recently been "converted" through the preaching of Benjamin Ingham and was telling everyone about her new happiness in Christ.

"Listen, Betty"—Selina sighed, pausing to find words to answer. Like many of England's eighteenth-century nobility, Selina Hastings, the Countess of Huntingdon, was a loyal member of the Church of England. She had always been more serious about her religious practice than her peers were, devoting herself to prayer and works of charity. But when, at thirty-one years of age, she saw Margaret's new-found joy and dramatic change of life, Selina realized that she was a stranger to a true relationship with God.[1] When she had heard Ingham's message declaring that good works alone could never earn God's favor, that sinners had to be born again and trust in Christ's work alone for salvation, her confidence in her own righteousness had been shaken. And now, Selina thought, few of the nobility at this evening's social gathering would even believe what she herself had recently experienced.

____

1. The contents of this chapter are adapted from Gilbert Kirby, *The Elect Lady* (East Grinstead, W. Sussex: Trustees of the Countess of Huntingdon's Connexion, ca. 1972), 1–80; Faith Cook, *Selina, Countess of Huntingdon* (Edinburgh: Banner of Truth, 2001), 34–395; and Alan Harding, *Selina, Countess of Huntingdon* (Werrington, Peterborough: Epworth, 2007), 26–68, except as otherwise noted.

"I don't need an explanation," Betty interrupted before Selina could continue. "I have heard more than enough of this 'new birth' talk from Margaret. Just promise me one thing."

"Anything, sister," Selina said, realizing that now was not the time to battle as strong a will as Betty's.

"Promise me," Betty said, "that before you leave tonight, you will talk to Bishop Bernard and get some sensible advice." Bishop Thomas Bernard was a clergyman on close terms with Selina's family.

"I promise I will speak with him," Selina reassured her.

Later that evening, Selina found Bishop Bernard sitting in a quiet corner of the hall at a side table with an empty chair across from him, as if he'd been expecting someone.

"Dear Selina, how good it is to see you," Bernard said in a way that hinted he and Lady Betty had been speaking about her. After a few minutes of exchanging some customary small talk, Selina abruptly changed the subject.

"Sir, I realize that my new outlook on religion is no secret," she began. "But the recent change in my life is not because preachers persuaded me. I have always maintained the most devout religious practice—"

"Yes, Selina," interrupted Bernard. "This is what surprises me. I'd always thought that among the nobility you were the closest to the kingdom of heaven."

"But that precisely was my problem," Selina continued. "I pridefully relied on my own righteousness but found that even the best of my works is not free from sin, and I could never earn God's favor. My outward religion turned into a source of emptiness. And then I saw the change in Margaret. I've never seen anyone with more peace and joy. I began to think that I would be willing to endure anything to come to the true knowledge of my Savior."

"But Selina, you remember how seriously ill you were just weeks ago," Bernard explained. "Many people when faced with the possibility of death become overly serious about spiritual matters. It seems to me that when your illness began to subside, these Methodist preachers came to your home and stirred up extreme emotions in you by their troubling words. Perhaps your overexcitement has yet to wear off. Your state of mind will calm in due time." Bernard was right that Selina's most recent sickness had been the worst in the history of her frequent illnesses, especially because she was pregnant. But the change in her life was hardly rooted in spiritual "overexcitement."

Selina realized it was impossible to get Bernard to understand, but she began: "My change in heart had nothing to do with recovering from my illness. In fact, my body was still sick when God healed my soul. What happened was that one evening, when my soul was in great distress at my spiritual poverty, my heart was filled with an irresistible desire to cast myself entirely on Jesus Christ for salvation. I asked God to lead me to trust in Christ's righteousness and not my own. When I stood up from my prayers, I instantly knew that I was a new woman. All my distress had disappeared in the shadow of the cross. My illness lingered for some days after, but though sick in body, I knew that by His wounds my soul had been healed."

Bernard shifted in his seat and adjusted his collar. "Well, I cannot pretend to understand what you experienced," he admitted. "But I will respectfully offer my advice to you, Countess. A person of your rank should not associate too closely with these Methodists or disclose too many of her feelings to them. Don't make any sudden changes in your way of life. Keep clear of emotional extremes—great despair on one side, or excessive zeal on the other. And limit the time you give to prayer or other spiritual commitments. Moderation will help you find that happy middle ground you once knew."

"Dear sir," Selina said loud enough to be overheard and standing up from her chair, "I hope never to 'find' that 'happy' middle ground again. I have put my hand to the plough. The Lord is at work and the Lord is at hand. I dare not slacken my hands in His vineyard. We must all be up and doing. Let us encourage each other, sir, to diligence and faithfulness."[2] She bade Bernard a good evening and walked away.

This was the last time Selina sought spiritual advice from the bishop.[3] And it was just the beginning of Selina's life of furthering gospel work in extraordinary ways in the eighteenth-century revival in England and beyond.

Early Life

Selina Shirley was born in 1707 in Staunton Harold, Leicestershire, England. She came from a distinguished family that traced its ancestry back to King Edward the Confessor, whose death in AD 1066 provoked the Norman invasion of England. Early eighteenth-century England was a place where the contrasts between rich and poor were sharp, crime was common, true religion was rare, and immorality was rampant among all classes.

---

2. Jacob Kirkman Foster, *The Life and Times of Selina, Countess of Huntingdon* (London: William Edward Painter, 1839), 1:79.

3. Bernard's comments above are taken from actual statements written in three letters he exchanged with Selina (July–October 1739).

Selina and her two sisters had a wealthy, aristocratic upbringing, but her childhood was filled with the pain of a broken family. When Selina was six years old, her parents separated due to disputes over money and her father's infidelity. Additionally, her father was embroiled in property disputes with her stepmother's family that continued unresolved until Selina was eighteen.

Selina was a serious-minded child. When she was nine years old, she witnessed a funeral service for a girl her age, which made a lasting impression on her. In her childhood years she was considered "God-fearing" and was known to hide herself in corners of the house privately to pour out the troubles of her heart to God. Her upbringing was preparing her to play the important role of a noble lady in society, but she was not impressed by the social functions and privileges of her high rank. When she could get away, she would retire to a quiet place to read her Bible.

Marriage and Conversion

On June 3, 1728, Selina was married to Theophilus Hastings, the ninth Earl of Huntingdon. Theophilus was a good match for Selina, who had prayed since childhood that she might marry into a serious-minded family. The two loved each other: Theophilus recognized her excellent character qualities, and Selina's affection for him was lifelong. Their first child,

Selina Hastings

Theophilus Hastings

Francis, was born in 1729 and was followed by George a year later. Five more children were born to the couple, but only three survived infancy. Selina's marriage, which gave her the title Countess of Huntingdon, brought her into an even wider circle of high society. Her preference, however, was to retreat to the quiet of her home, Donington Park. Though she sometimes hosted high-profile guests such as the composer George Frideric Handel, she more often could be found attending to the needs of the less-privileged individuals who made up the estate population.

Sometime in 1739, as Methodist ministers such as George Whitefield were boldly preaching the need for repentance, faith in Christ, a new birth, and a personal walk with Christ, Selina was converted. Her change in life was dramatic, and she openly confessed her new-found faith in Christ at every opportunity. Among the nobility, however, the word *Methodist* was an insult, and many of Selina's peers thought the Methodists had turned her into an "enthusiast" or fanatic. Yet her sister, Lady Margaret, who had been converted shortly before Selina, rejoiced and asked Methodist preacher Benjamin Ingham to visit the Earl and Lady Selina to further instruct them in the faith. Selina and her husband began to study the Bible, and soon a change was evident in Theophilus as well.

By 1742 Selina and her husband were regularly going to hear Whitefield, the Wesley brothers, and other Methodists preach in and around London. Selina invited many ladies of rank to these meetings but met with resistance to a message that many of the nobility considered to be beneath them. On one occasion, the Duchess of Buckingham told Selina that such preaching was offensive and insulting to the wealthy and the socially adept.

Selina also turned her home into a center of evangelism, bringing the gospel to all classes of people. While her drawing rooms were full of lords, ladies, philosophers, doctors, and poets, her kitchen was full of the poor whom she loved and served, and Congregationalist minister Philip Doddridge, author of the Christian classic *The Rise and Progress of Religion in the Soul*, noted that "Lady Huntingdon is quite a mother to the poor; she visits them and prays with them in their sickness."[4] She had a tremendous impact on the nobility and the poor alike, directing all to Jesus Christ as the only remedy for their sin and guilt. On the passage where Paul writes, "not many mighty, not many noble, are called" (1 Cor. 1:26), it is said that Selina remarked, "I owe my salvation to the letter 'm'; blessed be God, it does not say, 'any' mighty, 'any' noble; it says 'many' mighty, 'many' noble."[5]

Selina's life with Theophilus at Donington Park was happy, but soon dark clouds of trial filled her life. She had frequent illnesses and a difficult family life. Her father died a month after her first son was born, which made her responsible for ongoing property disputes with her stepmother's family. Around this time Selina's mother disowned her out of bitterness toward Selina's father. Of Selina's seven children, only one child, Elizabeth, outlived her, and even this child would eventually distance herself from Selina out of disagreement with her religious views. Not long after the death of two of her young sons, Theophilus died of a stroke in 1746, leaving Selina a single parent with a large family to care for. She was thirty-nine years old. Despite these losses and bereavements and the contempt of many in her social circle for her faith, Selina pressed forward undaunted. She was strengthened by the grace of God and the love of Christ in the power of the Holy Spirit to use her social position to advance the spread of the gospel.

Methodists and Chapels

After the death of her husband, Selina resisted the temptation to retreat quietly into retirement. Depending on God's strength, she cast herself fully into the work of the Lord.

Selina found herself in the middle of the eighteenth-century revival led by preachers such as George Whitefield, Howell Harris, Benjamin Ingham, and the Wesley brothers, John and Charles. They were dubbed Methodists because they stressed a "holy method" or disciplined way of Christian living. They were derisively called "enthusiasts" because they stressed the necessity of the Holy Spirit's work in salvation. For a long time, these Methodists were loyal to the Church of England and hoped to breathe spiritual life back into a national church that had fallen into dead, formal religion.

Soon after her conversion, Selina appointed George Whitefield as her chaplain, began a friendship with the Wesley brothers, and sought ways to support the growing

---

4. Foster, *The Life and Times of Selina*, 1:86.

5. Cited in Joseph Parker, *The People's Bible: Discourses upon Holy Scripture* (New York: Funk and Wagnalls Co., 1895), 26:191.

network of Methodist societies and preachers. Selina increasingly became a "cloak of protection" for Methodist preachers when Church of England authorities discountenanced them, broke up their meetings, or tried to bar them from evangelizing. As a result of Selina's influence, King George III sent her a letter declaring that "the King, as father and protector of the people, would permit no persecution to take place on account of religion; and that all magistrates shall be requested to afford protection to those who require it in the discharge of their religious observances."[6]

In addition to protecting preachers, Selina always watched for opportunities to begin new gospel works. Without the countess's influence, John Wesley might not have brought the gospel to the coal miners in 1742, who were described as lawless and violent, just as Whitefield had preached to the "unreachable" Kingswood coal miners a few years earlier.

Once, while visiting Brighton for her son Henry's health, Selina paid a visit to a soldier's wife who lay dying after giving birth to twins. Selina testified to her about her sinful state and the looming danger she faced if she died "unpardoned, unrenewed, and unwashed in the Savior's blood." The soldier's wife burst into tears under a sense of her guilt and misery. As she lay dying, she began to call on the name of the Lord with all the strength she could muster. Selina's words to the dying woman were overheard through a crack in the wall, and soon a small group of women, and later many townspeople, asked to hear the countess speak of the gospel. Months later, Selina found out that these people had formed a society in the town. Seeing a great gospel opportunity in Brighton, a popular health resort, Selina built her first chapel for use of the Brighton society right next to her own home in 1761. She paid for this chapel by selling her jewels for about a thousand pounds. Much evangelical preaching sounded forth from the chapel pulpit, and the response was so positive that six years later the chapel had to be enlarged. In 1774 it had to be rebuilt because the congregation again outgrew it.[7]

The countess continued to build chapels to serve as preaching stations in different locations for Methodist preachers. The second chapel Selina built was outside Brighton at Oat Hall to serve the country folk and farm workers who had a hard time coming into Brighton for services. William Romaine's ministry thrived at Oat Hall.

Selina built another chapel at a fashionable inland resort called Tunbridge Wells, along with others in Sussex and Bath, in 1765. More chapels followed, some making use of existing buildings that were repurposed as places of worship. From the 1760s onward, there was a remarkable work of the Spirit of God across the country, and Selina continued to put all of her considerable resources at the disposal of this revival.

The 1770s were some of Selina's most fruitful years. She made sure her chapels were continually supplied with gospel preachers. One of her ministers, John Berridge, encouraged her: "Go on, my dear lady, build and fight manfully…. Look upwards and press forwards. Heaven's eternal hills are before you, and Jesus stands with arms wide open

---

6. Alfred H. New, *Memoir of Selina, Countess of Huntingdon*, rev. ed. (New York: Protestant Episcopal Society for the Promotion of Evangelical Knowledge, 1858), 76–77. The letter is dated November 19, 1745.

7. It was an imposing structure in the middle of Brighton until it was demolished in 1969.

Selina's chapel in Bath
MIKE PEEL, CC BY-SA 4.0

to receive you."[8] By 1788 the countess was responsible for a network of 116 chapels. She also began to oversee several foreign missionaries whose work had a lasting impact in other lands.[9]

Trevecca College

The revival was spreading farther and faster than the first generation of aging but tireless revivalists could keep up with, making the demand for new preachers an urgent concern. When six students were expelled from Oxford as

___

8. Foster, *The Life and Times of Selina*, 2:95.

9. When George Whitefield died, he left his orphan house in Georgia to the care of the countess. Selina took a deep interest in the work, and in October 1772, three of her students were commissioned as missionaries to the American colonies. The orphan house was in a sad state when the missionaries arrived. They did what they could there, and also made evangelistic trips to other communities, spreading the gospel among both Native Americans and African Americans. Invitations for her missionaries to do further work came from all parts of the American colonies. This was the time shortly before the outbreak of the Revolutionary War, when feelings ran high in the colonies. Only months after her missionaries arrived, the orphanage in Georgia was destroyed by fire, either by lightning or by arson. The countess closed the Georgia mission project and called her missionaries to return home. After the war, the countess resumed overseeing missions work to the Native Americans. Many African Americans were also converted and took advantage of a government-chartered ship carrying slaves back to Africa, to Sierra Leone. At least half of the two thousand African Americans taken to Sierra Leone in 1792 were associated with the Countess of Huntingdon's Connexion. Fifty years later, in 1839, a Connexion church in Whitechapel was pleasantly surprised to get a visit from two members of a Connexion church across the globe in Sierra Leone, which England had forgotten about. The Connexion churches in Sierra Leone were never supported from the outside but were entirely self-supporting. It was not until 1899 that the first European "missionary" went to observe the work in that country.

Trevecca College
ENGRAVED BY JOSEPH CROSS

"enthusiasts" because they spoke of being born again and walking close to God, it became clear to Selina that there needed to be a better way to train ministers than sending them to Oxford and Cambridge, the only centers of higher learning in England at the time where men could train for the Anglican ministry. The countess began praying that God would bless a plan for a new school, a "nursery for preachers," to be built for the training of ministers for her chapels and beyond.[10]

God's answer to these prayers began unfolding in August 1768, when the countess found a building for the new school, Trevecca College, near Talgarth in Wales, where Welsh evangelist Howell Harris lived. The countess, along

___

10. In 1753, the countess had offered support for the establishment of the College of New Jersey, a school dedicated to the training of men for the Presbyterian ministry. This school would later become Princeton University. She also supported what would become Dartmouth College in New Hampshire.

with many evangelicals at the time, believed that the revivals they were witnessing may have been early signs of the return of the Lord and, therefore, that ministerial training needed to be efficient. Trevecca's curriculum thus did not focus on a heavy academic reading load, though it did include courses such as Greek, Latin, and church history. The course of study focused more on practical ministry, personal spirituality, and the work of preaching. Students would do itinerant ministry for weeks at a time or briefly supply the pulpit in one of the countess's chapels. Since Selina fed and clothed the students at her own expense, she also oversaw the candidate selection process, preaching assignments, and other daily matters involving the students.

One of the six students expelled from Oxford, Joseph Shipman, was among the first students at Trevecca College. John W. Fletcher was its first president and George Whitefield preached the opening-day sermon. Selina could write in 1776, "The Lord is powerfully at work by the College in most of the counties of England and Wales."[11]

Parting of the Ways

When John Wesley preached and published a sermon against predestination in 1740, George Whitefield answered with a sermon addressing Wesley's errors, causing a public dispute to break out between the men. The countess played the role of mediator between her two friends, urging them to strive for Christian unity, though she shared Whitefield's Calvinism and firmly disagreed with Wesley's Arminianism.

11. After the countess's death, the college was moved near London in 1791. In 1905 the college moved to Cambridge.

For a time, Selina was able to work with both Calvinistic and Arminian Methodists as she supported the work of the revival. However, in 1770 the Calvinistic and Arminian branches within the Methodist revival parted ways for good.[12]

For Selina this was a time of sadness and struggle. While these divisions were breaking partnerships and souring relationships, George Whitefield, one of Selina's most trusted chaplains, passed away in America. Now in her mid-sixties, the countess would begin to rely less on the input and guidance of her chaplains and more on her own convictions and decisions in the work ahead.

Driven Out of the Church of England

The bishops of the Church of England were generally hostile to Methodist preachers and often used their power to shut down unauthorized religious activities in the parishes they ruled.[13] They threatened to close the network of cha-

12. John Wesley publicly aired the doctrinal differences between his Arminian Methodists and the Calvinistic Methodists by publishing the *Minutes* from his twenty-seventh annual conference. A poor use of language in the *Minutes* led many to think Wesley was lessening the importance of the imputed righteousness of Christ for salvation. This misunderstanding, along with Wesley's unclear treatment of key doctrines and his active anti-Calvinism, led the countess to ban him from preaching in her chapels and to require all staff at Trevecca College to renounce Wesley's 1770 *Minutes*. The countess accused Wesley of stoking an Arminian-Calvinist divide and saw herself as one who always "sought to maintain peace and unity in the household of God." But division spread. In 1771 Joseph Benson, the language tutor at the college, resigned, unwilling to reject Wesley's *Minutes*. John Fletcher also resigned from the college's presidency in protest of Benson's departure and because of pressure from John Wesley to distance himself from the Calvinists.

13. One of Selina's strategies for working around the bishops'

pels Lady Selina had been building for decades, forcing the countess to leave the Church of England.[14] In 1782 she officially registered as a Dissenter. The countess and two ministers then drew up a confession of fifteen articles that combined the Westminster Confession with the Anglican Thirty-Nine Articles to guide her new denomination, now known as "The Countess of Huntingdon's Connexion."[15]

No longer a member of the Church of England, the countess was free to propose men from Trevecca as candidates for ordination without the bishops' permission. She still preferred, however, that those preaching in her chapels seek ordination in the Church of England. When Selina separated from the national church in 1782 there were 251 dissenting churches in England, but her daring move emboldened others to do the same, so that by the 1790s there were 832 dissenting churches.[16]

Death and Legacy

Even as Selina's body weakened with age and illness, her mind was as clear and quick as ever. She remained involved in the affairs of her college, chapels, and ministers up until the time of her death in June 1791, at the age of eighty-four.

Selina's impact on the success of the eighteenth-century English revival is remarkable. Without her involvement, the revival may never have gained the acceptance it did among the nobility. She used her high rank in society to advance the kingdom of God. In a time when the nobility was seen almost as a superhuman class of people, her support for the Methodist cause was a great source of encouragement for evangelical ministers.

---

authority in her effort to multiply evangelical preaching in England was to use her right as a noble lady to build private chapels attached to her houses and appoint preachers as "personal chaplains" to preach in them. When Selina opened Spa Fields chapel in Clerkenwell, London, in 1779, she appointed two preachers who ministered to a congregation of five thousand. The vicar of the nearby parish, however, began a legal attack against Selina's preachers in church courts. The judge sided with the vicar, arguing that a private chapel should serve only family and friends, not thousands of city dwellers. This decision was devastating, not only because Selina had to vacate the Spa Fields chapel but also because the future of every chapel she had established for evangelical preaching in the last forty years was now in jeopardy. The court decision meant that any local church official could silence any of Selina's preachers within his jurisdiction. Selina now had a difficult decision to make. Up to this point, she had been a loyal member of the Church of England, but now she faced losing all of her chapels unless she registered them as Dissenting churches and got protection under the Toleration Act of 1689. For a lady of her social rank, loyal to the Church of England, to become a Dissenter was almost unthinkable.

14. She said, "I am to be cast out of the church now, only for what I have been doing these forty years—speaking and living for Jesus Christ! And if the days of my captivity are now to be accomplished, those that turn me out, and so set me at liberty may soon feel what it is, by sore distress themselves, for those hard services they have caused me…. I have asked none to go with me—and none that do not come willingly to the help of the Lord, and by faith in the Son of God lay all at His feet—any other would do me no good, and He only knows these." New, *Memoir of Selina*, 399–400.

15. The countess's "Connexion" was represented by a large number of preachers, Dissenters, clergymen, and supporters. Concerned about

the continued support of her work after her death, she made out a will in 1790 that appointed four trustees (Thomas Haweis and his wife and Lady Anne Erskine and her husband) to be responsible for all the properties and operations in the Connexion. Until then, she had personally overseen every aspect of the work. Lady Anne, in particular, was suited for this role, as her thinking (courage and catholicity) was closest to the countess's. See https://www.cofhconnexion.org.uk/about-us for the current status of the Connexion.

16. Wesley's churches seceded in 1784, gaining the freedom to ordain their own ministers.

Regretfully, the countess's life experience as an aristocrat led her to be somewhat forceful in her personality and domineering in her leadership. Some criticized her for holding unbiblical sway over the affairs of the ministers, churches, and mission efforts under her care, sometimes making important decisions on the basis of nothing more than her personal opinion.[17] Some of her decisions such as banning Wesley from her chapels, though necessary for the truth's sake, weakened the overall evangelical cause.

Nevertheless, Selina was far ahead of her times in her unceasing pursuit of new ways of bringing the gospel to people of all classes, accomplishing an astonishing amount of work through many struggles, disappointments, and illnesses. She outlived her dear friend and chaplain, George Whitefield, and both of the Wesleys. Her early biographer Alfred H. New referred to her as the last of the revivalists.

Study Questions

1. What difficulties among her peers in her social rank did Selina have to face as she was following the upward call of God in Christ Jesus? What kinds of opposition can you as a follower of Christ expect in a world that may not understand the path God has for you?

2. What were some of the trials in Selina's life? What might a person of her rank and resources have done in response to such suffering? What did she do instead? What does this teach us about the power of God living in weakened vessels? Think of 2 Corinthians 4:7–9.

3. What are some ways in which the countess demonstrated generosity and sacrifice for the sake of the work of the gospel? In our age of Western prosperity, how can we better give of our resources for the spread of the gospel and the glory of God? Why is it so rare for Christians who have the most to give the most for the kingdom? Think of Luke 7:36–50.

4. How did Selina solve the problem of there being too few preachers to meet the demand of the eighteenth-century revival? What should this teach us about the power of the prayerful initiative of even one Christian?

5. Why is Selina described as a "reluctant" Dissenter? What can we learn from her in our day when many who experience difficulties in churches think of separating from the church as a first reflex rather than as a last resort?

---

17. One example was her single-handed dismissal of a popular preacher at Spa Fields, Thomas Wills, for expressing doubts about Selina's leadership.

Daniel Rowland

1711–1790

In the winter of 1735, Griffith Jones, renowned forerunner of the Welsh Great Awakening, was preaching in a churchyard in Cardiganshire, Wales.[1] A large crowd of men, women, and children, who could not fit in the church, listened attentively to the preacher even as the cold winter air swirled around them. But another wind was gathering force. Just as Christ said that "the wind bloweth where it listeth" (John 3:8), the Spirit of God was about to fall on an unsuspecting heart. With tears, Jones preached about repentance from sin and faith in Jesus Christ, warning the crowd that unless they were born again, it was impossible for them to enter heaven. Jones knew that only the Spirit could penetrate the rock-hard heart of man.

As Jones preached, he noticed one young man who seemed especially stiff-necked. This young man was acting restless, distracted, and rebellious, almost as if he was *trying* to disrupt the service. Surprisingly, the young man was an Anglican clergyman named Daniel Rowland, a curate in a nearby parish.[2] He was twenty-two years old and known by all to be a religiously lukewarm, worldly-minded jokester. Like many of his peers in the clergy, Rowland was hostile to those who preached the new birth and a Spirit-worked life change. He seemed to *want* Jones to know that he and his message were not welcome. The reason the congregation was meeting outside may even have been Rowland's doing.[3]

Griffith Jones (1684–1761)

---

1. This took place at either Llangeitho, Nantcwnlle, or Llanddewi Brefi parish. If it was in Llanddewi Brefi, Rowland would not have been curate but may have preached there on occasion.

2. A curate is a clergyman in the church of England charged with the care of souls in a church parish.

3. It was in the churchyard either because the crowds were too great or because the

Jones observed the young man for a moment. Then, pointing at Rowland, Jones exclaimed with an expression of gentle compassion, "Oh, for a word to reach your heart, young man!" Some in the crowd near Rowland glanced at him. Others silently prayed for him in their hearts. Rowland soon stopped acting rebellious and restless. For the rest of the sermon, he listened attentively and seriously. At first, Rowland felt ashamed as a clergyman to be called out for his misbehavior; but shame soon melted into conviction as the truth of Jones's message began to penetrate his heart.

After that day, Rowland would never be the same. Neither would Wales! No longer a mocker, Rowland wanted to be a follower and sought out Jones as his spiritual mentor. Once hostile to the gospel of Christ, Rowland was to become one of the greatest gospel champions that Wales has ever known.[4]

Early Life and Ministry Beginnings

Daniel Rowland was born in 1711 in Nantcwnlle,[5] South Wales. When he was a young child, he survived a near-death experience when a large stone fell from the top of a chimney onto a spot where he had been sitting by the fireplace a few minutes earlier.[6] Rowland was intelligent, lively, and

Daniel Rowland

athletic, but as a young man he was known for his levity and worldliness. He was short of stature but rugged and tough. When he was ordained as deacon in 1734 by the bishop of St. David's at Duke Street Chapel in London, he walked the nearly four-hundred-mile round trip from Wales to London and back. A short time afterward, he married Elinor, a pious farmer's daughter of Puritan-style upbringing.

Rowland's first ministry assignment was as a curate for the Llangeitho and Nantcwnlle parishes. His first sermons were nothing more than short essays on striving for moral

---

church was refused to Griffith Jones by the Rowland brothers, who were hostile to the gospel for some time.

4. Eifion Evans, *Daniel Rowland and the Great Evangelical Awakening in Wales* (Edinburgh: Banner of Truth, 1985), 33–34. For a summary of this book, see "Daniel Rowland," UK Wells, https://ukwells.org/revivalists /daniel-rowland.

5. This unusual spelling is possible because in the Welsh language *w* is a semi-vowel.

6. Evans, *Daniel Rowland*, 29.

goodness and keeping God's law. He was a stranger to God's grace.[7]

But when Rowland's life was turned upside down through the Spirit-worked preaching of the gospel, his own ministry was transformed. Rowland's wife, Elinor, was greatly encouraged by Rowland's change of heart and life. She reached out to Phillip Pugh, a godly minister and family friend, to help mentor Rowland along with Griffith Jones.[8]

The first thing to change about Rowland was that he began to study much harder to understand God's Word. Though burdened with the responsibility of running two farms and helping raise his newborn son, Rowland made time for diligent study. He nearly studied himself into exhaustion. Years later, his son confirmed that his father had memorized most of the Bible.

The second change was that Rowland began to preach thundering sermons on the law, sin, and hell. So fiery was his preaching that he became known as "the angry preacher." He was sharing his newfound personal conviction of the majesty of God and the reality of sin, but Phillip Pugh advised the newly converted preacher, "Preach the Gospel to the people, dear Sir, and apply the Balm of Gilead, the blood of Christ, to their spiritual wounds, and show the necessity of faith in the crucified Saviour."

"I am afraid," replied Rowland, "that I have not the faith myself in its vigour and full exercise."

"Preach on it," said Pugh, "till you feel it in that way; no doubt it will come. If you go on preaching the law in this manner, you will kill half the people in the country, for you thunder out the curses of the law, and preach in such a terrific manner, that no-one can stand before you." Rowland took the advice. He began inviting sinners to Christ by the free offer of grace in the gospel to be received by Spirit-given faith (Eph. 2:8–10).[9]

Once in these early days, a known troublemaker walked into one of Rowland's services intending on disrupting it. He defiantly stood up on a pew as Rowland began his sermon. Rowland went on preaching as usual. The words of truth were so heart cutting and convicting that the troublemaker soon sat down, sobbing, and the rest of the congregation was greatly convicted as well.[10]

Rowland and Welsh Methodism

The Great Awakening in Wales was a time of powerful conversions in great numbers through the preaching of Daniel Rowland and Howell Harris, who were dubbed Methodists.[11] Opponents to this revival were other "moderate" Welsh Anglicans, who called Christians only to outward religious observance and self-righteous morality, and Dissenters, who loved head knowledge and thought preaching

---

7. Evans, *Daniel Rowland*, 30–31.

8. Evans, *Daniel Rowland*, 38.

9. Evans, *Daniel Rowland*, 43.

10. Evans, *Daniel Rowland*, 39. Even this lopsided mode of preaching was used with great effect; see also p. 42.

11. The Great Awakening was becoming an identifiable movement within Wales. Jonathan Edwards's *Narrative of Surprising Conversions* reached England in 1737. Harris read it in 1738 and was amazed at the similarity of what was happening across the Atlantic. Soon, in 1739, George Whitefield sent him a letter describing revivals in and around London. The Welsh Methodists publicly identified with Whitefield's Calvinist theology in 1739. Ministers across the country were understanding that God was involved in an extraordinary work. Evans, *Daniel Rowland*, 91.

doctrine was the same as preaching Christ. Rowland and other Methodists, however, walked the narrow path between both errors, preaching a Spirit-worked change of heart in regeneration—a power "to make the living Christ real to the soul"—and the goal of living in "lively spirituality as well as strict orthodoxy and morality."[12]

People often misunderstood and persecuted the Methodists. When they preached that men had to be born again by the work of the Holy Spirit, people regarded it as fanaticism; when they declared that man is justified only by faith and not by works, many reacted from hurt spiritual pride; and when they taught that sanctification is an inward work of the Holy Spirit on the heart rather than the performance of outward duties and rituals, they were greatly offended to think their duties counted for nothing.[13]

Welsh Methodist leader Howell Harris heard Rowland preach in 1737, and the two instantly became friends and coworkers in the revival. Although Harris was not a clergyman, Rowland often let him preach in his parish. Both men held Griffith Jones to be their mentor.

As they worked together, large numbers of people were being converted through revivalists' preaching. They began setting up "societies," groups or bands of new converts in various locales organized to meet together for mutual edification. By 1740 there were over fifty societies in South Wales.[14] Harris traveled more frequently and widely—often to London and other English cities. While Rowland traveled to preach in different locations on occasion, he kept his ministry much closer to his home parish of Llangeitho.[15]

Unlike the Wesley brothers, Rowland, Harris, and the Welsh Methodists were Calvinists in their understanding of God's free grace in salvation. In 1739 Rowland preached from Ezekiel 33:11, saying, "Think not with the Arminians that you can be a devil today and a saint tomorrow; you cannot repent when you choose. Therefore, the time is *now,* because it is God's gift."[16] Thirty leaders of Welsh Methodism affirmed Calvinism as their unifying doctrine when they gathered in 1741 for an early association meeting. They also agreed to stay within the Church of England in Wales in order to reform it, unless it cast them out.[17] Rowland was soon recognized as the leader of the Welsh Methodists. George Whitefield visited Wales often, and Welsh and English Calvinistic Methodism were seen as one movement.

Persecution and Expansion

Since Methodism was unacceptable to many people in Wales, Harris and Rowland were regularly attacked by violent mobs. Someone once attempted to shoot Rowland. Another time he had to run for his life as people threw stones

---

12. Evans, *Daniel Rowland*, 185, 373.

13. Evans, *Daniel Rowland*, 375.

14. Evans, *Daniel Rowland*, 57, 71, 94, 120.

15. Rowland once reproved Harris in a (1742) letter, saying, "Don't you hear all the brethren in Wales crying out loudly, 'Help! help! help! Brother Harris, thou bold champion, where art thou? What, in London now, now in the day of battle?" Evans, *Daniel Rowland*, 100–101.

16. Evans, *Daniel Rowland*, 129.

17. Rowland came to an understanding of Calvinism independent of George Whitefield. Evans, *Daniel Rowland*, 157, 125. The Welsh Methodist association began to build society houses to avoid legal harassment. Unlike the English Methodists, the Welsh Methodists enjoyed doctrinal unity. Evans, *Daniel Rowland*, 228, 251.

The first Methodist association, chaired by George Whitefield and attended by Rowland and others

and attacked him with bats. Some even planned to blow up Rowland, but the plan was discovered and stopped.[18] Other Methodists such as Howel Davies and William Williams were persecuted by church courts that limited their activities or refused to ordain them even though they met all requirements. A frequent accusation against the Methodists was that they roamed the land and preached outside their parish bounds, which was a serious offense in the Anglican Church. Sadly, the Anglican backlash made Griffith Jones distance himself from Rowland and Harris, though he otherwise supported their work.[19]

In response to persecution, Rowland once preached from Romans 8:28: "O sinners! What do you mean by persecuting the people of God? If you propose to smother…the spark of fire which the Lord has kindled in our hearts, your purpose will never succeed…. It is fire from heaven; and the more the rain descends on it, the more it will blaze…. Let them alone: the Spirit of God in them is more than a match for hell and all its black battalions. These stars shine brightest when the night is darkest."[20] Rowland would soon find out just how correct this was.

By the start of 1743, as persecution intensified, Rowland's ministry became more powerful. Upon hearing Rowland preach, George Whitefield wrote, "The power of God…under the ministry of Mr. Rowland, was enough to make a person's heart burn within him. At seven in the morning I have seen, perhaps, 10,000 from different parts, in the midst of the sermon, crying 'glory,' 'praise,' ready to leap for joy."[21]

Rowland the Preacher

Rowland was known for such unusually powerful preaching that some people assumed that his sermons were written directly by inspiration of the Spirit! Once when someone recognized Rowland in a bookstore, he said to him, "What! Do you, the most eminent divine, come here to buy books? I thought you had the Spirit of God to study His Word and compose your sermon!" The fact was that Rowland was an avid reader of the Puritans and also relied on the work of contemporary theologians such as Ebenezer Erskine.[22]

Rowland also translated and promoted good books to help new converts cultivate a "truly Methodist mind" that was God-centered, Calvinistic, and engaged with the world. Rowland and William Williams published hymnbooks and translated into Welsh works such as John Bunyan's *Holy War*; Whitefield's sermon on Genesis 5:24, "Enoch Walked with God"; and Elisha Coles's *A Practical Discourse of God's Sovereignty.*

Rowland's preaching was simple and powerful. His sermons were brief and wisely applied a wide variety of biblical texts.[23] "There was such a vehement, invincible flame in his ministry" that it "dispelled and drove away the careless,

---

18. Evans, *Daniel Rowland*, 126, 162.

19. Evans, *Daniel Rowland*, 140–43, 149. Jones used to defend Rowland and Harris before the bishop, but now his departure made them even more vulnerable to persecution. For instance, Rowland was unjustly slandered in a newspaper article in 1741, accusing him of personally profiting from preaching. Evans, *Daniel Rowland*, 151.

20. Evans, *Daniel Rowland*, 119; see also Rowland, *Eight Sermons*, 87–96.

21. Evans, *Daniel Rowland*, 165.

22. Evans, *Daniel Rowland*, 118, 251, 358.

23. Evans, *Daniel Rowland*, 167–68.

worldly, dead spirit.... Eternity and its amazing realities were rushing into their minds."[24]

He would begin his sermons with a striking idea; then, after dividing the text, he would start with the first point. After glancing at his notes, he would preach at first in a calm, deliberate manner; soon his voice would rise with the conviction of the subject until "it resounded through the whole chapel! The effect on the people was wonderful; you could see nothing but smiles and tears running down the faces of all" as he applied "the glorious truths of the gospel." He would then "conclude with a few very striking and forcible remarks."[25]

An example of his experiential preaching is found in his sermon on Revelation 3:18:

If we sin, we shall not enjoy God's presence, and that is the heaviest judgment of all.... [Here are] the causes of our lukewarmness: complaints and murmurings and all spiritual distempers, and it is because we go out of Christ's righteousness. When we are out of His love we are full of sin. All things harden the wicked for hell and ripen the godly for heaven. When the distemper is in thy soul, thou art angry even with the stones of the way, and with thine own feet under thee, and this is when God hides His face. But when He returns again, all crosses and pain vanish. This is food for you that are spiritual, but nothing to you that are all flesh.... Because thou art so poor, come to

Christ. Do not say, "I am sinful and therefore depart from me!" That is Satan's doctrine.[26]

In another sermon on 1 Corinthians 7:35, Rowland observed that "lukewarmness and wandering thoughts are like stones that interrupt the channel. You shiver with cold, when God is a fire. You are hungering with famine and Christ is all food. You are thirsty and He is water to refresh you. Come up, then, nearer to God and don't stand off.... Give your soul to Christ that you may have victory over your sinful thoughts and not they over you. For this power is in grace to overcome all these: they can't stand before the Wind."[27]

Rowland preached that salvation is of God, not of man: "If God does not pluck us as brands out of the burning fire, by His free grace, and remove by His Spirit the veil of darkness and ignorance from our minds, none can be saved."[28]

Rowland's life was a picture of what the psalmist said: "I give myself unto prayer" (Ps. 109:4). For Rowland, prayer was sweet communion with God as well as a way to submit himself and his preaching to the power of the Holy Spirit. Due to the hardness of fallen man's heart, Rowland knew that without the Spirit's power, his ministry was nothing. "Mankind have brazen foreheads, adamantine necks, and ribs of marble around their hearts," he said. "They bleed not, they bend not, they blush not. Now the Word is a hammer, which breaks the rock within them; and the Holy Spirit is the Fire, which dissolves and melts it." Praying for the Spirit's grace to save sinners, Rowland also petitioned the Spirit

24. Evans, *Daniel Rowland*, 171–73.
25. Evans, *Daniel Rowland*, 360.

26. Evans, *Daniel Rowland*, 189.
27. Evans, *Daniel Rowland*, 193–94.
28. Evans, *Daniel Rowland*, 374.

to prepare him as a preacher. He often refused to preach until he felt that God had prepared him and his message.[29] So, before his public services, Rowland constantly prayed in private.

Once before a service at Llanbadarn Odwyn church, which sits atop a hill, the congregation could see Rowland leave his home and walk up the hill to the church. But as the people watched Rowland ascend the hill, they lost sight of him in a grove of trees. They waited; the time for the service passed. When some searched for him, they found him praying in the woods. He gladly told them of the sweet time of communion he had enjoyed with God and that he was now ready to preach.[30]

Friction and Flourishing

The relationship between Rowland and Harris teaches us that the world, the devil, and the flesh will always oppose great works of God. As Rowland and Harris worked closely together in revival, by early 1742, friction between them surfaced when Harris began struggling with pride, envy of Rowland, and disagreements over ministry. The two were able to keep working together until 1749, when Harris began to fall into unbiblical doctrines and practices. He began avowing direct guidance by God's voice, and he traveled with a woman who claimed to be a prophetess, though Harris himself was married. Rowland accused Harris of elevating "his own authority above that of Scripture, whether in matters of belief or behaviour." After the Welsh Methodist association meeting in 1750, the two men went their separate ways.

Howell Harris (1714-1773),
one of the leaders of the revival

Harris withdrew to isolation in his hometown, Trevecca, to lead a community of followers who lived and farmed together.[31] He resisted the pleas of the Wesley brothers and

---

29. Evans, *Daniel Rowland*, 373–74.

30. Evans, *Daniel Rowland*, 256–57.

31. "The great difference between Rowland and Harris, between Llangeitho and Trefeca [in the 1750s] is significant. People journeyed to Llangeitho to Rowland's powerful ministry fully resolved to return to live out their Christian lives in the place and calling chosen for them by God. Those who went to Trefeca did so with the intention of withdrawing from the world into a spiritual community." Rowland took the fight to enemy territory; Harris kept the fight in his soul and in those who joined him. So "Rowland displayed the God-centered quality of a

other friends to humble himself and come back to the work of revival.[32]

While Harris was in isolation, Welsh Methodists continued the revival work in harmony under Rowland's leadership. In 1751 Rowland preached with Whitefield to vast crowds in Bristol. From the 1750s into the early 1760s, Rowland's ministry expanded and flourished.[33] In the early 1760s, God also brought Harris to greater humility. Harris said that he was ready to come out of isolation and serve the work of the revival again, viewing himself to be "less by millions of degrees than Whitefield, the Wesleys, and Rowland."[34]

The year 1773 saw both a sunset and a sunrise in Welsh Methodism: Howell Harris died and Thomas Charles was born again to eternal life. Harris had been an untiring, zealous preacher of the gospel. His life was one of struggle for the sake of the gospel against persecution, opposition, and even his own heart. In the year that this warrior of faith finished his labors, God raised up another. Thomas Charles was converted under Rowland's preaching at Bala in Gwynedd. God used Charles mightily to advance biblical literacy and further spread the gospel in Wales.

In the early 1760s, the Welsh revival began to languish and grow cold. But in 1762 God used a combination of Rowland's ministry; the work of some young, less-experienced preachers; and a new hymnal published by William Williams to renew the fading revival. Rowland's sermon on Revelation 3:20, "The Redeemer's Voice," sparked this renewal. In it he called people to a renewed dependence on God:

> O conscience! awake from thy deadly stupor and ponder…on the height and depth of redeeming love…. Though you have lost the power of obeying, and, like Samson, are shorn of your strength, yet with God all things are possible. When He said, "Let there be light," there was light. When He sends out His Word, He can heal you. His Spirit can quicken your dead souls, and enliven your dullest frames…. It is His voice alone that has this vivifying power in all ages of the world. Let not ministers, therefore, think they can convert souls by their gifts and persuasive eloquence…. It is the Holy Spirit that convinces the world of sin.[35]

The revival now advanced more powerfully than ever, spreading throughout all parts of Wales. Crowds in the tens of thousands regularly attended the preaching of the Word. Rowland commented that he had never seen revival on this scale before.[36]

Sometimes God allows His work to diminish in order to rebuke our pride, lukewarmness, or conflicts with one another. God is always able and ready to renew revival. Those who serve the gospel must always be careful to depend on God and not themselves.

---

vigorous Calvinism, while Harris practiced a more subjective and individualistic Pietism." Evans, *Daniel Rowland*, 295.

32. Evans, *Daniel Rowland*, 277–80, 285–95.

33. Evans, *Daniel Rowland*, 298.

34. Evans, *Daniel Rowland*, 305–6.

35. Evans, *Daniel Rowland*, 309–12.

36. Evans, *Daniel Rowland*, 314–15, 323.

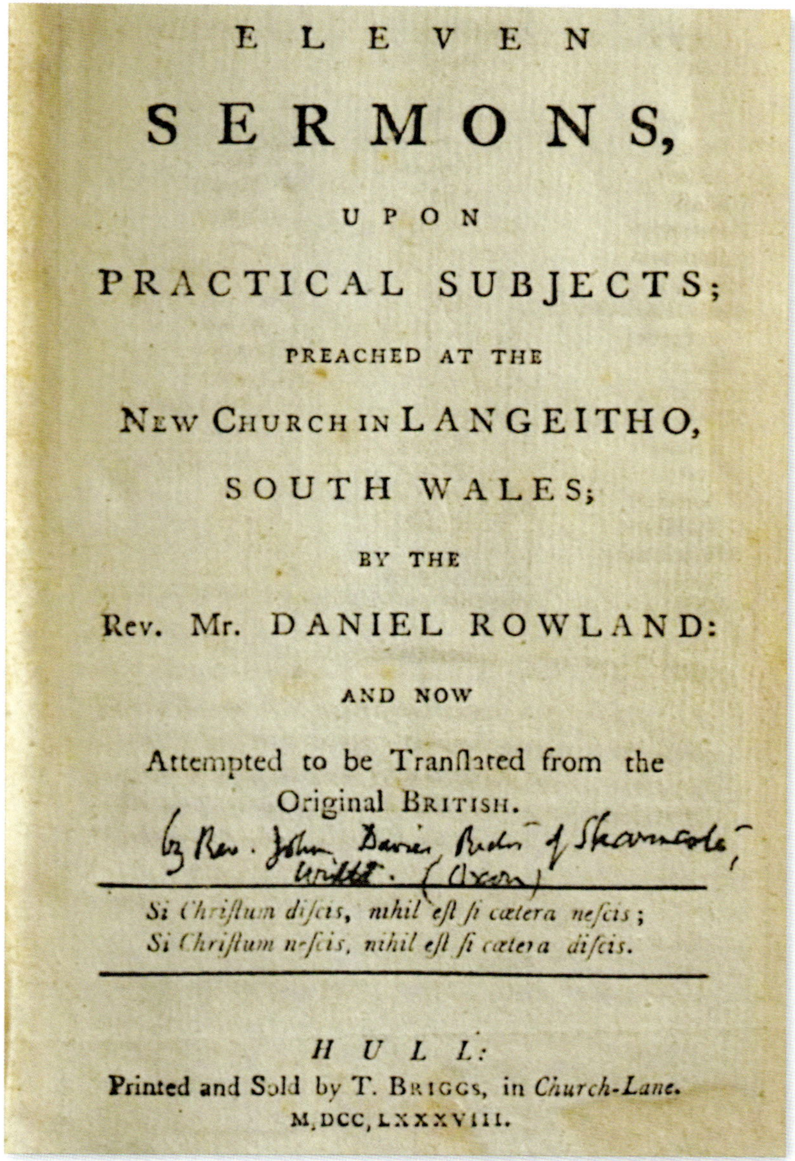

ELEVEN SERMONS,

UPON

PRACTICAL SUBJECTS;

PREACHED AT THE

NEW CHURCH IN LANGEITHO,

SOUTH WALES;

BY THE

Rev. Mr. DANIEL ROWLAND:

AND NOW

Attempted to be Translated from the
Original BRITISH.

by Rev. John Davies, Rector of Skarncole, writer. (Oxon)

Si Christum discis, nihil est si cætera nescis;
Si Christum nescis, nihil est si cætera discis.

HULL:
Printed and Sold by T. BRIGGS, in *Church-Lane.*
M,DCC,LXXXVIII.

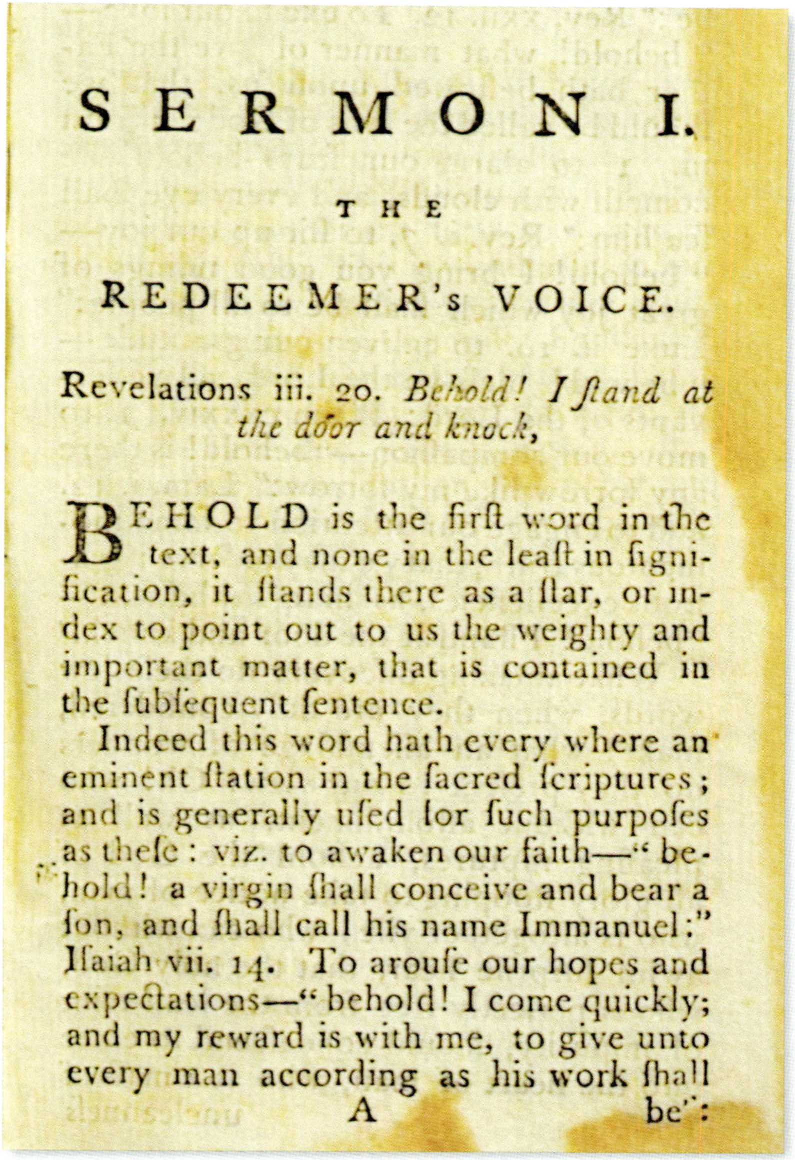

SERMON I.

THE

REDEEMER's VOICE.

Revelations iii. 20. *Behold! I stand at
the door and knock,*

BEHOLD is the first word in the text, and none in the least in signification, it stands there as a star, or index to point out to us the weighty and important matter, that is contained in the subsequent sentence.

Indeed this word hath every where an eminent station in the sacred scriptures; and is generally used for such purposes as these: viz. to awaken our faith—"behold! a virgin shall conceive and bear a son, and shall call his name Immanuel:" Isaiah vii. 14. To arouse our hopes and expectations—"behold! I come quickly; and my reward is with me, to give unto every man according as his work shall be":

A

Some of Rowland's published sermons, including "The Redeemer's Voice"

Trials and Opportunities

While God was raining showers of blessing on the revival, He was preparing Rowland to face one of the hardest trials of his life. In 1763 Rowland's supervising bishop replaced him as curate of Llangeitho and Nantcwnlle with a man named William Williams. Rowland was now out of a job! His congregation, however, overwhelmingly supported him and had a chapel built nearby, where they continued to sit under his ministry.

In 1768 Rowland met Lady Selina, the Countess of Huntingdon, when her ministerial training college was opened in Trevecca. From that time on, Rowland participated in many of the school's anniversary preaching conferences. Rowland also began occasionally preaching in England on behalf of the countess. In 1777 the countess wrote, "One of our Welsh ministers, Mr. Rowland, has been at Bristol and set it all on fire." The countess used her influence to help Rowland get the position of chaplain to the Duke of Leinster. This brought Rowland some needed extra income and brought his preaching to the ears of the nobility. This position also helped Rowland build permanent chapels for Methodist societies in Wales, which helped secure the influence of Welsh Methodism into the future.[37]

As Rowland's influence grew, so did his opportunities. In 1769 he was offered a very well-paid position in a parish in England that would have raised his standard of living and solved his frequent money troubles. When Rowland's flock in Llangeitho heard of the offer, they tearfully pleaded with him to stay among them. So, Rowland made the difficult decision to decline the offer. But John Thornton, who made the offer, wrote to Rowland's son, Nathaniel, "I had a high opinion of your father before, but I have now a still higher opinion of him, though he declines to accept my offer.… It is not a usual thing with me to allow other people to go to my pocket, but tell your father, that he is fully welcome to do so whenever he pleases."[38] Thornton offered his "pocket" to Rowland anytime, which suggests that God was looking after his money problems after all, without Rowland having to leave his beloved flock!

Trials come upon us in the Christian life, but God's faithful dealings with Rowland encourage us to persevere in God's work even when the pressures on us seem to multiply.

End of Life and Legacy

In the years 1780–1781, Rowland's ministry was as powerful as ever, especially in Llangeitho, from which the blessings radiated outward into South Wales. People from all over Wales made their way to Llangeitho, some traveling fifty to eighty miles to get there, sometimes even braving persecution on their journey.[39]

In the late 1780s, as he reached his late seventies, Rowland's health began to fail. Two Sundays before his death, he said to his church, "I am almost leaving, and am on the point of being taken from you. I am not tired *of* work, but *in* it.… My heavenly Father will soon release me from my labours, and bring me to my everlasting rest. But I hope he will continue his gracious presence with you after I am gone."[40]

---

37. Evans, *Daniel Rowland*, 335–38.

38. Evans, *Daniel Rowland*, 327.

39. Evans, *Daniel Rowland*, 352–53.

40. J. C. Ryle, *The Christian Leaders of the Last Century; Or, England a Hundred Years Ago* (London: T. Nelson and Sons, 1869), 194.

A statue of Daniel Rowland in Llangeitho
ROGER KIDD, CC BY-SA 2.0

Lady Huntingdon arranged for a miniature to be painted of Rowland, and it was finished just a week before he died on October 16, 1790. He was seventy-nine and left a legacy of fifty-five years of fruitful gospel labor behind him.

A week before his death when someone reminded Rowland of his fifty-five-year gospel ministry that saw thousands converted and over one hundred pastors mentored, Rowland replied, "It is nothing." Although the countess collected his journals and other important documents in order to have his biography written, she died only a year after Rowland, and all the papers were lost. The biography was never written. All the efforts of ministers, Rowland once said, are like little streams that finally disappear into the ocean and are "swallowed up and lost in the great deep for ever…in the everlasting ocean of love and glory!"[41] Some of his last words to his family were, "I die as a poor sinner, depending fully and entirely on the merits of a crucified Saviour for my acceptance with God."[42]

Edward Morgan said that Rowland always tried to learn four main lessons in his life: "To repent without despairing; to believe without presuming; to rejoice without levity; to be angry without sinning."[43]

41. Evans, *Daniel Rowland*, 382–83.
42. Evans, *Daniel Rowland*, 363–64.
43. Evans, *Daniel Rowland*, 359.

1. What were the circumstances of Daniel Rowland's conversion? What should this teach us as those who preach the Word or sit under the preaching of the Word?

2. Describe some of the first "baby steps" Rowland made as a newly converted minister. What strikes you about the ways he was growing and changing?

3. How were Welsh Methodists different from Anglicans and Dissenters? Why do you think people were so offended at the Methodists' message?

4. What were some of the challenges Rowland faced in ministry? How can friction between Christians, persecution, and even our struggle with remaining sin dampen the work of God? What should we be careful to do when involved in God's work?

5. What were some of the unexpected opportunities God opened for Rowland throughout his life? What does this teach us about perseverance?

6. Which of the four life lessons Rowland tried to live by affects you the most? Why?

~ 5 ~

George Whitefield

1714–1770

One frigid Saturday afternoon in February 1739, twenty-five-year-old George Whitefield walked with a young gentleman named William Seward on the road to Kingswood, an isolated mining community near Bristol.[1]

"We can still turn back, Mr. Whitefield," said Seward, trying to control the tremor in his voice. "In weather as cold as this, people would scarcely venture outdoors to gather firewood, let alone to listen to outdoor preaching."

Whitefield looked at Seward with a calm smile on his face. He knew it was not the weather that worried the young man but the coal miners who lived at Kingswood. Here men, women, and children, clothed in rags and living in filthy shacks or holes in the ground, worked the dangerous, dirty coal mines.

Return of the Miners
CONSTANTIN MENUNIER

They were known as tough, violent, and immoral people. The drunkenness and chaos of Kingswood would sometimes spill over into Bristol when wild mobs of coal miners would storm the city, steal from stores and homes, and

---

1. William Seward was a wealthy widower who was greatly useful in financing many aspects of Whitefield's ministry.

terrorize its citizens. The people looked on the coal miners with disgust and fear, and the coal miners distrusted anyone from the outside.

"My heart aches for the poor coal miners," Whitefield replied. "They are like sheep without a shepherd. Besides, the gospel is the power of God unto everyone who believes," he continued. "Let's see what the Lord may accomplish today through His powerful gospel."

"You are right," said the young man. "May the Lord give His Word success."

As they ascended a hill that would bring them into Kingswood, one thought did worry Whitefield. It was not the coal miners' reputation that troubled him but his authorities in the Church of England who prohibited outdoor preaching unless a minister was evangelizing in an unreached mission field. Wherever Whitefield went, he always tried to respect this rule by first asking the bishop of the district for permission to preach in area churches. If his request was rejected, he would either preach at indoor gatherings of local laypeople called "religious societies" or in the jails.[2] But now he felt that God was leading him to preach

Whitefield Preaching in Moorfields
E. CROWE

outdoors, and since the Bristol clergy had closed their church doors to him, he turned to the open fields of Kingswood and the coal miners.

Whitefield reckoned that he was not breaking church rules against preaching outdoors, for he considered the coal miners an unreached people on a new mission field. *Some may censure me*, he thought, *but if I thus pleased men, I should not be the servant of Christ.*[3]

As Whitefield and Seward paused at the top of the hill overlooking Kingswood, they saw smoke rising from the shacks and hovels where hundreds of needy folk lived. The sight filled Whitefield with the urgency of the message he was about to preach, and any fear of offending Church of England

---

2. Religious societies were gatherings of laypeople seeking spiritual revival, first organized by theologian Anthony Horneck in the 1670s in London.

3. Arnold Dallimore, *George Whitefield: The Life and Times of the Great Evangelist of the 18th Century Revival* (Edinburgh: Banner of Truth, 1970), 1:256.

clergy disappeared. The two men entered Kingswood and began inviting people out of their pits and shacks to gather for the preaching of the gospel. A group of over two hundred assembled as Whitefield took his stand on a grassy mound and began to preach on John 3:3: "Except a man be born again, he cannot see the kingdom of God."[4] Whitefield declared that Jesus Christ came for sinners such as they were, who had no righteousness of their own.

As he preached, many of the coal miners were brought under deep conviction of sin. Their tears formed white gutters as they streaked down their coal-blackened cheeks, and many repented of their sins. The Spirit of God was drawing many to faith in Christ. At his second preaching at Kingswood, five thousand were in attendance; at his third, ten thousand. Thousands of coal miners' lives were transformed by the gospel, and plans were made for a school to be built for the children in Kingswood.

But while Whitefield was thus winning many souls for Christ, he gained many enemies among the clergy for his outdoor preaching. Nonetheless, he

<hr>

4. Robert Philip, *The Life and Times of George Whitefield* (Edinburgh: Banner of Truth, 2007), 101.

The Bell Inn
GEORGE MORLAND

pressed on in the face of strenuous opposition, just as he would do throughout his thirty-three years of unshakable commitment to gospel ministry.

From Serving Tables to Studying at Oxford

George Whitefield was born in 1714 to a large family in Gloucester, England. His father died when he was two, so his mother raised him as she ran the family business, a hotel or "public house" called the Bell Inn. After his mother remarried, the frequent financial troubles his stepfather brought on the family interrupted Whitefield's education, though he was an able student and gifted in public speaking. He once had to leave school for over a year to help with the family business, serving tables and cleaning rooms. Whitefield learned responsibility through work, and his time serving drinks at the pub to local workers taught him how to relate to ordinary people. During evenings after work, he would read his Bible and compose sermons, with a seemingly far-fetched dream to enter the ministry someday. Any hope of his going to university seemed beyond the family's means until his mother learned that he could attend Oxford as a "servitor"— a poorer student who did menial work and ran errands for the richer students in exchange for financial aid—while trying to study whenever possible. At eighteen years of age, Whitefield eagerly began his studies at Pembroke College, Oxford.

Whitefield's Conversion and Doctrine

In 1733, about a year into his studies, Whitefield was invited to join the Holy Club, a student organization that promoted holiness through strict religious devotion and good works, led in part by

The Holy Club
MARSHALL CLAXTON, © SALFORD MUSEUM & ART GALLERY

classmates John and Charles Wesley. Whitefield immersed himself in the activities of the Holy Club as a way of trying to win God's favor and approval. But soon he sensed that all he gained was spiritual pride. He could not be sure that God accepted his works.

When Charles Wesley gave Whitefield a copy of Henry Scougal's *The Life of God in the Soul of Man*, he began a journey that resulted in his true conversion by the grace and work of the Holy Spirit. Reading the book, Whitefield realized his problem and thus stated, "I must be born again or be damned. I learned that a man may go to church, say his prayers, receive the sacrament, and yet not be a Christian." As he held the book, he prayed, "Lord, if I am not a Christian, or if I am not a real one, for Jesus Christ's sake show me what Christianity is, that I may not be damned at the last."[5]

A time of deep spiritual struggle followed, with sleepless nights, fasting, isolation, and continual prayer that interrupted his studies and weakened his health until finally, in April 1735, he confessed, "God was pleased to remove the heavy load, to enable me to lay hold of His dear Son by a living faith.… Oh, with what joy unspeakable…when the weight of sin went off and an abiding sense of the pardoning love of God and the full assurance of faith broke in upon my disconsolate soul!"[6]

Early on, Whitefield's walk with Christ and his heart for evangelism were fueled by Calvinism, the doctrines of God's free, sovereign grace to save His elect. Whitefield reports, "About this time God was pleased to enlighten my soul, and bring me into the knowledge of His free grace, and the necessity of being justified in His sight *by faith only*.… [William] Burkitt's and [Matthew] Henry's *Expositions* were of admirable use to lead me into this, and all other Gospel truths."[7] But Whitefield would also declare that he did not learn these doctrines from Calvin but from Jesus and Paul.

Beginnings in Ministry and Preaching

As Whitefield neared the completion of his bachelor of arts degree, it had become his practice to visit prisoners and the poor to teach them the Bible and do charitable works. He took every opportunity to share his faith. "God forbid I should travel with anybody a

George Whitefield
PORTRAIT BY JOSEPH BADGER
© PRESIDENT AND FELLOWS OF HARVARD COLLEGE

---

5. From a sermon, "All Men's Place," cited in Dallimore, *George Whitefield: The Life and Times*, 1:73.

6. George Whitefield, *George Whitefield's Journals* (Edinburgh: Banner of Truth, 1998), 89.

7. Whitefield, *Journals*, 62.

quarter of an hour," he said, "without speaking of Christ to them." Whitefield's joyful, serious pursuit of Christ was so noticeable that his friends and even the bishop of Gloucester encouraged him to enter the ministry, though he hadn't yet met the minimum age requirement of twenty-three. Whitefield felt the Lord's call to minister to souls, but applying for ordination as a deacon (the first level of ministry in the Church of England) made him fearful, for he did not take the solemn responsibility of ministry lightly. "I have prayed a thousand times," he said, "till the sweat has dropped from my face like rain, that God…would not let me enter the Church before he called me and thrust me into his work."[8] Whitefield believed God was preparing him for some great work, but he felt that "the Devil sees it and is permitted to beset me."[9]

Whitefield was ordained in 1736 and preached his first sermon in the church of his hometown of Gloucester, which deeply affected most of the three hundred attendees. He returned to Oxford to pursue a master's degree and would have settled into a quiet, scholarly life. But he continually received requests to preach in London, Bristol, and other places. These ministry opportunities won him much attention and admiration, particularly for his gift of preaching, and invitations for positions in London promised him a life of comfort and prestige, a sure escape from the financial uncertainty he had grown up with. Whitefield reflected, "Had it not been for my compassionate High Priest, popularity would have destroyed me."[10] Rather than securing a prestigious position for himself, Whitefield received a letter from John Wesley, who had been in the British colony of Georgia a year, inviting him to come serve as a missionary there. "Upon reading [Wesley's letter], my heart leaped within me, and, as it were, echoed to the call."[11]

While he waited for his opportunity to go abroad, he kept up a busy preaching schedule in various churches, stressing the doctrine of regeneration from John 3: "Ye must be born again." Several of his sermons were published during this time, but the most widely circulated sermon was "The Nature and Necessity of Our New Birth in Christ Jesus."[12] The clergy criticized him for what they despised as "religious enthusiasm"—that is, Whitefield's emphasis on regeneration and true conversion, evidenced by a transformed life in Christ by the power of the Spirit.

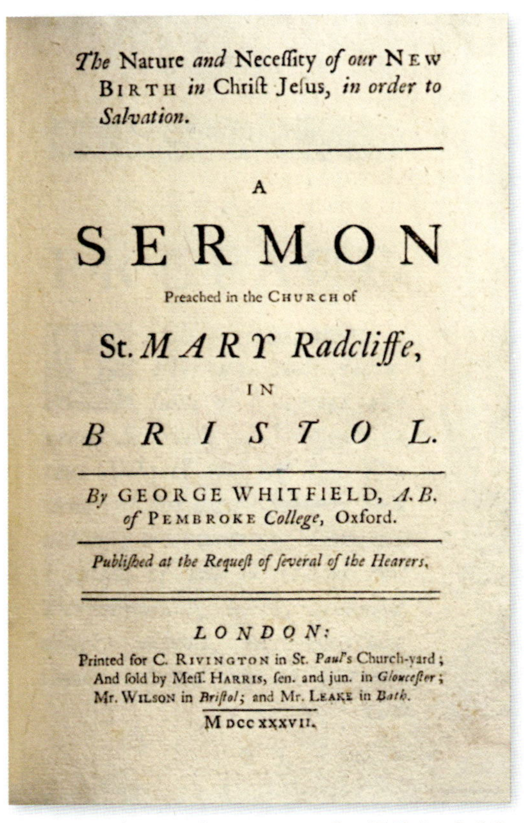

A popular early sermon by Whitefield

8. George Whitefield, "The Good Shepherd," cited in Dallimore, *George Whitefield: The Life and Times*, 1:86.

9. Diary entry, June 8, cited in Dallimore, *George Whitefield: The Life and Times*, 1:94.

10. Whitefield, *Journals*, 89.

11. Whitefield, *Journals*, 80, in Dallimore, *George Whitefield: The Life and Times*, 1:107.

12. Dallimore, *George Whitefield: The Life and Times*, 1:345.

Churches began closing their pulpits to him. A lady once asked him, "Mr. Whitefield, why do you always preach on that text, 'Ye must be born again'?" (John 3:7). He answered, "Because, madam, you must."

The Spiritual Condition of England

Why did many church leaders dislike Whitefield's preaching on the doctrine of the new birth? We can explain this partly by considering the diminished quality of social, moral, and religious life in England during the time of Whitefield, in what Bishop Benson called "degenerative days."[13] Masses of people crowded the cities, living in filth and squalor. Public drunkenness was widespread as gin houses selling cheap alcohol—even to children—stood on almost every block. The slave trade was active with slave ports in Liverpool and Bristol. Prostitution was rampant, and the books and plays of popular culture glamorized the practice. Animal torture was promoted via cruel sports such as cockfighting and bearbaiting. The clergy of the Church of England were theologically barren, many embracing deism, or a rationalistic disbelief in the supernatural.[14] Church authorities were often more interested in politics and keeping people in their proper social classes than in biblical, doctrinally grounded, heartfelt gospel ministry. Outside of Anglican circles, dissenting Christians, heirs of the Puritans such as Presbyterians, Congregationalists, and Baptists, were either corrupt in doctrine or else too restricted by official policies to effect meaningful change.[15] Negative experience with radical sects such as the Society of Friends ("Quakers") had inculcated widespread distrust of excessive zeal or "religious enthusiasm." Therefore, when Whitefield preached the necessity of being born again, his message irritated the hard hearts of many unconverted and ineffective pastors and clergy members comfortable with the way things were.

Serving God in America

In 1738 Whitefield set sail for Georgia in a company of three ships transporting soldiers to the colonies. Whitefield served as a military chaplain to the soldiers and sailors on his ship. He cheerfully and persistently busied himself with caring for the sick; leading daily prayers, devotions, and hymn singing; exhorting people one-on-one; and, of course, preaching. In this way he slowly won the respect of all on board, eventually leading many to Christ, and was honored with the people's tearful goodbyes when the ships arrived in Georgia in October 1739. Around this time, the Wesley brothers were sailing back to England from Georgia, filled with a sense of failure in their missionary labors and a growing realization that they themselves were not yet converted.

Whitefield immediately went to work in Georgia setting up schools, donating essential supplies he brought with him from England to those in need, preaching the Word, leading worship, and promoting hard work and orderliness among the settlers. His heart was struck by the many homeless, orphaned children living in terrible conditions,

---

13. Arnold Dallimore, *George Whitefield: God's Anointed Servant in the Great Revival of the Eighteenth Century* (Wheaton, Ill.: Crossway, 1990), 43.

14. Deists attempted to rely on logic and reason as authorities over religion, faith, and Scripture. Many of them believed in the existence of God as a logical necessity but denied that He gave laws or got involved in His creation. Thomas Paine and Benjamin Franklin were deists.

15. Phil Arthur, "The Life and Ministry of George Whitefield," unpublished conference talk, 2014.

and he considered it his duty to establish an orphanage he would later call Bethesda ("House of Mercy").[16] This first mission to Georgia, which lasted only three months, inspired a vision for ministry in America that would bring him back six more times, enabling him to preach in all thirteen colonies and oversee the development and operation of the Bethesda orphanage. Beset with many financial and administrative difficulties, the Bethesda project developed slowly but eventually provided housing and education for more than one hundred orphans in Whitefield's lifetime. On his second visit to America the following year, starting in Philadelphia, Whitefield launched an extensive preaching tour in the colonies. In Northampton, Massachusetts, Jonathan Edwards had him stay at his home as his guest, and in Philadelphia, Whitefield began a lifelong friendship with Benjamin Franklin. His preaching played a major role in the First Great Awakening, the revival that spread to such an extent in Britain and its colonies that "by 1750 virtually every American loved and admired Whitefield and considered him their champion."[17]

Closed Doors, Open Fields

While Whitefield was in Georgia, his popularity in England continued to spread through the influence of his printed sermons, but the number of clergy who opposed him and closed their churches to him also grew. In 1739, upon returning to England from a second trip to America, Whitefield received his second stage of ordination as a priest and immediately began preaching in churches open to him and in the religious societies in London and Bristol, intending to raise money for the orphanage. Facing more and more closed church doors, however,

Benjamin Franklin,
one of the Founding Fathers of the USA
PORTRAIT BY JOSEPH DUPLESSIS

Whitefield was encouraged to try outdoor or "field preaching," following the example of a Welsh preacher, Howell Harris, who had been evangelizing outdoors in Wales with great success and with whom Whitefield had been exchanging letters. It was the coal miners of Kingswood, Bristol, who would hear Whitefield's first outdoor sermon.

---

16. Dallimore, *George Whitefield: The Life and Times*, 1:206–7.

17. Harry Stout, quoted in Michael Haykin, "George Whitefield: A Man of Focus from the Eighteenth Century," *Thrive: The EB Online Magazine*, fall 2014, https://www .thrive-magazine.ca/qry/page.taf?id=27&_function=atcldetail&sbtatcl_uid1=229& _nc=cc66fb41e0e26c9efc864205b28c08b7.

Whitefield went from Bristol to London to continue preaching and raising funds for the orphanage in Georgia, remarking, "If the churches are closed against me, bless God, the fields are open."[18] He preached first in a north London park called Moorfields to a crowd of ten thousand and then in a large field in south central London called Kennington Common, where great numbers of poor people typically gathered: "men, women, and children—unwashed and ignorant, wicked and diseased, a vast host of whom it might be said, 'No man cared for their souls.'"[19] It was feared by some that these preaching opportunities could incite mob activity, but the crowds were always silent as they listened to Whitefield proclaim the Word of God. His efforts won so many that Moorfields and Kennington Common became central locations of Whitefield's London ministry.

Whitefield's Preaching

In a time when no microphones or amplification systems were available, it is remarkable that Whitefield could preach to crowds in the tens of thousands, a fact that was documented by Benjamin Franklin, who determined by measurement that Whitefield's voice reached thirty-five thousand people when he preached in Philadelphia. Whitefield's preaching was biblical, simple, sincere, and colorfully dramatic, and it had a ring of divine authority that flowed from his personal experience with Christ. He had encountered the living God, experienced the strictness and spirituality of His law, felt God's holy displeasure at sin and His justice in punishing sinners, and, seeing himself as an unworthy debtor

freed by God's grace, spoke powerfully and eloquently from a heart filled with love for Christ and for the spiritual welfare of sinners. "I am persuaded," he wrote in his journal, "the generality of preachers talk of an unknown and unfelt Christ. The reason why congregations have been so dead is, because they have had dead men preaching to them."[20]

The Wesleys: Partnership and Division

Around this time, Whitefield invited the Wesley brothers to assume leadership of the work in Bristol, and after showing John how to preach outdoors, Whitefield went to London. Whitefield and the Wesleys had become known as Methodists because of their association with the disciplined, orderly "holy method" of living promoted by the Holy Club they led at Oxford. After a short time of partnering with Whitefield's work in Bristol, however, John Wesley decided (by casting lots) to preach and later publish a sermon against predestination. This grieved Whitefield, not only because the doctrines of sovereign grace had become precious to him as his life's experiences and trials ripened and sweetened his theological understanding of them but also because he saw Wesley diverging from the focus of evangelism and causing unnecessary division.[21] Whitefield, in an attempt to prevent Wesley from publishing the sermon, wrote, "Sir, if you have

18. Whitefield, *Journals*, 230, 257.

19. Dallimore, *George Whitefield: The Life and Times*, 1:288.

20. Whitefield, *Journals*, 471.

21. In a later letter to Wesley, he wrote, "The more I examine the writings of the most experienced men, and the experiences of most established Christians, the more I differ from your notion about not committing sin, and your denying the doctrines of election, and final perseverance of the saints.… God Himself, I find, teaches my friends the doctrine of election." Dallimore, *George Whitefield: The Life and Times*, 1:492–93.

any regard for the peace of the church, keep your sermon on predestination. But you have cast a lot!… Indeed, I desire all the success you can wish for. May you increase, though I decrease! I would willingly wash your feet.… Oh, wrestle, wrestle, honoured sir, in prayer, that not the least alienation of affection may be between you and your obedient son and servant in Christ."[22]

Wesley argued that predestination was the enemy of evangelism. Whitefield tried to help Wesley better understand the doctrine, writing, "Though I hold Particular Election, yet I offer Jesus freely to every individual soul."[23] Wesley, however, was not so easily persuaded. Besides, he benefited from the doctrinal divide since he gained his own following of people who adhered to his distinctive Arminian teaching on the way of salvation and the pursuit of sinless perfection. This allowed him to become the head of his own branch of Methodism known as Wesleyanism.[24] But this

division weakened the progress of the evangelical revival and emboldened its enemies, making it necessary in 1741 for Whitefield to leave a mission trip in America early to contain or repair the damage Wesley was doing in England.

A first important step, which he took with hesitation, was to publish a letter he had written to Wesley correcting the doctrinal errors in his sermon against predestination. Both in the letter and in his demeanor, Whitefield maintained the character of a peacemaker, often appealing to the Wesleys for unity and refusing to preach against them. "Let my name be forgotten," said Whitefield. "Let me be trodden under the feet of all men if Jesus may thereby be glorified. Let my name die everywhere. Let even my friends forget me if by that it means the cause of the blessed Jesus may be promoted."[25] Whitefield refused to create a denomination around himself, and in 1749 he removed himself from the direct management of the Calvinistic Methodist societies in England. He shifted his focus exclusively to itinerant gospel preaching. These changes eased the tension between him and the Wesleys but never completely restored their relationship.

Whitefield's Character

Whitefield's cheerful, humble, and wholeheartedly devoted character revealed itself in the difficulties he faced. A woman from New York once remarked, "Mr. Whitefield was

---

22. Dallimore, *George Whitefield: The Life and Times*, 1:387

23. From a letter dated October 10, 1741. Another letter to Wesley reads, "Dear sir, what a fond conceit it is to cry up *perfection*, and yet cry down the doctrine of *final perseverance*! But this and many other absurdities you will run into, because you will not own *Election*. And you will not own election because you cannot own it without believing the doctrine of *Reprobation*. What then is there in reprobation so horrid? I see no blasphemy in holding that doctrine, if rightly explained. If God might have passed by all, He may pass by some. Judge whether it is not a greater blasphemy to say, 'Christ died for souls now in hell.'" Dallimore, *George Whitefield: The Life and Times*, 1:575.

24. Doctrine had always been one of Wesley's weaknesses: "Wesley had entered a realm that was new to him—that of evangelical doctrine—and in which he was as yet quite unlearned. In this, the Reformers and Puritans would have proved valuable teachers, but he had turned not to them but to the Moravians, and as a result his approach had become largely an empirical one. Failing to see the Scriptural teaching of his

constant *standing* in Christ, he concerned himself with his day-by-day *state* in Christ, and the fluctuations that he experienced caused his uncertainty." Dallimore, *George Whitefield: The Life and Times*, 1:197. Eventually he would depend on evangelical doctrine, but at this stage, he was quite unlearned in it.

25. Arthur, "Life and Ministry of George Whitefield," 25.

so cheerful that it tempted me to become a Christian."[26] As a young man, he did not let his early success and popularity blind him to his deep need for spiritual and doctrinal growth, and so he often wrote to more experienced Christians such as Ebenezer and Ralph Erskine, William Law, and Jonathan Edwards for counsel. Later in life, Whitefield humbly reflected on certain statements he had made as a younger man that were not helpful: "I find that I frequently wrote and spoke in my own spirit, when I thought I was writing and speaking by the assistance of the Spirit of God."[27]

Whitefield refused to lift his voice in self-defense against false accusations or smears by his enemies, writing, "Thou shalt answer for me, my Lord and my God. A little while and we shall appear at the judgment seat of Christ. Then shall my innocence be made clear as the light and my dealings as the noonday."[28] Someone who took Whitefield's side in the division with Wesley asked him, "Do you expect to see John Wesley in heaven?" Whitefield answered, "No, I shan't see Wesley in heaven." But he explained, "He will be so much nearer the throne than I. He will be obscured by the blaze of glory from the throne. No, I shan't see him."[29] What a beautiful example of honoring or preferring others more than ourselves!

Whitefield's choice of a wife helps us understand his single-hearted devotion to God's work. In November 1741,

at twenty-seven years old, he married a thirty-six-year-old widow, Elizabeth James, describing her as one who was "neither rich in fortune nor beautiful as to her person, but I believe a true child of God, and would not, I think, attempt to hinder me in his work for the world."[30] She would serve him faithfully until her death two years before Whitefield died.

Burning Out for God: Whitefield's Life and Death

From the time he was twenty-two until he died at fifty-five, Whitefield lived at a breathtaking pace, preaching several times a day, at least in his earlier ministry, wherever he was. He woke at four each morning for an hour of prayer and Bible reading, preached at five o'clock, preached two to three more times in the day, wrote letters, counseled spiritual seekers, ended each day preaching to whomever happened to be where he was staying, and was in bed by ten o'clock.[31] It is estimated that he preached eighteen thousand times in his life.

When he was not preaching, he was traveling to preach elsewhere or else to recover his ministry-battered health at remote places like Holland or Bermuda, where he continued preaching. In addition to preaching for his two societies in London and ministry throughout England, he made frequent trips to Wales, fifteen to Scotland, two to Ireland, and seven to America. On his last trip to America, in ill health and

26. Arthur, "Life and Ministry of George Whitefield."

27. Haykin, "George Whitefield."

28. Whitefield, *Journals*, 213, in Dallimore, *George Whitefield: The Life and Times*, 1:229.

29. Arthur, "Life and Ministry of George Whitefield."

30. Letter to Gilbert Tennent, in Dallimore, *George Whitefield: The Life and Times*, 2:110. Cited in Dallimore, *George Whitefield: God's Anointed Servant*, 113.

31. John D. Woodbridge, ed., *Great Leaders of the Christian Church* (Chicago: Moody, 1988), 295–300.

in desperate need of rest, he arrived at Exeter, New Hampshire, where he preached at the request of the people. Exhausted but journeying on, he passed away the next day, September 30, 1770, at Newburyport, Massachusetts.

When he died, Whitefield was the best known and most loved preacher in the American colonies and highly regarded in the United Kingdom as well. He was regarded as the greatest English-speaking preacher and revivalist of the eighteenth century. God was pleased to use his sermons for the "new birth" of many thousands of people. Only eternity will reveal the full impact of his ministry for the conversion of the lost, the maturation of the saints, and the glory of God's worthy name.

A statue of Whitefield in Philadelphia

1. What important truth was Whitefield brought to understand before his conversion? How have you understood this to be true in your life?

2. What spiritual struggles did God allow Whitefield to experience before his conversion? How might these experiences have helped him in his work caring for souls? What kinds of experiences have you had in fleeing the world, the flesh, the devil, empty religiosity, or comfortable presumption?

3. How did the division between Whitefield and Wesley develop? What should this teach us about unity with one another as we serve God together?

4. Read some of Whitefield's letters responding to Wesley's errors about predestination. How can Whitefield's teaching help you or others you know work through a correct application of this crucial doctrine?

5. Is it surprising to hear that many church leaders disliked Whitefield's preaching on the doctrine of the new birth? What biblical doctrines may be out of vogue in the religious landscape of our day, and how should we respond?

6. Are Whitefield's enemies correct in thinking he was too enthusiastic about religion and revival? Or is Whitefield simply taking seriously the urgency of the gospel seen in the apostle Paul? Where do we stand in our sense of urgency for revival and passion for the progress of the gospel?

Samuel Davies

1723–1761

Samuel Davies

"The suburbs of heaven." So one man described the worship of God led by the prince of colonial preachers, Samuel Davies. The short but widely influential life of Samuel Davies began November 3, 1723, in New Castle County, Delaware. His parents were earnest Christians of Welsh extraction, his father a plain farmer, hardworking but far from wealthy, from "utter obscurity," as Davies later described his early life. Looking back, Davies referred to himself as "a son of prayer," his mother, Martha Davies, having especially asked the Lord to give her a son, as Hannah in the Bible had done (1 Sam. 1:9–13). And like Hannah, this mother also named her son Samuel.

At an early age, Samuel showed a lively tenderness toward the things of God and soon became and continued to be throughout his life the most unsparing judge of his own life as a Christian. His parents placed him under the tutelage of the saintly Samuel Blair at his "Log College" across the Delaware River in

Log College building
PRESBYTERIAN HISTORICAL SOCIETY

Pennsylvania. Blair trained some of the most important Christian leaders early America produced. After completing his studies at "the gate of heaven," as Davies later described Blair's Log College, at only twenty-three years of

age, he began his life as a Presbyterian evangelist, receiving the first license to preach as a dissenting minister in colonial Virginia where the Church of England was "by law established." In 1746 he married and soon after began his missionary work in the backwoods. After only a year of ministry, feverish and sick from overwork, he rode a hundred miles home on horseback, only to find his pregnant wife struggling for her life. She and their son died only days later.

After months of grief and ill health, Davies answered a call to become minister of the Presbyterian congregation in Hanover, Virginia. Davies continued itinerant preaching at various remote meetinghouses in the wilderness of western Virginia. Eventually he served seven congregations, traveling up to 250 miles a month on horseback and preaching upward of twenty sermons each month, all while in poor health.

War Preacher

The western frontier of the colony of Virginia when Davies arrived was a dangerous region for European settlers. The French and their Indian allies threatened the colony with war. In July 1755, British general Edward Braddock's redcoat army embarked on a campaign to drive back the French and Indian forces from the western borders of Pennsylvania and Virginia. General Braddock led an expedition to capture Fort Duquesne and take control of the upper reaches of the Ohio River. Braddock's troops were wholly unprepared for the "skulking way of war" practiced by these hostile forces, who avoided pitched battles and would lie in wait behind rocks and trees, their muskets at the ready. Braddock's force was attacked and nearly massacred. After having four horses shot out from under him, Braddock himself was shot in the chest; he died four days later on July 13, 1755.

What was a gospel minister of numerous widely scattered congregations under imminent threat of slaughter to do? Davies comforted and encouraged his people—and he kept on preaching. To his Hanover congregation on July 25, 1755, Davies delivered one of his famous war sermons, in which he said, "Let me earnestly recommend to you to furnish yourselves with arms and put yourselves into a position of defense. What is that religion good for that leaves men cowards on the appearance of danger? And permit me to say that I am particularly solicitous that you, my brothers of the dissenters, should act with honor and spirit in this juncture, as it becomes loyal subjects, lovers of your country, and courageous Christians."[1]

Davies's reputation as an able and gifted preacher had spread throughout the colonies; he had numerous invitations to take up pastoral duties in far safer places to minister. But he remained resolved and loyal to his people and to Virginia. He wrote,

> If I consulted either my safety or my temporal interests, I should soon remove my family to Great Britain or the northern colonies…. And yet I must declare that after the most calm

The burial of General Braddock

1. Maurice W. Armstrong, "The Dissenting Deputies and the American Colonies," *Church History* 29, no. 3 (September 1960), https://www.cambridge.org/core/journals/church-history/article/abs/dissenting-deputies-and-the-american-colonies/D15E6E86BD3FD72FFD49F3E9F2B6FF05.

and impartial deliberation, I am determined not to leave my country while there is any prospect of defending it. Certainly, he does not deserve a place in any country who is ready to run from it upon every appearance of danger. The event of the war is yet uncertain but let us determine that if the cause should require it, we will courageously leave house and home and take the field.[2]

That very day, hearing Davies's call, a company of colonists with rifles at the ready enlisted in Hanover. On August 17, Davies preached a stirring sermon to the new recruits from the text "Be of good courage, and let us play the men for our people" (2 Sam. 10:12). Davies told these new recruits about "that heroic youth, Colonel Washington, whom I cannot but hope Providence has hitherto preserved in so singular a manner for more important service."[3]

By May 8, 1758, the French and Indian War had reached a fever pitch. There was an urgent need for more men to enlist and defend the colony. To his Hanover congregation, Davies preached another war sermon:

> May I not reasonably insist upon it that the company of soldiers be made up this very day before we leave this place. Methinks your king, your country, nay, your own interest command me: and, therefore, I insist upon it…. Oh! For the influence of the Lord of

Montcalm after the Battle of Carillon (Ticonderoga)
HENRY ALEXANDER OGDEN

armies, the God of battles, the Author of true courage and every heroic virtue, to fire you into patriotic and true soldiers this moment, young and hardy men, whose very faces seem to speak that God and nature formed you for soldiers.[4]

As he came to the conclusion of his sermon, Davies spoke these stirring words: "Ye that love your country, enlist, for honor will follow you in life or death in such a cause. Ye that

<hr>

2. Henry Alexander White, *Southern Presbyterian Leaders* (New York: Neale Publishing, 1911), 50.

3. Jane Hampton Cook, "The Mystery of Survival: HW Bush, George Washington and Living Life to the Fullest," The Hill, December 12, 2018, https://thehill.com/opinion/white-house/420963-the-mystery-of-survival -hw-bush-george-washington-and-living-life-to-the/.

4. White, *Southern Presbyterian Leaders*, 50.

love your religion, enlist, for your religion is in danger. Can Protestant Christianity expect quarter from heathen savages and French papists? Sure in such an alliance, the powers of hell make a third party. Ye that love your friends and relations, enlist, lest ye see them enslaved and butchered before your eyes."[5]

Once again, the needed recruits stepped forward moments after Davies completed this war sermon. So effective were the Presbyterian recruits in the French and Indian War that the Anglican Church in Virginia relaxed more of its regulations against Dissenters and Nonconformists. Thereafter, Presbyterianism had more freedom, especially in the western part of Virginia, all as a result of the Lord using Davies's oratory in his war sermons.

Presbyterian in Anglican Territory

In 1619 the Virginia House of Burgesses established the Church of England as the only lawful church in the colony. There were inevitable tensions between Presbyterian ministers and the clergy of the established church. Davies, however, was very much aware of potential conflict and did all he could not to cause trouble. In a letter to the bishop of London, who ruled the churches in Virginia, Davies wrote,

> In all the sermons I have preached in Virginia, I have not wasted one minute in exclaiming or reasoning against the peculiarities of the established Episcopal Church, nor so much as assigned the reasons of my own non-conformity. I have not exhausted my zeal in railing against the established clergy, and exposing their imperfections, some of which lie naked to

my view, or in deprecating their characters. The plain truth is a general reformation must be promoted in this colony by some means or other, or multitudes are eternally undone, and I see, alas, but little ground to hope for it from the generality of the [Anglican] clergy here.[6]

Davies went on to declare his principal desire, to preach the gospel "of Jesus in its life and power."[7] But traveling on horseback through the wilderness, in all weathers, to preach sometimes four or five times on Sabbath days took its toll on Davies's health. With the unstinting help and encouragement of his second wife, Jane Holt, Davies's health for a time improved, and he found renewed strength and great pleasure in his calling. He wrote, "I am as happy as perhaps creation can make me. I have a peaceful study, the venerable dead are waiting in my library to entertain me. I very much question if there is a more calm, placid, and contented mortal in Virginia."[8] God's Spirit moved in response to Davies's prayers and faithful preaching, and many nominal Christians in Virginia were converted to Christ under his ministry.

Additionally, Davies was a leader in proclaiming the gospel to the indigenous tribes and to the African slave population in Virginia. His congregations grew and included both aristocratic gentlemen and ladies and their black slaves together praying, singing psalms and hymns, and hearing the preaching of God's Word in one place. In Davies's

---

5. White, *Southern Presbyterian Leaders*, 51.

6. White, *Southern Presbyterian Leaders*, 106.

7. White, *Southern Presbyterian Leaders*, 106.

8. Douglas Bond, *Mr. Pipes Comes to America* (Arlington Heights, Ill.: Christian Liberty Press, 2001), 35.

congregations, the bread and wine of the Lord's Supper were distributed equally to black and white hand alike. One man described being among the devout and ethnically diverse worshipers in Davies's congregations as residing in "the suburbs of heaven." Under Davies's influence, literacy and education spread, and a whole generation of black slaves grew up learning to read the Bible and other Christian books. Davies encouraged wealthier white Christians to supply good books, which black Christians received with deep gratitude.

Preaching before a King

Davies's part in the Great Awakening was abruptly interrupted when the Presbyterian Synod of New York, encouraged by George Whitefield, urged him to join Gilbert Tennent in a fundraising voyage to Britain to raise support for a new ministerial training college. American Presbyterians placed a high priority on an educated clergy. Founded in 1747, the College of New Jersey at Princeton had a singular purpose: to train young men for the ministry of the Word in the growing Presbyterian congregations throughout the colonies. But there was a great need for more funding for the institution.

Arriving in London on December 25, 1753, Davies soon found English Presbyterianism to be cold and formal. It was almost as if they wanted to be Anglicans, and most Presbyterians he met objected to his preaching on the doctrines of grace and the biblical system of theology known as Calvinism. While English Presbyterian pulpits were largely closed to Davies, he did meet a young Presbyterian preacher from Scotland named John Witherspoon, who greatly impressed Davies and Tennent as a faithful man of

God and an able preacher of the gospel. Witherspoon was later called, in 1768, to be the sixth president of Princeton, and in 1776 he became the only Presbyterian minister to sign the Declaration of Independence, one of the reasons the British scornfully referred to the American War for Independence as "The Presbyterian Parson's War." It was Davies's meeting of Witherspoon on this voyage that led to these later important developments.

While preaching in Britain, Davies discovered that Baptists received him with appreciation, but they were able to offer little financial support for the college. George Whitefield and John and Charles Wesley, however, offered considerable support for a building to house the college.

Davies preached whenever, wherever, and to whomever he could. Word spread about the young preacher's skills as an orator, and eventually Davies came to the attention of the King of Great Britain. Shortly thereafter, twenty-nine-year-old Davies was summoned to deliver a sermon at the royal chapel before King George II and his court.

The story is told that while Davies preached before His Majesty, the king frequently whispered to his advisers to the left and the right of his throne. Disconcerted, Davies finally halted and said, "When the lion roars, the beasts of the forest all tremble; and when King Jesus speaks, the princes of the earth should keep silence."[9] Whether or not this is an accurate report of his words before the monarch, there is no doubt that Davies understood that the faithful preaching of the Word of God *is* the Word of God. Davies finished his sermon before a silent and attentive king.

-----

9. White, *Southern Presbyterian Leaders*, 49.

King George II
PORTRAIT BY ENOCH SEEMAN

After the sermon, the king seemed unoffended by Davies's boldness and offered an explanation. He told Davies that he was so astonished at the young preacher's giftedness he felt compelled to comment on it to his advisers. The king then generously contributed funds from his royal coffers for the founding of the new college. Davies had high regard for George II and wrote a eulogy when the king died in 1761, calling him "George, the mighty, the just, the gentle, and the wise."

Nassau Hall and the Prayer Room

After a tumultuous voyage across the Atlantic, Davies's ship dropped anchor off the coast of America, where the little ship strained and lurched at anchor in a violent Atlantic gale for another three long weeks. Once ashore in Plymouth Harbor, though weary from his voyage, Davies mounted a horse for the long ride back to Hanover, where he immediately resumed his ministry.

With the money raised for the College of New Jersey, the trustees first set funds aside for men preparing for gospel ministry who were too poor to pay for their education. After that, they used funds to erect the first building. Nassau Hall, named in honor of the Protestant king of England, William III of Orange-Nassau, would serve for many years as the center of Presbyterianism in the region. In its day, Nassau Hall, which housed the entire college, was the largest academic building in the western hemisphere. And during the War of Independence, it would play an important role. Troops from both the American colonial army and the British forces used it for a garrison and a hospital. In 1777, at the Battle of Princeton, British soldiers fleeing George Washington's troops took cover inside her thick stone walls and chopped up pews for firewood. The British were finally driven from the hall when colonial cannon fire shook the stout building. One cannonball, as the story is told, crashed through the walls and decapitated a portrait of

George II, former king of England. Congress commissioned the celebrated artist and patriot soldier Charles Willson Peale to paint a battle portrait of George Washington. As a symbolic gesture, they placed Washington's new portrait in the frame of the beheaded portrait of the king of Great Britain. Late in the war, in 1783, Nassau Hall housed the Continental Congress and briefly served as the new nation's capital. A cannon used at the Battle of Princeton is on display on the lawn in front of Nassau Hall today.

Some of the greatest men in American history have taught, preached, and studied at Nassau Hall. George Whitefield once preached a sermon there at five o'clock in the morning. James Madison, father of the US Constitution, was a student at the College of New Jersey and would have heard gospel preaching at Nassau Hall daily during his years of study. No other individual deserves as much credit for raising the funds to build the first Princeton building—and, for a time, the only building—as the young Presbyterian minister, Samuel Davies.

Preacher and College President

The second president of Princeton was the son-in-law of the celebrated preacher Jonathan Edwards, Aaron Burr Sr. (not to be confused with the Aaron Burr who later shot and killed Alexander Hamilton in a duel). Burr served for nine years and died in 1757. The trustees appealed to Jonathan Edwards to accept their call as the next president of the college. Edwards came to take his new duties in 1758. After being inoculated against smallpox only a few months after becoming president, Edwards died of smallpox, leaving the young institution again without a leader. The trustees turned to Davies. He at first refused, but the trustees exerted

NASSAU HALL, PRINCETON COLLEGE.

considerable pressure, and in 1759 Davies at last accepted the call.

Davies served as president for only eighteen months. During his short time, however, Davies understood that preaching to the young men preparing to be ministers of the gospel was one of his chief duties. His clear, passionate preaching filled Nassau Hall several times a week during the year-and-a-half of his presidency. Imagine the many young preachers who heard Davies's words: "The world is dying all around you. And can you rest easy in such a world, while unprepared for eternity? Awake to righteousness now, at the gentle call of the gospel, before the last trumpet gives you an alarm of another kind!"[10]

In a sermon delivered January 1, 1760, Davies preached from Romans 13:11: "Knowing the time, that now it is high time to awake out of sleep: for now is our salvation nearer than when we believed." His opening comment on the text was a line borrowed from Isaac Watts, "'Time, like an ever-running stream,' is perpetually gliding on, and hurrying each of us into the boundless ocean of eternity!" Later in the sermon, Davies particularly called on the complacent churchgoer to come to repentance and true faith:

> This day let us put this question to our hearts: "What am I? Am I a humble, dutiful servant of God? Or am I a disobedient, impenitent sinner? Am I a disciple of Christ in reality? Or do I only wear his name, and make an empty profession of his religion? Whither am I bound? For heaven or for hell? Which am I most fit for in temper? For the region of perfect holiness or for that region of sin and impurity? Shall I stupidly delay the determination, until it is passed by the irrevocable sentence of the Supreme Judge, before whom I may stand before this year is at a close? Alas, if it should then be against me, my doom will be remediless! But if I should now discover my case to be bad, blessed be God, it is not too late to alter it. I may yet obtain a good hope, through grace, though my present hope should be found to be that of the hypocrite!"[11]

---

10. Samuel Davies, *Sermons on Important Subjects* (Boston: Lincoln and Edmands, 1811), 1:380.

11. Samuel Davies, *Sermons on Important Subjects* (London: for W. Baynes, by J. F. Dove, 1815), 3:339.

Several prominent American patriots credited the significant influence of Samuel Davies on their lives and work, including Dr. Benjamin Rush, signer of the Declaration of Independence, who wrote, "The only means of establishing and perpetuating our republican forms of government is the universal education of our youth in the principles of Christianity by means of the Bible."[12] Another Founding Father greatly influenced by Davies was Patrick Henry of Virginia. Henry regularly attended Davies's Hanover congregation with his mother during his childhood and youth, and he became a noted orator in his own right. He is famously remembered for rising to his feet and declaring his zeal for the cause of American independence with the words, "Give me liberty, or give me death!"

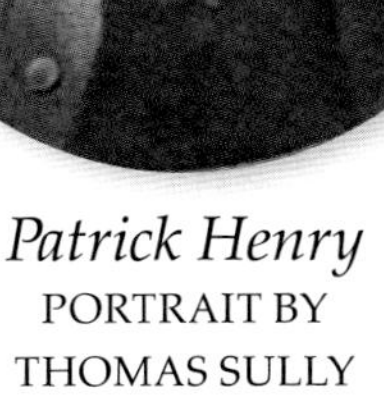

Patrick Henry
PORTRAIT BY
THOMAS SULLY

Preacher and Hymn Writer

Samuel Davies was a preacher par excellence. With divine unction, he preached biblically, doctrinally, experientially, and practically. He excelled at preaching about the heinousness of sin and the depravity of man, the glories of Christ and His substitutionary atonement, and the Spirit's saving

---

12. Benjamin Rush, *Essays: Literary, Moral and Philosophical* (London, 1806), 112.

work in the soul of sinners. He preached the marks of grace clearly and extolled God's mercy to penitents. In sermons titled "The Gospel Invitation," "Sinners Entreated to Be Reconciled to God," and "The Divine Mercy to Mourning Penitents," he fully and freely proclaimed God's amazing gospel offer in Christ to the greatest of sinners. Dr. Martyn Lloyd-Jones believed that Davies was the greatest preacher America ever produced. His three volumes of sermons have been reprinted often, most recently by Reformation Heritage Books in 2021.

Hundreds, if not thousands, of people were converted under Davies's fourteen-year ministry. He was mightily used of God in Virginia, especially during the Great Awakening. He has long been regarded as the southern revivalist counterpart to Jonathan Edwards in the north. The two evangelistic revival preachers deeply respected each other as ministers and valued each other's preaching. When Edwards's church in Northampton dismissed him, Davies requested his assistance in the revival transpiring at that time in Virginia.[13]

One of the books Davies loved to use in his worship services was Isaac Watts's *Psalms of David Imitated*, first published in America in 1729, by printer Benjamin Franklin. Presbyterians from an English background quickly took up Watts's version in preference to the Scottish Psalter so dear to Presbyterians from Scotland and Ireland. The popularity of Watts's hymns dislodged the Psalms of the Bible from the exclusive place of honor they had held in public worship since the Reformation, and they opened the gates for numerous hymns produced in the nineteenth century.

George Whitefield used Watts in his evangelistic preaching around the colonies, and so did Davies, who gave away many copies of Watts to needy Christians in his wide parish. Davies described how his own kitchen would be filled with African American Christians who loved worshiping God with psalms and hymns at any time of the day or night. He wrote, "Sometimes when I waked about two or three o'clock in the morning, a torrent of sacred harmony poured into my chamber and carried me away to heaven."

Davies himself wrote sixteen hymns, his most famous being "Great God of Wonders":

Great God of wonders! all Thy ways
Are matchless, godlike and divine;
But the fair glories of Thy grace
More godlike and unrivaled shine,
More godlike and unrivaled shine.

    Who is a pard'ning God like Thee?
    Or who has grace so rich and free?
    Or who has grace so rich and free?

In wonder lost, with trembling joy
We take the pardon of our God;
Pardon for crimes of deepest dye,
A pardon bought with Jesus' blood,
A pardon bought with Jesus' blood.

    Who is a pard'ning God like Thee?
    Or who has grace so rich and free?
    Or who has grace so rich and free?

---

13. See W. H. Foote, *Sketches of Virginia* (1850; repr., Richmond, Va.: John Knox Press, 1966).

O may this strange, this matchless grace,
This godlike miracle of love,
Fill the whole earth with grateful praise,
And all th'angelic choirs above,
And all th'angelic choirs above.

> Who is a pard'ning God like Thee?
> Or who has grace so rich and free?
> Or who has grace so rich and free?[14]

Preaching His Own Funeral Sermon

It is said that Davies preached his own funeral sermon at Nassau Hall. His New Year's Day sermon, delivered on the first day of 1761, came from the text in Jeremiah 28:16, "This year thou shalt die." He wanted to alarm careless and unconverted hearers with the shortness of life; he told them that it was highly probable that death might meet some of them that very year. "Perhaps I may die this year," he said, as he urged them to repent and make good use of their lives, living each day of the coming year for Christ. One month later, Samuel Davies died, aged only thirty-seven years.

Davies's dear mother was by his side as he fell asleep in Jesus. "There is the son of my prayers," she said, "but there is the will of God and I am satisfied." Appropriately, his funeral service was conducted in the Prayer Room of Nassau Hall, where he had preached his own funeral sermon only one month before. Imagine Davies's "trembling joy" seeing his pardoning God face-to-face and, no longer in the suburbs of heaven but in heaven itself, hearing "all th'angelic choirs above."

----

14. Samuel Davies, "Great God of Wonders!," in *Trinity Hymnal* (Suwanee, Ga.: Great Commission Publications, 1991), 82.

Study Questions

1. What lessons can you learn from Samuel Davies as a "war preacher"?

2. What was Davies's principal desire in life? How did he fulfill this as a minister of the gospel? In what ways is he a role model also for ministers—and, in a sense, for every Christian—still today?

3. How does Davies's rebuke of King George II reveal the fear of God in him? If the fear of God means to esteem God's smiles and frowns more than the smiles and frowns of people, how should this influence the way we live?

4. What practical lessons can we learn from Davies's short tenure as college president?

5. Why do you think Dr. Martyn Lloyd-Jones called Davies the greatest preacher America has ever known?

6. How does Davies's famous hymn, "Great God of Wonders," reveal his Reformed convictions about genuine religious experience?

~ 7 ~

John Newton

1725–1807

Ship in a Storm
NICHOLAS POCOCK

"The ship is foundering!" At the dreaded cry, horror filled twenty-three-year-old John Newton's heart. "We're all lost!"

It was March 10, 1748. John awoke in the night to the plunging and lurching of the *Greyhound* caught in a violent storm. The trading vessel had been too long at sea and was badly in need of dry dock and repairs. Water began filling the hold beneath John's pitching hammock. "We're all lost!" Others took up the cry. John heard his own terrified voice among the rest. What he feared most had come upon him.

Sea Captain's Son

Born in 1725, John Newton enjoyed the loving nurture of a godly mother, while seeing little of his sea captain father. From his earliest days, his mother

John Newton

taught him Scripture verses and the poems and hymns of Isaac Watts, and she often told him he would grow up to preach the gospel. When John was seven, however, she died. His father soon remarried and placed John in a boarding school, where he spent several miserable years making friends with boys who taught him to swear and cheat.

Finally, eleven-year-old John convinced his father to take him on a voyage as cabin boy, a course of life that proved most hurtful to John. He quickly learned the crude, sinful ways of seamen and forgot all his dear mother had taught him. For several years his father endured John's unruly ways. At last, his father, weary of his incorrigible son, found John a berth on another ship.

Given several days' leave before sailing, John left to visit friends of his mother in Kent. There he met Mary Catlett and fell deeply in love. He deliberately overstayed his leave, returning three weeks after the ship sailed. His father was furious when he heard the news. It would not be the last time John failed to return to his ship on schedule, and his father nearly disowned him the next time it happened.

At eighteen, John was conscripted into the navy on a British man-of-war, HMS *Harwich*, and was eventually made a midshipman, a junior officer in training to command a ship one day. He squandered this new beginning by rebelling against the authority of his captain and, while on leave again, overstayed a visit to Mary's family. Later, sent ashore at Plymouth on a mission to round up deserters, John took to his own heels and deserted. The British Navy was relentless in punishing deserters. John was captured and flogged, and the captain had him thrown below in irons. In utter disgrace, he was demoted to common seaman.

Brooding at sea, he watched the swirling waves and considered throwing himself overboard. He couldn't swim and would have surely drowned. His bitterness grew so great he even plotted to kill the captain. Then one day, the *Harwich* stopped in mid-ocean, availing itself of an opportunity to get rid of undesirable men by transferring them to an African trading vessel. Few doubted who would be chosen. John found himself discharged from the navy in the midst of the sea and left to his fate as a disgraced and unwanted sailor on a trading ship.

John immediately fell in with coarse and foul men and soon made himself hated by yet another captain. Somehow, in the midst of his loose living, he enjoyed writing poetry, but not ennobling poetry. He wrote a vulgar song mocking the captain and "sinned with a high hand," as he referred to it, by teaching the rebellious lyric to the entire ship's company.

A Slave in Africa

Having run afoul of another captain, John decided to jump ship and remain in Africa to make his fortune. Promised a partnership in the rounding up of black slaves, he entered the service of a white slave trader living on a small island off the west coast of Africa. There he offended the slave trader's African wife, who began mocking and abusing him. He became ill, and might have starved to death under the cruelty of his master's wife, if it were not for the pity of the African slaves.

John went on a trip with his master and was falsely accused of theft. His master had him chained to the ship deck whenever he went ashore, leaving John exposed to the open skies for days at a time. He was given a meager ration of rice and allowed to catch fish to feed himself. Even after the voyage when they returned home, John's master continued to keep him chained.

To keep his sanity in this hopeless condition, John read the only book available, *Euclid's Geometry*. He drew diagrams in the sand, eventually mastering the mathematical principles of the book. Though humiliated living the life of a slave, his heart remained hard and unrepentant.

One day, when John was laboring to plant lime trees, his master came by and mockingly said that perhaps one day John would become an English sea captain and return to this place to pluck some of the limes. Neither of them knew at the time that one day that very thing would take place.

Rescued on the Greyhound

After some time, John was released from bondage and became the business partner of another slave trader. John enjoyed some worldly success in this wicked work and might have chosen to remain there, but God had other plans. One of John's coworkers happened to be on the beach when an English ship, the Greyhound, passed by. The man used smoke signals to invite the ship to stop and do business. The man was astonished when the ship's captain inquired about John Newton. Providentially, the captain had been sent by John's father to find his son and bring him back to England. Later John marveled at God's sovereignty in directing the ship right to his obscure island surrounded by thousands of miles of ocean and the long African coast.

John worked as a seaman on board his new home, the *Greyhound*, and again, scorning God's mercy to him, he reverted to his old ways as a blasphemer of God. After trading along the coast, the ship sailed for England. Wind and current required them to sail across the Atlantic and north to Newfoundland, where they provisioned the ship with fish.

Too long at sea without repair, the *Greyhound* did her best, but all feared that the ship would not hold if a storm arose. On that fateful night in March, the dreaded storm overtook them with a vengeance. Pitching violently in the rising waves, the vessel was taking on too much seawater far too rapidly. John heard the cries of his fellow seaman: "The ship is sinking! We're all lost!" He joined in the terrified cry.

As John climbed up the companionway, in the chaos, the captain promptly sent him back below for a knife. The man just behind John stepped on deck in John's place, and immediately a wave swept him overboard into the churning seas, beyond recovery. Another vicious wave wrenched planking from one side of the ship, and howling winds tore sails and shattered masts and spars. The beleaguered trading vessel plunged into the troughs of massive waves. At every plunge, John expected her to sink into the depths— and he with her, never to rise again.

For the first time, John cried out, "Lord, have mercy on us!" The storm raged for days while every man, desperate for his life, took turns pumping water out of the sinking ship. While lashed to the helm, John, the great blasphemer—now crying for mercy—feared that God would not forgive so vile a sinner as he.

Later, frantically pumping, John recalled all he'd learned from his mother about Jesus's death for sinners and how those in distress should put their trust in Him. Wiping the briny sea spray from his face, John cried, "Can these things be true?"

The worst of the storm lasted eleven days. Without her cargo of heavy beeswax, the poor *Greyhound* would have surely foundered, but the crippled ship sailed on, her crew famished and exhausted. As the storm subsided, John discovered a Bible and read Luke 11:13: "If ye then, being evil, know how to give good gifts unto your children: how much more shall your heavenly Father give the Holy Spirit to them that ask him?"

Looking hard at the pages of the book in his hands, John concluded, "If this book is true, the promise in this passage is true likewise." He began earnestly praying, asking God to give him the Holy Spirit. As he prayed, his spiritual despair gave way to hope. He read on. While meditating on the story of the prodigal son, he was impressed by the father running to greet his wayward son, and the parable gave him greater confidence in the heavenly Father's love for His children.

Their food stores all ruined by the storm, the crew was emaciated. Just when John wondered if they had been spared by the storm only to die of starvation, he heard the cry of the seaman on watch, "Land, ho!"

Once in port, John made his way to the nearest church. Falling on his knees, he worshiped the Lord and offered heartfelt thanksgiving for his deliverance. By the regenerating power of the Holy Spirit, John repented wholeheartedly of his sinful, misspent life and embraced by faith the merits and mediation of Christ as his Savior for his salvation. Overjoyed with the sweet freedom of forgiveness of sins, he pledged his life in service to God, to be the Lord's forever and only the Lord's.

Growing in Grace

Now in Christ, John's appetites changed. No longer enslaved to rebellion and blasphemy, he studied the Bible and other Christian books, preparing for a life dedicated to God.

A slave ship

Newton, now a responsible and dutiful sailor, was eventually given command of a trading vessel. After another voyage, John proposed to Mary, and, in 1750, they became husband and wife. Deeply devoted to his beloved wife and now captain of a slave ship, John wrote Mary more than two hundred letters on his last sea voyages. She kept every one of them.

Knowing how vile sailors' lives were, John knew that only Christ could set them free from such a life. Concerned for their spiritual welfare, he gathered them on the decks of the ship for public worship every Lord's Day. Longing for the education he never had, Newton studied Latin and mathematics on board the ship. He soon decided that Cicero and the Latin poets, though valuable, taught him not a word of Jesus, and he committed himself to reading more authors who did.

Life as a sea captain in the eighteenth century was a dangerous and toilsome life. John quelled a mutiny and thwarted several slave insurrections on his ship. But then the Spirit of God began working on his awakened conscience. He suddenly saw the appalling inhumanity of the slave trade. How could he, a Christian, make his living buying and selling human beings? This thought, combined with a desire to be at home with Mary and his growing interest in ministering the gospel, led him to leave the sea and become a tide surveyor in Liverpool.

Gospel Ministry in Olney

Recalling how his mother longed for him to be a minister of the gospel, Newton spent the next ten years studying the Scriptures, listening to the preaching and counsel of George Whitefield, and seeking ordination as an Anglican minister. Perhaps due to his disreputable past (who wants a blasphemer and slave trader for his pastor?) the local bishop rejected Newton as a minister.

Finally, with the help of Lord Dartmouth, a Christian nobleman who used his resources and influence to promote the gospel, Newton was called to be curate, or assistant, to the vicar in the little market town of Olney in the county of Buckinghamshire. John and Mary Newton set up house in the old vicarage between the village and the parish church of Saints Peter and Paul, which had been built in the early fourteenth century.

From 1764 to 1779, Newton ministered by loving the working poor, by exemplifying godliness and faithful preaching, and by writing hymns for the children in his congregation. God brought such large numbers to faith in Christ through Newton's ministry that the church had to be enlarged. Many traveled from far and wide to hear the story of a slave-trading infidel turned gospel minister. John and Mary took the duty of hospitality seriously and extended it to anyone who walked more than six miles to church. So many took advantage of that offer, that warmhearted Mary often prepared large meals for guests on the Lord's Day.

The previous curate had arranged the study so that his back was to the town and he could look out on the beautiful scenery of the medieval church and the river winding through pastoral farmland. When Newton arrived, he switched the arrangement of the pastor's study. He turned his desk so that he looked out at the tenement housing of the poor. As a constant reminder of his desperate need of God's grace, and that he had been a slave himself, Newton had two verses installed above the mantel: "Since thou wast precious in my sight, thou hast been honourable" (Isa. 43:4) and "Thou shalt remember that thou wast a bondman in the land of Egypt, and the LORD thy God redeemed thee" (Deut. 15:15).

In the mystery of God's providence, John and Mary Newton, though they deeply loved children, never had any of their own. Newton wanted to reach the children of Olney for Christ, so he gathered them together on Thursday afternoons for Bible stories and singing. He attracted as many as two hundred children with his sea stories, paper ships, and hymns. He even gave cash prizes for those who memorized Scripture passages and hymns. He gathered their parents midweek for Bible study and prayer and taught them his hymns, often adding a new one each week.

Marks of Newton's Ministry

Knowing that it was the sovereign grace of God alone that had justified a wretch such as he, and that it was that same grace at work in the sometimes slow process of sanctifying him, Newton's ministry to his flock was marked by love, gentleness, and patience. But he was a minister in the Church of England, in which he observed, "Errors abound on all sides, and every truth of the gospel is either directly denied or grossly misrepresented."[1] Newton, therefore, was deeply committed to contending for the faith, but he feared that

Olney Vicarage
T. SULMAN

some ministers "delivered truths in a raw, unguarded manner."[2] While some of his fellow Bible-believing ministers threw themselves into theological controversy, Newton was reluctant to enter the public debates. "Few writers of controversy," Newton cautioned, "have not been manifestly hurt by it. Controversies are productive of little good. They provoke those whom they should convince, and puff up those whom they should edify."[3]

Newton's alternative to public controversy in his day, such as the one instigated by John Wesley against the Calvinism of his colleagues, George Whitefield and Augustus Toplady, was faithfully and winsomely to expound the Word of God. There was no doubt about his Reformed soteriology. "I

---

1. John Newton, *Selected Letters of John Newton* (Edinburgh: Banner of Truth, 2011), 115.

2. Iain Murray, *Heroes* (Edinburgh: Banner of Truth, 2009), 105.
3. Newton, *Selected Letters*, 115.

William Cowper
PORTRAIT BY WILLIAM BLAKE

The Olney Hymns

In 1767 God brought William Cowper, one of England's greatest poets, to reside near Newton's home at the old vicarage. Cowper, who suffered with debilitating depression, found solace in gardening and collecting a menagerie of animals for pets. And he wrote poetry, some of the finest in the language.

Newton put his new friend Cowper to work writing hymns based on the Bible, to be sung by the children and adults who attended the midweek meetings at the parish hall. The two poet friends often wrote in what Cowper called his "verse manufactory," a small summer house in his garden. When Cowper would fall into depression, Newton would come to his side, pray, read Scripture with him, and urge him to write more hymns. Which Cowper did! "God Moves in a Mysterious Way," one of his best-loved hymns, explores the incomprehensible ways of God's sovereignty and goodness in the vicissitudes of the Christian life. "Sometimes a Light Surprises the Christian While He Sings" is a contemplative hymn on how God comforts bewildered Christians who continue in praise and adoration of God even in the darkness.

The two friends published the *Olney Hymns* in 1779, a collection of sixty-eight hymns by Cowper and 280 by Newton for the "faith and comfort of sincere Christians." Newton's greatest hymn is something of an autobiographical versification of God rescuing him "through many dangers, toils, and snares" by His amazing grace. It remains one of the best-loved hymns in the Christian church.

> Amazing grace—how sweet the sound—
> That saved a wretch like me!
> I once was lost, but now am found—
> Was blind, but now I see.
>
> 'Twas grace that taught my heart to fear,
> And grace my fears relieved;
> How precious did that grace appear
> The hour I first believed!

am an avowed Calvinist," wrote Newton, and then added, "The doctrines of grace are essential to my peace; I could not live comfortably a day, or an hour, without them."[4] But he was determined to avoid the irony of lacking grace as he proclaimed the doctrines of grace. One of the ways he did it was by adorning Calvinist doctrine in the many hymns he wrote with William Cowper.

---

4. Murray, *Heroes*, 102–4.

Newton's versification of Psalm 87
set to a tune by Joseph Hadyn

Thro' many dangers, toils, and snares,
I have already come;
'Tis grace has brought me safe thus far,
And grace will lead me home.

And when this flesh and heart shall fail,
And mortal life shall cease,
I shall possess within the veil
A life of joy and peace.

When we've been there ten thousand years,
Bright shining as the sun,
We've no less days to sing God's praise
Than when we'd first begun.

Another marvelous hymn Newton wrote is a loose versification of Psalm 87, a hymn with strength, conviction, and unshakable resolve. "Glorious Things of Thee Are Spoken" is full of God's covenantal care for His children. Just as Israel's enemies waged war against her, so Christ's enemies war against His church, but "with salvation's walls surrounded," Christians may "smile at all [their] foes." Newton, herein, gives us a versified sermon, a poetic theology, extolling the glories of membership in Christ's church, concluding with a thrilling stanza of consecration:

Savior, since of Zion's city
I, through grace, a member am,
Let the world deride or pity,
I will glory in Thy name.
Fading are the world's best pleasures,
All its boasted pomp and show;
Solid joys and lasting treasures
None but Zion's children know.

The Great Anti-Slavery Meeting
THOMAS HOSMER SHEPHERD

As biblical, substantive, and precious as many of New-ton's hymns are, it needs to be noted that he never wanted his hymns sung in public worship in the church as a substitute for the singing of the Psalms.

Additional Writings

Newton wrote much more than his renowned hymns. In addition to his hymns, the six-volume set of *The Works of John Newton* reprinted by Banner of Truth contains more than one hundred of his most important and best-known sermons, his renowned autobiography *Out of the Depths*, more than three hundred of his edifying letters that are packed full with experiential and practical wisdom, his reflections on various topics, his thoughts and abolitionist views on the slave trade together with other political and social treatises, and additional miscellaneous writings—nearly four thousand pages of material in all. *The Works of John Newton* also contains Richard Cecil's excellent, moving biography of Newton, first published two years after Newton died. This biography includes considerable fascinating information on Newton's life and reflections on his legacy and influence.

Newton's remarkable letters are known as *Cardiphonia: or, The Utterance of the Heart*—so named upon William Cowper's suggestion to the author—and they are truly the voice of a seasoned pastor's heart. They have made a profound impact on thousands of readers over the years since they were first published. Of *Cardiphonia*, C. H. Spurgeon wrote, "In few writers are Christian doctrine, experience, and practice more happily balanced than in the author of these letters, and few write with more simplicity, piety, and force."[5]

Final Years and Death

In Newton's last years of ministry, he was called to St. Mary Woolnoth Church in London, a few blocks away from St. Paul's Cathedral. There he wrote, preached, and cared for the poor, and there he laid to rest his beloved wife, Mary.

Meanwhile, the celebrated William Wilberforce became friends with Newton and invited him to speak against the slave trade before Parliament. With Newton's help, Wilberforce presented a bill that would forever abolish slavery in all British dominions. In 1788 Newton wrote *Thoughts upon the Slave Trade*, in which he detailed the cruelty and inhumane conditions on board slave ships. In the pamphlet he offered a heartfelt "confession, which…comes too late…. It will always be a subject of humiliating reflection to me, that I was once an active instrument in a business at which my heart now shudders."[6] He went on further to confess that during his years as a slave captain, "I was greatly deficient in many respects…. I cannot consider myself to have been a believer in the full sense of the word, until a considerable time afterwards."[7] With Newton's support, Wilberforce's bill ending the British slave trade was passed into law by Parliament in 1807.

John Newton died December 21, 1807, and was buried with his wife at St. Mary Woolnoth, London. But in 1893, when tunnels or "tubes" for London's famed Underground Railway were being dug underneath the churchyard where the Newtons were buried, their remains were exhumed and

<hr>

5. C. H. Spurgeon, *The Sword and the Trowel*, August 1866, 382.

6. Adam Hochschild, *Bury the Chains: The British Struggle to Abolish Slavery* (Basingstoke: Pan Macmillan, 2005), 130–32.

7. John Newton, *Out of the Depths*, ed. Dennis Hillman (Grand Rapids: Kregel, 2010), 84.

reinterred back in the Olney churchyard. Newton's own words appear on their sarcophagus: "JOHN NEWTON. Clerk. Once an infidel and libertine a servant of slaves in Africa [he] was by the rich mercy of our LORD and SAVIOUR JESUS CHRIST preserved, restored, pardoned and appointed to preach the faith he had long laboured to destroy. Near 16 years as Curate of this parish and 28 years as Rector of St. Mary Woolnoth."[8]

One of the last recorded things Newton said before he died provides a simple but profound summation of his gospel ministry: "My memory is nearly gone, but I remember two things, that I am a great sinner, and that Christ is a great Savior."[9] He had preached this message for more than forty years, and his hymns proclaim the same gospel truths today.

8. As read by the author from the tombstone in St. Peter's and St. Paul's parish churchyard in Olney, Buckinghamshire, England.

9. John Newton, *Wise Counsel: John Newton's Letters to John Ryland Jr.*, ed. Grant Gordon (Edinburgh: Banner of Truth, 2009), 401.

Study Questions

1. What were some of the ways John Newton showed his rebellion against God in his youth? What are some of the ways you are tempted to rebel against God?

2. When John Newton thought his ship was about to sink, he felt that he was lost. What particular memories did God's Spirit bring to his mind in his distress?

3. Looking back on his life, Newton did not believe he was a true believer in Jesus Christ when he continued with slave trading. Is it possible for someone to be a true Christian and a slave trader? What are biblical examples of believers who were used of God but who needed a great deal of progress in sanctification and growth in grace in their lives?

4. What were specific ways Newton ministered to the special needs of his friend William Cowper? Who are people you know who need special grace from others in their lives? How could you be used of God to encourage them in the things of God?

5. How did Newton go about proclaiming the doctrines of grace? Why did he avoid controversies?

8

Lemuel Haynes

1753–1833

Lemuel halted at the edge of the field, wiping sweat from his brow. He rested wearily against the plow that was secured to the yoke of oxen standing in front of him. The oxen were exhausted too. Sweat glistened on their sides in the afternoon sunlight. This first day of June was hotter than usual for Massachusetts, and Lemuel's strength was drained by his long day working under the sun. It was often tiring to be an indentured servant on Deacon Rose's family farm.[1]

Slave labor
HENRY P. MOORE

---

1. Indentured servanthood was different from slavery. Indentured servants would often regain independence after serving a set term of labor. Also, it was relatively normal for poor people in general—whites and blacks—to serve terms of indentured servanthood.

Lemuel looked up again to the western horizon. The ominous clouds he had seen a few minutes earlier were getting closer and darker. Based on past experience, Lemuel figured he had about twenty minutes to get the oxen and equipment put away before the storm broke.

"Com' on, Abner. Git up now, Joab." Lemuel coerced the two oxen toward the rugged barn on the other side of the property. As they drew near to the barn, he unhitched the yoke from the plow. Leaving the plow to rest in the grass outside, he led the yoke of oxen together into a shady corner pen in the barn, carpeted with fresh straw.

Lemuel looked out the window just as the dark clouds blotted out the light of the sun. The leaves of the trees began to rustle wildly as the storm drew nearer. He fumbled around, trying to take the yoke off the necks of the oxen in the dim light. Finally, he succeeded in his task. He slung the heavy yoke up on one shoulder and climbed carefully over the gate of the pen to put the yoke away.

By this time, thunder rumbled with increasing frequency and intensity. Lemuel laid the yoke in its proper place and ran to the door of the barn, hoping to beat the rain. Right as he came to the door, a terrifying flash of light filled the sky. Lemuel dropped to his knees and covered his eyes. Stunned and trembling, he thought, *If the fearsome attack of this thunderstorm is just a small part of God's normal working, how terrible must the final judgment of God be against sinners!*

Lemuel immediately thought back to a similar event that had happened several years before. While Mr. and Mrs. Rose had been away from the house, a storm just like this had unexpectedly broken over the forests and fields, shrouding the land in deep shadow. The rain had pelted the ground without mercy. The fire of heaven had filled the sky. The crack of thunder had shaken the earth, as though it could dislodge its inhabitants. That lonesome, fearful evening was the first time that Lemuel had understood the reality of God's power and judgment.

Lemuel once again trembled at the solemn reality of God's wrath as he stood a moment longer in the doorway of the barn. A straggling chicken scrambled across the yard to the chicken coop as a wall of rain swept across the farm. Lemuel took a deep breath and dashed through the pounding rain to the back door of the house. He ducked quickly inside and clambered into a back hallway of the house, dripping water. As he paused to catch his breath, Mrs. Rose came out of the kitchen to welcome him.

"Lemuel, so glad you made it in! I was concerned you'd be caught out in the field. The rainstorm came up so quick!" Mrs. Rose came and put a motherly arm around Lemuel's shoulder and gave him a gentle squeeze. She didn't mind the damp imprint he left on her blouse.

"Ma'am," Lemuel stated, grateful for Mrs. Rose's gentle care. She was the closest thing to a mother he'd ever known. He paused, his mind still racing with thoughts of God's holy dominion. "The Lord hasn't brought the end yet. I suppose there's still time for an unworthy sinner like me to find Jesus."

Mrs. Rose took a step back and looked thoughtfully into Lemuel's eyes. "Lemuel, we're real grateful to have you in the home—Mr. Rose and I are so glad that the Lord opened the way for you to come and help out 'round here. He doesn't make mistakes. Just *seek ye first the kingdom of God and His righteousness*—I trust the Lord has a good plan for you."

"I hope so, ma'am." Lemuel nodded with a grateful smile and trundled off to his bedroom to gather some dry clothes. Once he had changed, Lemuel settled into his favored corner by the chimney to read by the light of the fire. As he read through a sermon by Jonathan Edwards, Lemuel could not help but feel the weight of God's majesty again. He was convinced that God had all splendor and power, but he struggled to believe that the mercy of God could be for him. As the firelight grew dim, Lemuel laid the book aside and prayed. Timidly, yet earnestly, he asked that God would grant him confident faith—faith that Jesus's work would even reach down to a humble sinner like him and save him.

Lemuel Haynes

The Father's Care of the Fatherless

In July of 1753, a baby was born in West Hartford, Connecticut. The father was black, possibly held as a slave by one of the local landowners. The mother was white, possibly from a prominent family in town. The baby was Lemuel Haynes. Tragically, the mother saw the complexion of the child and refused to keep him. Even later in life, when Haynes attempted to come back into contact with his biological mother, she would not acknowledge him.

Though he was abandoned at birth by his mother and father, Haynes had a Father who did not abandon him. The Lord provided him with a godly home where he would be prepared for a lifetime of fruitful ministry. At the age of five months, Haynes was taken in by Mr. and Mrs. David Rose to be an indentured servant in their household. Mr. and Mrs. Rose were devout Calvinistic Congregationalists who lived in the rural town of Granville, Massachusetts. Even though Haynes was a household servant, the Rose family (Mrs. Rose especially) treated him as part of the family. Haynes would later say that Mrs. Rose "had peculiar attachments to me: she treated me as though I was her own child. I remember a saying among the neighbors, that she loved Lemuel more than her own children."[2]

Haynes regularly attended church with the Rose family. While he heard the warnings and promises of God's Word throughout his childhood, a number of experiences in his early life impressed these truths on his heart. On two different occasions, Haynes came near to death. The first

2. Timothy Mather Cooley, *Sketches of the Life and Character of the Rev. Lemuel Haynes, A.M.: For Many Years Pastor of a Church in Rutland, Vt., and Late in Granville, New-York* (New York: J. S. Taylor, 1839), 30.

time, he nearly drowned when learning to swim in a local river. The second time Haynes came near to death was when an angry ox pursued him and nearly gored him with its horns. In both instances, God provided a friend who was able to bring rescue at just the right time. These events helped to convince Haynes of God's special providence for His people.[3]

At a different time, when Haynes was home alone in his youth, a violent storm suddenly sprang up. Haynes was convinced that God's judgment against the earth had come. He recognized with terror the vast power of God and the certain judgment of the wicked in hell. Thunderstorms continued to bring Haynes to humble thoughtfulness throughout his life afterward.[4] Though Haynes was very conscious of God's power, he struggled to believe that the grace of God was attainable for him. When he was about twenty years old, he witnessed a spectacular display of the Northern Lights, which prompted a renewed terror in him of God's coming judgment. Haynes was deeply affected by this incident, and he began reflecting on the weighty matters of eternity with great urgency. At last, while sitting under an apple tree several days

Seeing the Northern Lights gave Haynes a sense of God's power and judgment

later, he experience the joy of *personal* forgiveness and access to God through the work of Christ.[5] Though he would struggle with assurance of his salvation in various seasons of his life after this, he would often return to that apple tree to remind himself of the hope he had found in Christ.[6]

The Preparation of America's First Black Minister

Throughout his term as an indentured servant, Haynes was a reliable worker. Just as Joseph showed great ability in managing all of Potiphar's house,

---

3. Cooley, *Sketches of the Life and Character*, 33–34.

4. Cooley, *Sketches of the Life and Character*, 32.

5. John Saillant, *Black Puritan, Black Republican: The Life and Thought of Lemuel Haynes, 1753–1833*, Religion in America (Oxford: Oxford University Press, 2003), 14; D. Sherman, *Sketches of New England Divines* (New York: Carlton & Porter, 1860), 273.

6. Cooley, *Sketches of the Life and Character*, 41.

Haynes proved that he could be trusted with all the cares of the household, including purchasing livestock on Mr. Rose's behalf. Though Haynes's labor around the farm was a full-time job, he still managed to gain a decent education through careful management of his time. Even after he had spent a full day doing manual labor in the fields, Haynes would trudge over to the schoolhouse and gather the lessons he had missed that day in order to teach himself. Resolved to learn as much as he could, he spent his evenings in the chimney corner of his house, memorizing Scripture and doing schoolwork by the light of the crackling fire. Through these long evenings of independent study, he managed to become well educated, and he gained local admiration for being self-taught.[7]

When the time of his indentured servanthood expired, Haynes left the Rose family farm and became involved with colonial militia activities in 1774. He participated in multiple military exercises, including the capture of Fort Ticonderoga from the British in 1776.[8] It was during this time that he gained a deep respect for George Washington and the principles of a free republic. Late in 1776, however, he contracted an illness and was discharged from the army. He returned home to the Rose family farm to work and write. It was during this time that Haynes decided to try his hand at writing poetry, social commentary, and sermons.

Saturday evenings, it was common practice in the Rose family to gather together in preparation for Lord's Day worship. Haynes would select a sermon written by such men as John Owen, Richard Baxter, Jonathan Edwards, or Philip Doddridge

Haynes was influenced by Jonathan Edwards and other Puritan-minded men

---

7. Saillant, *Black Puritan, Black Republican*, 13.

8. Saillant, *Black Puritan, Black Republican*, 15.

and read it aloud.[9] The frequent reading of robust, heart-searching sermons by Puritan-minded, evangelistic men undoubtedly was influential in sharpening Haynes's biblical insight. In the same biblical, experiential manner, Haynes wrote out his first sermon on John 3:3, "Jesus answered and said unto him, Verily, verily, I say unto thee, Except a man be born again, he cannot see the kingdom of God."[10] And on the next Saturday evening, when Haynes pulled out a sermon to read for the Rose family, it wasn't the usual published sermon. Instead, Haynes read his own sermon. At the end of the reading, Mr. Rose expressed his appreciation for the message and attempted to guess who had written it, supposing it had been written by the great evangelist George Whitefield.[11] Haynes eventually admitted it was his own. From that point onward, his family urged him to enter pastoral ministry.

Though an opportunity arose for Haynes to study at Dartmouth College, he instead moved to Connecticut in 1779 and began training for the ministry under two ministerial mentors, Daniel Farrand and William Bradford. Both Farrand and Bradford helped Haynes to learn Latin and to gain biblical language skills. After a brief season of rigorous training, Haynes became licensed to preach in 1780.[12]

After obtaining a license to preach, he received a call from his former church back in Granville, Massachusetts. He preached regularly there for five years. Prior to his arrival, a young woman in the congregation, Elizabeth Babbit, had been experiencing a season of spiritual distress. Under the preaching of Haynes, however, she was greatly encouraged in her faith. Her deep appreciation for Haynes grew conspicuously, and it soon became known to Haynes that she had affectionate feelings for him. On September 22, 1783, Lemuel and Elizabeth were married. Over the next twenty years, they would enjoy the blessing of raising ten children.

After preaching for five years at his home church in Massachusetts, in 1785 Haynes became an ordained minister in the Congregational church. He was the first black man in the United States to be formally ordained as a pastor.[13]

Pastoring the Prejudiced

The Congregational church ordained Haynes as a minister-at-large while he was providing long-term pulpit supply at a church in Torrington, Connecticut. However, the church in Torrington never officially accepted him into the pastorate. A significant part of their objection to Haynes involved prejudice against his skin color.[14]

9. Lemuel Haynes, *May We Meet in the Heavenly World: The Piety of Lemuel Haynes*, Profiles in Reformed Spirituality (Grand Rapids: Reformation Heritage Books, 2009), 6; Sherman, *Sketches of the Life and Character*, 270; Luke Walker, *Lemuel Haynes: The Black Puritan*, Wrath and Grace Biographies (Richfield, Minn.: Wrath and Grace Publishing, 2017), 17.

10. Cooley, *Sketches of the Life and Character*, 49.

11. Cooley, *Sketches of the Life and Character*, 48–49.

12. Helen MacLam, "Introduction: Black Puritan on the Northern Frontier," in *Black Preacher to White America: The Collected Writings of Lemuel Haynes, 1774–1833*, by Lemuel Haynes, ed. Richard Newman (Brooklyn, N.Y.: Carlson Pub., 1990), xxi.

13. MacLam, "Introduction: Black Puritan," xxi; Haynes, *Black Preacher to White America*, xv.

14. Thabiti M. Anyabwile, *The Faithful Preacher: Recapturing the Vision of Three Pioneering African-American Pastors* (Wheaton, Ill.: Crossway, 2006), 19.

The Declaration of Independence
JOHN TRUMBULL

It was not easy being a black pastor in predominantly white churches. Haynes was poignantly aware of the evils of slavery and the prejudice it promoted against people of his skin color. Following the Declaration of Independence in 1776, he wrote an essay titled "Liberty Further Extended" in which he argued that the United States should truly uphold the rights of "life, liberty, and the pursuit of happiness" for *all* people, including blacks. His main point in writing was to argue that a black slave "may justly challenge, and has an undeniable right to his liberty: consequently, the practice of slave-keeping, which so much abounds in this land [America], is illicit."[15] Appealing to Acts 17:26, he noted that all men were essentially one "species," and, as such, all men should be equally given the same rights and governed by the same laws.[16] Haynes noted that according to God's own law, manstealing was a clearly heinous crime punishable by death.[17] Though he knew that some slave owners argued that blacks were descended from Canaan and "destined by the almighty to slavery,"[18] Haynes powerfully rejected this falsehood and argued that any "middle wall of partition" that had formerly divided the nations has been broken down with the arrival of Jesus Christ.[19] He conceded that slavery was still practiced in the New Testament after the arrival of the gospel. Arguing from 1 Corinthians 7:21, however, Haynes pointed out that Paul clearly identified freedom for the slave as the ideal ultimate reality.[20]

Haynes's arguments were not only directed against nonbelievers. Some of the people who supported slavery and colonization were fellow Congregationalists and Calvinists. Calvinists all agreed that God governed all people, things, and events by His sovereign providence. Yet some Calvinists wrongly claimed that slavery was *good* because God was using it providentially to bring pagan Africans into lands where they could hear the gospel. People who argued this way thought that the ends justified the means. Haynes, however, knew that stealing and enslaving was inherently wrong according to God's Word. He turned to Romans 6:1 and asked the probing question: "Shall we continue in sin, that grace may abound?" The answer was clearly no.[21] Haynes was confident that God would sovereignly work out all things to bring about His good purposes—even despite evil practices like the transatlantic slave trade. However, he denied the conclusion that Christians should, therefore, support ongoing slavery.[22] Haynes rightly taught that God's sovereign providence did not remove the responsibility men had to obey the clear commands of Scripture.

This essay, which would have been very controversial in that era, was never published during Haynes's lifetime. It is unclear whether the essay remained unpublished due to his own reluctance or whether it was due to being refused by potential publishers. In any case, Haynes was an early voice in the American church to show how the gospel ultimately undermined slavery.

After two years of ministering in the Torrington church without being welcomed as their pastor, Haynes finally

15. Haynes, *Black Preacher to White America*, 19.

16. Haynes, *Black Preacher to White America*, 19.

17. Haynes, *Black Preacher to White America*, 23. See Exodus 21:16.

18. Haynes, *Black Preacher to White America*, 24.

19. Haynes, *Black Preacher to White America*, 25. See Ephesians 2:13–15.

20. Haynes, *Black Preacher to White America*, 25–26.

21. Haynes, *Black Preacher to White America*, 26–27.

22. Walker, *Lemuel Haynes*, 31.

received a formal call to pastor a church in 1788. He and his family moved to Rutland, Vermont, where he became the first black minister of an all-white congregation at the age of thirty-five. During his time in Rutland, in 1804, Haynes received an honorary master's degree from Middlebury College to recognize his contributions as a gospel minister. He was the first black man to ever receive an honorary degree from an American college.[23]

Commitment to Gospel Vitality

Prior to Haynes entering the pastorate, a major controversy had surfaced in the Congregational church concerning revival. During the First Great Awakening, which had occurred about forty years earlier, New England had seen great spiritual transformation. Many people were converted due to evangelistic preaching, and during these revivals it was not uncommon for people to respond to the preaching of the gospel with visible emotional reactions. A faction of "Old Light" Congregationalists developed in the church that believed such revivals were disorderly and were nothing more than demonstrations of emotional excess. Old Light ministers also tended to support a controversial practice known as the half-way covenant, which allowed church members who couldn't profess they were saved and their children to receive the sacraments of the church. As a result of this practice, many New England churches were filled with outwardly moral church members who lacked inward signs of saving grace.

Haynes rejected the Old Light position and identified as a "New Light" Congregationalist, following closely in the theological footsteps of Jonathan Edwards. Haynes supported itinerant preaching to advance the gospel and believed that the half-way covenant normalized spiritual deadness. At the same time, Haynes was helpfully moderate in his New Light position. He was wary of superficial emotionalism that could sometimes accompany revivalist meetings and was careful to stress the importance of true, Spirit-worked change in human hearts through the preaching of God's Word.[24]

The Old Light-New Light debate was an ongoing point of controversy that afflicted the churches of New England throughout Haynes's ministry. The Granville, Massachusetts, church split over this issue during his youth. The Torrington, Connecticut church split over the same controversy in 1785 during his two-year term filling the pulpit. The Rutland, Vermont church even split over this issue in 1797, after he had been preaching there for nearly a decade. After the Rutland church's schism, Haynes continued on as the pastor of the West Rutland parish, which was theologically conservative. The East Rutland congregation ultimately embraced the half-way covenant and tended toward spiritual nominalism.

The need for ministry throughout western Vermont was great at this time. Though thousands of settlers had moved west of the Green Mountains, only four or five Congregational ministers were present there to care for their souls. Many of these settlers had been influenced by a cultural shift known as the Enlightenment. Instead of bringing light, however, the Enlightenment ironically had brought

---

23. MacLam, "Introduction: Black Puritan," xxviii.

24. Anyabwile, *Faithful Preacher*, 19; Lemuel Haynes, "A Prayer for New Birth (1776)," in *Conversations with God: Two Centuries of Prayers by African Americans*, ed. James Melvin Washington (New York: Harper Perennial, 1995).

confusion and darkness to many American churches. People influenced by the Enlightenment began to discredit the importance of divine revelation and claimed that people could uncover truth by using their own reason and senses. Prominent men began to deny the God of Christianity in order to teach deism. Many settlers around Rutland, Vermont, were influenced by the deism of the American patriot Ethan Allen. Haynes was well suited intellectually and spiritually to minister in this difficult climate.[25]

The Enlightenment had negative impacts on more than just laymen. As Americans became increasingly influenced by the Enlightenment, some ministers even began to teach serious errors, such as Unitarianism[26] and Universalism.[27] On one occasion Haynes even had to deal with a Universalist preacher speaking in his home pulpit. In June 1805, some local residents invited a notorious Universalist named Hosea Ballou to give a message at the West Rutland meetinghouse. Though Haynes had already made alternative plans for the day, friends persuaded him to come and counter Ballou's remarks. Ballou preached from 1 John 4:10–11: "Herein is love, not that we loved God, but that he loved us, and sent his Son to be the propitiation for our sins. Beloved, if God so loved us, we ought also to love one another."[28] Ballou

claimed that God's love was so great that God would punish no one with eternal death and hell; rather, everyone would ultimately be saved.

Having only minutes to prepare, Haynes showed his sharp wit by improvising a sermon in response to Ballou's heresy. Haynes's sermon would become publicly embarrassing to the Universalist cause for decades. He selected Genesis 3:4 as his text: "And the serpent said unto the woman, Ye shall not surely die." From this text, Haynes argued that the very first Universalist preacher was Satan. Though Satan taught a popular message among sinners, saying that the wages of sin is life,[29] his Universalist message was presumptuous and false. The word of God, on the other hand, had declared "in the day that thou eatest thereof thou shalt surely die" (Gen. 2:17). Those who believed the preaching of Satan were enemies of the gospel. But those who saw the truth would live according to the rightness of God's words, "Go ye into all the world, and preach the gospel to every creature. He that believeth and is baptized shall be saved; but he that believeth not shall be damned" (Mark 16:15–16).[30]

Haynes's satirical sermon against Universalism was circulated in the Americas and Europe and was printed

---

25. Cooley, *Sketches of the Life and Character*, 78.

26. Unitarianism denies the doctrine of the Trinity, often on the grounds that it defies human logic. Unitarianism is essentially synonymous with Socinianism, in which God is presented as being one in every sense, denying the divinity of Jesus Christ and the Holy Spirit.

27. Universalism teaches a doctrine that appeals to human logic and yet contradicts Scripture: that God's love will result in the ultimate salvation of all people from death and hell.

28. MacLam, "Introduction: Black Puritan," xxix; William Buell Sprague and Timothy Mather Cooley, eds., *Annals of the American Pulpit:*

Or, Commemorative Notices of Distinguished American Clergymen of Various Denominations from the Early Settlement of the Country to the Close of the Year Eighteen Hundred and Fifty-Five with Historical Introductions (New York: Robert Carter & Bros., 1857), 2:179.

29. Compare with Romans 6:23.

30. Haynes, *Black Preacher to White America*, 105–11; Cooley, *Sketches of the Life and Character*, 283.

on dozens of occasions over the next six decades.[31] Haynes became an important voice arguing for basic evangelical doctrines in his generation. In light of God's certain and eternal judgment against impenitent sinners, he proclaimed the necessity for people to be born again by the Holy Spirit, to repent of all their sins, to place their faith in Jesus Christ, and to love walking in God's ways.[32] What about you? Do you know these four things by personal experience?

Personal Wit and Family Worship

Haynes's clever and penetrating thinking was evident in his preaching, but he also had a reputation for giving sharp, witty responses in the affairs of daily life. On one occasion, the congregants of a local parish asked Haynes to help them. They were pastored by a young minister who seemed irresponsibly unwilling to pursue marriage. Though the minister would listen to his congregation's caring encouragements with agreement, the minister procrastinated and would take no action. Haynes set up a meeting with the young minister and explained to him how starting a family would help him to better understand the pastoral needs of his congregation. The young man nodded his agreement and replied, "I understand, Mr. Haynes, that you have some very fine daughters." Haynes replied without hesitation, "I have sympathy for you and for your parishioners; but, really, I have taken great pains to educate my daughters, and much care to prepare them for usefulness, and I hate to throw them away."[33]

On a different occasion, Haynes was confronted by a man who spoke against the authority of the Bible. He pressed Haynes to give proof for why he believed the Bible. Haynes responded, "Why sir, the Bible, which was written more than a thousand years ago, informs me that I should meet just such a man as yourself." The unbelieving man asked Haynes to explain himself, to which Haynes said, "Why, sir, the Bible says…'In the last days, scoffers shall come, walking after their own lusts.'"[34]

Haynes was committed to leading his family spiritually. Morning and evening, he would gather with his wife and children for family worship. Each member of the family would have an open Bible, and Haynes would read from the Septuagint or the Greek New Testament. Whenever a passage was read, Haynes would ask for his family to give an interpretation, saying, "I want light: who of you can give any?"[35] He would give everyone an opportunity to respond, from the youngest to the oldest. If no one was able to articulate a proper response, he would sometimes respond playfully, "You give darkness rather than light on the subject."[36] Haynes was dearly loved by his family. The Lord was pleased to work through his ministry to his family, and all ten of his children grew up to profess faith in Christ.

Ministry and Politics

Haynes ministered in Rutland, Vermont, for thirty years. Historians have at times referred to him as "the Black

---

31. Haynes, *Black Preacher to White America*, 105; Sprague and Cooley, *Annals of the American Pulpit*, 2:179.

32. Haynes, *May We Meet in the Heavenly World*, 31–35.

33. Cooley, *Sketches of the Life and Character*, 128–29.

34. Cooley, *Sketches of the Life and Character*, 129. Haynes referenced 2 Peter 3:3.

35. Cooley, *Sketches of the Life and Character*, 281–82.

36. Cooley, *Sketches of the Life and Character*, 282.

Puritan" since his preaching style was similar to the Puritans of England and New England—biblically anchored, expositionally profound, experientially stirring, and immensely practical. As one of his close friends later wrote, "Never did he wait to inquire whether a particular doctrine was popular. His only inquiries were, 'Is it true? Is it profitable? Is it seasonable?'"[37]

Though Haynes was not afraid to teach unpopular doctrines, he did not teach in order to be divisive. Instead, many of his fellow ministers recognized him as a gifted peacemaker, and he was regularly asked to serve on local church councils when congregations needed help resolving disputes. When moderating one particular crisis that was tearing apart a rural church in Vermont, Haynes pleaded with his fellow believers, "How painful the thought that the Redeemer would be wounded in the house of his friends!"[38]

Haynes's loyalty to Christ and his faithful preaching brought substantial numerical and spiritual growth to the church in Rutland. Despite all these labors, however, his congregation dismissed him from serving as pastor in 1818, when Haynes was sixty-five. The reason for Haynes's dismissal is unclear, but it may have been due to his political sentiments.[39]

Haynes preaching in church

Haynes lived during a time when there was substantial political upheaval in America. During his life, the American colonies became an independent nation, and many a man clamored to form the young republic after his own image. Like many Congregational ministers of his day, Haynes believed that the domains of politics and religion

---

37. Cooley, *Sketches of the Life and Character*, 79.

38. Cooley, *Sketches of the Life and Character*, 149.

39. Cooley, *Sketches of the Life and Character*, 171–72;

MacLam, "Introduction: Black Puritan"; Sprague and Cooley, *Annals of the American Pulpit*, 2:180. Anyabwile, *Faithful Preacher*, 19–20.

could not be entirely divided from each other.[40] Haynes understood that God's Word should be formative in shaping how Christians understand everything, including politics.

Haynes at times advocated publicly for a Federalist political position, which may have eventually caused dissent among his congregation in Rutland. He came to recognize pastorally that political issues could cause great disruption for the church and could distract from more foundational spiritual concerns. Writing to a friend, Haynes noted, "Dissensions about politics have had an unfavorable influence on religion, as they have greatly tended to alienate the affections of the people from each other." Despite his strong political convictions, however, Haynes knew that his hope was not ultimately in politics. When his political hero George Washington suddenly died, Haynes concluded, "May it teach us to stop trusting in man, whose breath is in his nostrils."[41]

Haynes's last home in South Granville, New York
DANIEL CASE, CC BY-SA 3.0

---

40. MacLam, "Introduction: Black Puritan," xxvi.

41. Cooley, *Sketches of the Life and Character*, 85.

Desiring a Better Country

After leaving Rutland, Haynes was soon called to serve a church in Manchester, Vermont, where he ministered effectively from 1818 to 1822. Toward the end of this time, though, his health began to decline. Haynes, now sixty-nine years old, encouraged the church in Manchester to find a younger minister. Rather than retiring, however, Haynes then took up a call to serve a church in Granville, New York, where he pastored for the remaining eleven years of his life, running the race faithfully to the very end (Heb. 12:1–2). Under Haynes's persistent ministry, the Granville church added eighty new members who professed faith in Christ.

Living in rural New England at this time was fraught with hazards, and the possibility of death was constant. Over the course of his ministry, Haynes preached at least 520 funeral services.[42] He regularly preached that all of life should be lived in light of ultimate realities. If this was true for the layperson, it was especially true for the minister. In *The Character and Work of a Spiritual Watchman*, Haynes listed several ways that eternity must shape a minister's activities: A minister looking to heaven (1) examines his own heart carefully, (2) is diligent in his duties, (3) recognizes that he is accountable to God, (4) preaches with urgency and plain speech, and (5) is attentive to the spiritual condition of the congregation.[43] Haynes lived in these ideals as a minister, husband, and father—and this focus on eternity also influenced how Haynes interacted with America's politics and the abolition of slavery. He sought the welfare of his earthly country because he caught sight of a heavenly country where holy men and women enjoyed total righteousness and lasting joy in God's presence.

Haynes died on September 28, 1833, at the age of eighty, having spent more than five decades preaching the glorious doctrines of God's grace. He had been a faithful shepherd for his wife and children, for the congregations he had pastored, and for his fellow countrymen. After his death, a small note was found among Haynes's writings recording an epitaph he wished to be placed on his tombstone. Its contents effectively display the evangelical piety of a faithful minister:

> Here lies the dust of a poor hell-deserving sinner, who ventured into eternity trusting wholly on the merits of Christ for salvation. In the full belief of the great doctrines he preached while on earth, he invites his children, and all who read this, to trust their eternal interest on the same foundation.[44]

---

42. Haynes, *May We Meet in the Heavenly World*, 14.

43. Haynes, *Black Preacher to White America*, 49–51.

44. Cooley, *Sketches of the Life and Character*, 312.

1. How did Lemuel Haynes use his time as a young man? In light of eternity, what are ways you can make good use of your time?

2. Why is it a bad idea to trust in what people can comprehend or sense more than we trust in God's Word?

3. Is God's anger against sin incompatible with God's love? How might God be loving us by forbidding and punishing sin?

4. Why might Universalism seem so appealing to people? In what ways does Universalism discourage repentance and obedient faith?

5. Can religion and politics be totally separated from each other? Is there anything in life that God's Word is unable to speak to?

6. Some Calvinists in New England used theology to defend their practice of slavery instead of letting Scripture shape their practices. Are you doing the same thing in some areas of your life?

7. When Lemuel Haynes was dismissed from the Rutland, Vermont, church, he was likely tempted to abandon the ministry. How can you respond to rejection and discouraging events with continued confidence and fruitful activity?

8. How do eternal realities impact the way you live as a student, family member, friend, citizen, church member, employee, and neighbor?

9

Andrew Fuller

1754–1815

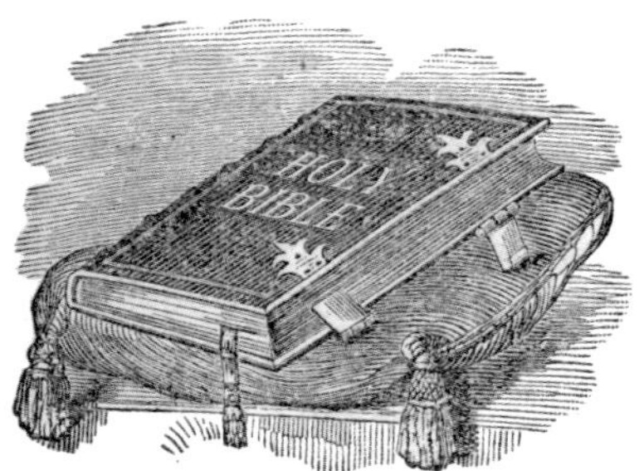

William Wilberforce (1759–1833), the great evangelical politician who led the fight against the slave trade and slavery, loved having people over to his house for breakfast or a cup of tea. In fact, he made it a rule never to omit "any opportunity to become acquainted with any good or useful man."[1] This meant, as his sons later observed, that his house was "seldom free from guests," some of whom would arrive early enough in the day to join Wilberforce at his breakfast and all of whom would provide a field for Wilberforce's remarkable conversational skills.[2] Among the guests whom Wilberforce received at his home was the Baptist theologian Andrew Fuller (1754–1815), whose theological abilities Wilberforce deeply admired.[3]

On one occasion, Wilberforce endeavored to quickly introduce Fuller to one of his sons after his

William Wilberforce, the great abolitionist
PORTRAIT BY H. ROUSSEAU

arrival had been announced. "You know Andrew Fuller?" he asked him. "No, I never heard his name," came the reply. "Oh, then you must know him," Wilberforce said. "He is an extraordinary man, whose talents have raised him from a very low condition." Fuller came in. Wilberforce later noted that the

---

1. William Hague, *William Wilberforce: The Life of the Great Anti-Slave Trade Campaigner* (London: HarperCollins, 2007), 506.

2. Robert Isaac Wilberforce and Samuel Wilberforce, *The Life of William Wilberforce* (London: John Murray, 1839), 3:388.

3. Wilberforce and Wilberforce, *Life of William Wilberforce*, 3:389.

Baptist author was "a man of considerable powers of mind" but looked like a blacksmith.[4] True to Wilberforce's description, Fuller lacked formal education beyond the basics of reading and writing. Yet, by God's grace, his talents enabled him to become, as Charles Haddon Spurgeon (1834–1892) once put it, "the greatest [Baptist] theologian" of the nineteenth century.[5]

What brought forth such praise from Wilberforce and Spurgeon? One factor was the books Fuller wrote—for example, one that ably refuted deism, which expressed Enlightenment thinking about God, or another book that gave a thoroughly biblical response to the hyper-Calvinism of his day, which damaged quite a number of English Baptist communities during the eighteenth century.[6] The latter, in turn, led to Fuller's extensive involvement as the secretary of what came to be called the Baptist Missionary Society, whose most famous missionary was one of Fuller's closest friends, William Carey (1761–1834). In fact, as the missions scholar Harry R. Boer observed, "Fuller's insistence on the duty of all men everywhere to believe the gospel," which he taught especially in his works against hyper-Calvinism, "played a determinative role" in forming "Carey's missionary vision."[7]

Andrew Fuller
STAINED-GLASS PORTRAIT,
FULLER BAPTIST CHURCH, KETTERING, ENGLAND

---

4. Wilberforce and Wilberforce, *Life of William Wilberforce*, 3:389.

5. Gilbert Laws, *Andrew Fuller: Pastor, Theologian, Ropeholder* (London: Carey Press, 1942), 127.

6. For Fuller's response to deism, see *The Gospel Its Own Witness* (1800), and for his reply to hyper-Calvinism, see *The Gospel Worthy of All Acceptation* (first edition, 1785; second revised edition, 1801).

7. Harry R. Boer, *Pentecost and Missions* (Grand Rapids: Eerdmans, 1961), 24.

Lessons from Fuller's Conversion

The youngest of three brothers, Andrew Fuller was born on February 6, 1754, at Wicken, a small agricultural village in Cambridgeshire, England, to Robert Fuller (1723–1781) and his wife, Philippa Gunton (1726–1816). His parents rented and worked a succession of dairy farms.[8] When Fuller was seven years of age, his parents moved to the village of Soham, about two and a half miles from Wicken. Once settled in Soham, they joined themselves to the Calvinistic Baptist work in that locality. The pastor of the work was John Eve (d. 1782), who was a hyper-Calvinist, or, as Fuller put it, one "tinged with false Calvinism" in his teaching.[9] Many years later Fuller remembered how Eve's preaching "was not adapted to awaken [the] conscience" and "had little or nothing to say to the unconverted."[10] Thus, despite the fact that Fuller regularly attended the Baptist church, he gave little thought or heed to the sermons he heard.

When Fuller was fourteen, though, he began to entertain thoughts about the meaning and purpose of life. Yet the hyper-Calvinism that formed the air he had breathed since his earliest years proved to be a real barrier to his coming to Christ. It maintained that in order to flee to Christ for salvation, the "warrant" that a person needed to believe that he or she would be accepted by Christ was a subjective one. Conviction of one's sinfulness and deep mental anguish as a result of that conviction were popularly regarded by hyper-Calvinists as such a warrant. From this point of view, these experiences were signs that God was in the process of converting an individual. This perspective on conversion was a direct result of the argument that the Scriptures invite only those sinners who are sensible of their sin to believe in Christ. The net effect of this teaching was to place the essence of conversion and faith not in believing the gospel "but in a persuasion of our being interested in its benefits." Instead of attention being directed away from one's sinful and needy self toward Christ, the convicted sinner was only turned inward on himself or herself to search for a variety of evidences that he or she was being converted.[11] Eventually, though, Fuller decided, "I will trust my soul, my sinful, lost soul in his [that is, Christ's] hands—if I perish, I perish!" So it was in November 1769 that Fuller found peace with God and rest for his troubled soul in the crucified Christ.[12]

His personal experience prior to and during his conversion ultimately taught him three things in particular about conversion. First, there was the error of maintaining that only those sinners aware of and distressed about their spiritual state have a warrant or right to come to Christ. Against this perspective Fuller would later argue that the gospel exhortation to believe in Christ was a sufficient enough warrant to come to the Lord Jesus. Second, genuine faith is Christ-centered, not just a curving inward on oneself to see if there was any desire to know Christ and embrace His salvation. Finally, Fuller recognized that true conversion is

---

8. Andrew Gunton Fuller, "Memoir," in *The Complete Works of the Rev. Andrew Fuller*, ed. Joseph Belcher (Harrisonburg, Va.: Sprinkle, 1988), 1:1. For details of Fuller's family, see Andrew Gunton Fuller, *Andrew Fuller* (London: Hodder and Stoughton, 1882), 11–12.

9. Fuller, "Memoir," in *Works*, 1:2, 12.

10. Fuller, "Memoir," in *Works*, 1:2.

11. Andrew Fuller, *Strictures on Sandemanianism, in Twelve Letters to a Friend*, in *Works*, 2:563–64. See also E. F. Clipsham, "Andrew Fuller and Fullerism: A Study in Evangelical Calvinism," *The Baptist Quarterly* 20 (1963–1964):103.

12. Fuller, "Memoir," in *Works*, 1:5–6.

rooted in a radical change of the affections of the heart and manifests itself in a lifestyle that seeks to honor God.[13] These insights into the nature of true conversion are still of vital significance today.

Learning about Divine Sovereignty and Human Responsibility
In the spring of 1770, following his conversion, Fuller was baptized and joined the church at Soham. Later that year, though, the church was sorely divided over the question of whether sinful men and women had "the power—to do the will of God and to keep themselves from sin." The controversy in the Soham church over this issue eventually led to Pastor Eve's resignation from the church in October 1771.[14] Fuller later commented that though this controversy deeply troubled him, it was ultimately the means of leading him into "those views of divine truth" that later made their appearance in his major published works.

In January 1774 the church asked him to regularly fill the pulpit. Sixteen months later, Fuller was ordained as the second pastor of the Soham church. The church consisted of forty-seven members and met for worship in a rented barn. It was not until 1783, a year after Fuller had been called to Kettering Baptist Church in Northamptonshire, that the church had the finances to erect a more permanent building.

During this first year of ministry, Fuller's time was largely taken up with reading and study. Since Eve's preaching was the only model he had ever had, he preached like Eve and refused to urge the unconverted to come to Christ.

Kettering Baptist Church, now called Fuller Baptist Church
BURGESS VON THUNEN, CC BY-SA 2.0

But he was increasingly dissatisfied with the reasoning of hyper-Calvinism. He began to sense that his "preaching was anti-scriptural and defective in many respects." But he saw no easy solution to his problem. He felt he was having to feel his way slowly "out of a labyrinth."[15]

Meanwhile, Fuller was also immersing himself in the works of two authors: the well-known evangelist from the previous century, John Bunyan (1628–1688), and John

13. Clipsham, "Andrew Fuller and Fullerism," 106–7.

14. Fuller, "Memoir," in *Works*, 1:10. The controversy is described in Fuller, "Memoir," in *Works*, 1:8–10.

15. Fuller, "Memoir," in *Works*, 1:13.

John Bunyan
PORTRAIT BY THOMAS SADLER
© NATIONAL PORTRAIT GALLERY, LONDON

great and good man," he was not as clear as Gill regarding the gospel. However, as Fuller studied the writings of other sixteenth- and seventeenth-century authors, in particular those of the Puritan theologian John Owen (1616–1683), he noted that they, too, gave "free invitations to sinners to come to Christ and be saved." In other words, Fuller discerned that with regard to preaching there was a definite difference not only between Bunyan and Gill but more broadly between sixteenth- and seventeenth-century Calvinism and that of the hyper-Calvinists of the early eighteenth century.

To help resolve his questions about hyper-Calvinism, Fuller began to write a treatise,

Gill (1697–1771), one of the leading eighteenth-century Calvinistic theologians. Fuller found much that was helpful in Gill's systematic theology but was deeply troubled by the evident differences between Gill and Bunyan. Both were ardent Calvinists, but whereas Bunyan recommended the free offer of salvation to sinners without distinction, Gill did not. Initially Fuller wrongly concluded that though Bunyan was "a later titled *The Gospel Worthy of All Acceptation*, for his own instruction. A preliminary draft of the work was written by 1778 and completed in 1781. Two editions of the work were published in Fuller's lifetime. The first edition, published in Northampton in 1785, was subtitled *The Obligations of Men Fully to Credit, and Cordially to Approve, Whatever God Makes Known, Wherein Is Considered the Nature of Faith in Christ, and the Duty of Those Where the Gospel Comes in That Matter*. The second edition, which appeared in 1801, was more simply subtitled *The Duty of*

Sinners to Believe in Jesus Christ, a subtitle that well-expressed the overall theme of the book. Substantial differences were evident between the first edition of 1785 and the second edition of 1801, which Fuller freely admitted and which primarily related to the doctrine of particular redemption. The work's major theme remained unaltered, however: "Faith in Christ is the duty of all men who hear, or have opportunity to hear, the gospel."

This epoch-making book sought to be faithful to the central emphases of historic Calvinism while at the same time attempting to leave preachers with no alternative but to drive home to their hearers the universal obligations of repentance and faith. Fuller expressed his position well in an article of the statement of faith he made at his induction into the pastorate of the Baptist church at Kettering, Northamptonshire, in 1783:

> I believe it is the duty of every minister of Christ plainly and faithfully to preach the gospel to all who will hear it;…and that it is their [i.e., the hearers'] duty to love the Lord Jesus Christ and trust in him for salvation.… I therefore believe free and solemn addresses, invitations, calls, and warnings to them to be not only *consistent*, but directly *adapted*, as means, in the hand of the Spirit of God, to bring them to Christ. I consider it as a part of my duty which I could not omit without being guilty of the blood of souls.[16]

Critical in Fuller's method of inquiry after truth in these early years was his rigorous commitment to the Bible as the unerring Word of God. As his close friend John Ryland (1753–1825) wrote in his memoirs of Fuller, "He had fewer means of assistance from men and books than he might have had elsewhere; but he was obliged to think, and pray, and study the Scriptures, and thus to make his ground good."[17] A personal covenant written by Fuller in 1780 thus speaks of his "determination to take up no principles at second-hand, but to search for everything at the pure fountain of [God's] Word."[18] Fuller was never afraid to go back to the Scriptures and, on the basis of God's inerrant Word, question what passed for orthodoxy. This did not mean that Fuller did not seek to learn from other Christian authors. We have noted his reading of John Bunyan, John Owen, and John Gill. In many ways, the American theologian Jonathan Edwards (1703–1758) was his theological mentor. But the thinking of all of these men was tested by the inerrant Scriptures.

The Gospel Worthy of All Acceptation involved Fuller in much unwanted controversy. Not long after the publication of the book, Fuller was challenged in print by two London hyper-Calvinists, William Button (1754–1821) and John Martin (1741–1820). It is noteworthy that, despite their attacks on Fuller, both Button and Martin subsequently had friendly relations with him. Button, for instance, was a firm supporter of the Baptist Missionary Society from its early years until his death. And Martin, in 1797, could speak of his sincere respect for Fuller. While penning a response to the former of these two Baptist pastors, Fuller found himself under attack by a representative from the other end of the

16. A. C. Underwood, *A History of the English Baptists* (London: Carey Kingsgate Press, 1956), 163–64.

17. John Ryland, *The Work of Faith, the Labour of Love, and the Patience of Hope, Illustrated; in the Life and Death of the Rev. Andrew Fuller* (London: Button & Son, 1818), 43.

18. Ryland, *Work of Faith*, 129.

theological spectrum—namely, the General (i.e., Arminian) Baptist Dan Taylor (1738–1816).

Later, Fuller was to describe his own theological position, which some dubbed "Fullerism," as "strict Calvinism." He sought to differentiate it from hyper-Calvinism, which was "more Calvinistic than Calvin," and from moderate Calvinism, which was essentially the theological perspective of the Puritan Richard Baxter (1615–1691) and which Fuller considered as "half Arminian." Fuller reckoned strict Calvinism to be "the system of Calvin." Fuller's theology, which today some call "evangelical Calvinism," was that of his close friend William Carey as well as his later admirer C. H. Spurgeon. His theological view was able to combine a vigorous passion for the salvation of sinners and the missionary advance of the kingdom of God with a profound confidence in the sovereignty of God.

Lessons from Fuller's Other Controversies

The critical role Fuller played in this controversy did not preclude his engaging in other vital areas of theological debate. In 1793 he issued an extensive refutation of the Unitarianism of Joseph Priestley (1733–1804) in *The Calvinistic and Socinian Systems Examined and Compared, as to Their Moral Tendency*. Due to the vigorous campaigning of Priestley, Unitarianism, which denied the Trinity and the deity of Christ, had become a leading form of serious error within England in the last quarter of the eighteenth century. Fuller's rebuttal of Unitarianism aptly displays the Christ-centered nature of eighteenth-century Baptist thought. Fuller ably showed that the early church made the divine dignity and glory of Christ's person "their darling theme."

Joseph Priestley

Then, in 1800, Fuller published *The Gospel Its Own Witness*, a definitive eighteenth-century response to deism, in particular that of the pamphleteer Thomas Paine (1737–1809). This work was one of the most popular of Fuller's books, going through three editions by 1802 and several reprintings in the next thirty years. Wilberforce considered it to be the most important of all of Fuller's writings. The work has two parts. In the first, Fuller compares and contrasts the moral effects of Christianity with those of deism. The second part of the book aims to demonstrate the divine origin of Christianity from the general consistency of the Scriptures.

Fuller engaged in yet another vital controversy with a group of men and women called Sandemanians, the followers of Robert Sandeman (1718–1771), who distinguished themselves from other eighteenth-century evangelicals by a predominantly intellectual view of faith. They became known for their main theological tenet that saving faith is "bare belief of the bare truth." In a genuine desire to exalt the utter freeness of God's salvation, Sandeman had sought to remove any vestige of human reasoning, willing, or desiring in the matter of saving faith. In his *Strictures on Sandemanianism* (1810), Fuller makes a couple of important points. First, if faith did concern only the mind, then there would be no way to distinguish genuine Christianity from nominal Christianity. A nominal Christian mentally assents to the truths of Christianity, but those truths do not grip the heart and reorient his or her affections. Second, the knowledge of Christ is a distinct type of knowledge. Knowing Him, for instance, involves far more than knowing certain things about Him, such as the fact of His virgin birth or the details of His crucifixion. It involves an ardent desire for fellowship with Him and a delight in the sweetness of His presence.

In all three of these controversies, each of which can be traced back to the influence of Enlightenment rationalism, Fuller revealed himself to be a pastor-theologian very much in touch with the worldview of his culture. Fuller did not spend his energy, for example, primarily fighting battles that had occupied many of his seventeenth-century Puritan forebears—namely, struggles about ecclesiological issues. If Fuller can teach us anything about the defense of Christian truth, it is that we must be ever alert to the challenges that confront Christianity in our particular circumstances.

Fuller's Christ-Centered Spirituality

Finally, in our day when both those within the church and those outside of it are fascinated by spirituality, Fuller's piety has much to teach us. Take, for instance, his conviction that the cross of Christ lies at the very heart of Christianity. The cross, Fuller maintained in 1802, is "the central point in which all the lines of evangelical truth meet and are united." Just as the sun is absolutely vital for the maintenance of the solar system, so "the doctrine of the cross is to the system of the gospel; it is the life of it."[19] Fuller would forthrightly declare that the atoning death of Christ is nothing less than "the life-blood of the gospel system."[20] From another perspective, the preaching and teaching of Christ crucified can be compared to "a golden link which, if laid hold of, draws with it the whole chain of evangelical truth."[21] In sum, the cross is "the grand peculiarity and the principal glory of Christianity" and is all but equivalent to the gospel itself: "The doctrine of salvation through the blood of Christ…is, by way of eminency, called the gospel."[22]

Given this view of Christ's death, it is no surprise to find Fuller asserting that it has been the doctrine of the cross that "God, in all ages, has delighted to honour." Wherever times

---

19. Andrew Fuller, *The Calvinistic and Socinian Systems Examined and Compared, as to Their Moral Tendency*, in *Works*, 2:182.

20. Andrew Fuller, *Letters on Systematic Divinity*, in *Works*, 1:687.

21. Andrew Fuller, *The Common Salvation*, in *Works*, 1:411.

22. Fuller, *Calvinistic and Socinian Systems*, in *Works*, 2:181; *The Believer's Review of His State*, in *Works*, 1:303.

of spiritual vitality and vigor have been enjoyed by the church—"times of great revival," as Fuller termed them—there the atoning work of Christ has held an exalted place. Fuller noted that this doctrine was central to the Reformation and that the Reformers gave it a place of prominence. It was the leading theme of the Puritans and Fuller's spiritual forebears, the nonconformists of the seventeenth and early eighteenth centuries.[23] In his own day, the missionary triumphs of the Moravian missionaries in the West Indies, among the Eskimos, and especially in Greenland had been triumphs of the cross: the "doctrine of the atonement by the death of Christ…forms the great subject of their ministry."[24]

Fuller's writings are filled with reflection on the blessings wrought by Christ's death. He insisted, for instance, that the cross is the only way for sinners to be reconciled to a holy God. When Fuller was asked in 1798 to draw up a brief account of his early spiritual pilgrimage, he noted that at the time of his conversion he was brought to the conviction that "God would be perfectly just in sending me to hell, and that to hell I must go unless I were saved of mere grace." "Mere grace," he went on to explain, entailed the relinquishing of "every false confidence"[25] and trusting solely in the death of Christ for one's salvation. The laying down of His life on the cross, he wrote on another occasion, is "the only hope of a lost world, the only medium of acceptance with God, and the only admissible plea in our approaches before him."[26]

23. Fuller, *God's Approbation of Our Labours*, in *Works*, 1:190; *Common Salvation*, in *Works*, 1:412; *Calvinistic and Socinian Systems*, in *Works*, 1:121; *Decline of the Dissenting Interest*, in *Works*, 3:486.

24. Fuller, *Calvinistic and Socinian Systems*, in *Works*, 2:128.

25. Fuller, "Memoir," in *Works*, 1:5.

26. Fuller, *Truth the Object of Angelical Research*, in *Works*, 1:665.

Fuller the Pastor

Alongside these literary endeavors, Fuller exercised a significant pastoral ministry at Kettering. During his thirty-three years at Kettering, from 1782 to 1815, the membership of the church doubled and the number of "hearers" grew to over a thousand, necessitating several additions to the church building. Fuller was first and foremost a pastor, and he constantly sought to ensure that his many other responsibilities did not encroach on those related to the pastorate.

Two examples aptly display his pastoral heart. After Fuller died, there was found among his possessions a small book titled *Families Who Attend at the Meeting, August, 1788*. In it he wrote, "A Review of these may assist me in praying and preaching." Then, among his letters there is one dated February 8, 1812, written to a wayward member of his flock, of which the following is an excerpt: "When a parent loses… a child nothing but the recovery of that child can heal the wound. If he could have many other children, that would not do it.… Thus it is with me towards you. Nothing but your return to God and the Church can heal the wound."

Fuller's Family

Fuller's first wife was Sarah Gardiner (1756–1792). Married on December 23, 1776, she and Andrew subsequently had eleven children, of whom seven died in infancy—three at Soham and four at Kettering.[27] Of the other four, two predeceased their father, Sarah (1779–1786) and Robert (1782–1809). Fuller could rejoice that the other two children from this first marriage, John and Mary, both knew and loved the

27. Ryland, *Work of Faith*, 269–70.

*Deathbed Portrait
of a Child*
JOHANNES THOPAS

Lord.[28] Fuller's first wife died giving birth to their eleventh child on August 23, 1792.[29]

Two years later, Fuller married Ann Coles (1763–1825), a pastor's daughter. When Fuller's mother, Philippa, heard of her son's impending second marriage, she told him that she wished his "poor children well." "Have you any reason to fear the contrary?" her son asked her. Philippa Fuller admitted she didn't, but she reckoned that she herself would "not have made a good step-mother." Fuller, ever the plain speaker, replied to his mother, "And so from thence you judge that others will be the same. For my part I am persuaded now that I should be a kind father to any family put under my care."[30]

---

28. Thomas Ekins Fuller, *A Memoir of the Life and Writings of Andrew Fuller* (London: J. Heaton & Son, 1863), 148.

29. For his first wife's final days, see Ryland, *Work of Faith*, 286–91.

30. Fuller, *Andrew Fuller*, 74–75.

He and Ann had six children. Of these six, three, all daughters, died in infancy.[31] Another, also called Sarah (1797–1816), died just over a year after her father. The remaining two were sons, Andrew Gunton, who wrote a number of biographical studies of his father, and William.

All told, then, Fuller had seventeen children, of whom ten died in infancy and one other before she was ten. This startling figure is typical of this era, where it is estimated that one in two English children did not reach their tenth birthday.

Final Days and Fuller's Confidence

When Fuller died on May 7, 1815, his funeral was attended by an immense crowd. The wife of John Keen Hall (d. 1829), Fuller's successor, wrote of this event in a letter: "The rush of people was astonishing; it was supposed there must be 2,000 persons. The galleries were propped in several places to prevent any accident." At Fuller's request, his old friend John Ryland preached the funeral sermon. Based on Romans 8:10, it included not only an insightful exposition of this Pauline text but also a brief account of Fuller's final days. Noteworthy is the following declaration made by Fuller in his last letter to Ryland, which the latter read at the end of his funeral sermon:

> I have preached and written much against the abuse of the doctrine of grace, but that doctrine is all my salvation and all my desire. I have no other hope than from salvation by mere sovereign, efficacious grace through the atonement of my Lord and Saviour. With this hope I can go into eternity with composure.[32]

Study Questions

1. What kind of ministry did Fuller sit under as a young boy? What are some problems with hyper-Calvinism?

2. How was Fuller converted? What important lessons do we learn from his conversion?

3. Why did Fuller write his book *The Gospel Worthy of All Acceptation*? What is the main argument of the book?

4. How did Fuller view the Bible?

5. What other controversies was Fuller involved in? What does deism teach? And what does Unitarianism teach? And what is Sandemanianism?

6. Why was the death of Christ important to Fuller? How did he view it?

7. What kind of pastor and father was Fuller?

8. What can we learn from Fuller's last words?

---

31. For a short account of the death of one of these three, Ann, see Ryland, *Work of Faith*, 295–96.

32. Ryland, *Work of Faith*, 355.

~ 10 ~

Thomas Charles of Bala

1755–1814

Mary Jones (1784–1864), a young girl from the countryside in North Wales, was on a mission. She was desperate to get her very own Bible.

Through the Bible studies at the Methodist Society Mary had been attending, God had planted within her heart a seed of desire for Himself. By the time she was eight, her faith came alive and blossomed. When Mary was ten, she learned to read the Bible in Welsh through the Sunday schools that had been organized throughout Wales. Captivated by the Bible stories she had learned, and hungry for more, Mary would walk two miles to her neighbor's house to read the Bible there, memorizing what she could before returning home. The only other Bible in town was in the parish church. This limited access to God's Word could not satisfy Mary's hunger for it. She needed a Bible of her own. Being from a very poor family, however, she could not afford one.

Undeterred, ten-year-old Mary began working—mending clothes, selling eggs, and babysitting. She saved every penny she earned for six years. When she had enough to buy a Bible, sixteen-year-old Mary went into her village but found no Bibles for sale there. Then she heard that the famed preacher, Rev. Thomas Charles, was selling Bibles in the town of Bala.

So, one morning in 1800, Mary said goodbye to her mother and set out toward Bala, walking barefoot for twenty-five miles across rugged mountain terrain, carrying her shoes in a bag to keep them clean. She arrived at Bala in the evening, tired and hungry. The next morning,

Mary walking two miles to read a Bible

she put her shoes on her sore, swollen feet; ran to Thomas Charles's house; and knocked on the door.

"Good morning, Miss. What can I do for you?" said Charles, appearing in the doorway.

"Sir," Mary exclaimed with beaming face, "I heard you are selling Bibles. I wish to buy a Bible of my very own!"

"I am so sorry, my dear," said Charles. "But I have no more Bibles to sell."

Mary was sure she misheard. She was about to ask Charles to repeat what he said. But she found no words, only tears. She felt crushed and began to weep. "I'm sorry…I just…" she started, but her words turned to sobs.

"Now, now, my dear—what is it?" Charles asked.

Mary began to explain, pausing between sentences to wipe away her tears, that she had been working and saving her earnings since she was ten and that this was the day she had been waiting for. As Charles listened, he was moved, and his own tears began to well up. His life's work of bringing the gospel to the Welsh people seemed to hinge on what he would do in this moment. *I dare not send her away empty-handed*, Charles thought. Then he remembered that his stock of Bibles was not quite exhausted.

"You wait right here, Miss," Charles said, quickly disappearing into his home. When he returned to the doorway, he handed Mary a thick book with a beautiful white cover.

"I don't understand," Mary began, feeling the weight of the Bible in her hands. "I thought you—"

"This was my last Bible. I was keeping it for someone who bought it. But now it is yours!" Charles declared.

Mary could hardly believe that she was holding her very own copy of God's Word—a 1799 Welsh edition. Six

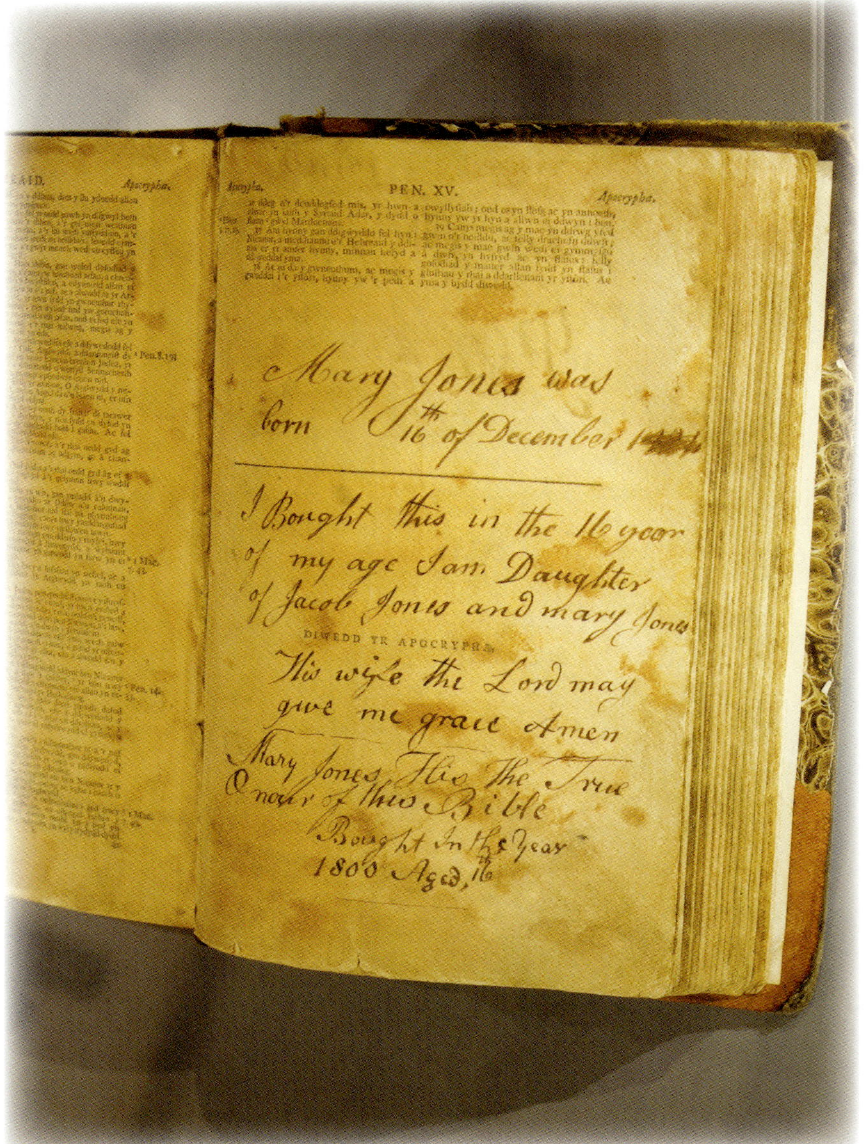

Mary's Welsh Bible
PHOTO BY ROBIN LLWYD AB OWAIN, CC BY-SA 3.0

years of hard work finally paid off! She paid for the Bible with her hard-earned savings and started home, singing lines from a popular Welsh hymn:

> This is Jesu's dear Bible,
> Precious gift of God's right hand;
> There we find the rule for living
> And the path to Canaan's land;
> There we read our ruin's story,
> Eden's sad and sorry loss;
> There we find the way to glory
> Through my Jesus and His cross.

When Mary returned home, she penned her name, age, and date of birth inside one of the Bible's pages, and added, "Mary Jones His [is] The True Onour [owner] of this Bible. Bought In the Year 1800."[1] Thomas Charles had long known that Bibles were very scarce in Wales in those days, but his efforts to supply them had met with little success thus far. But now Mary's determination to get a Bible in the face of extreme poverty filled Charles with new zeal to end this problem once and for all. "I must not now rest until I have found a way to fill the country with God's Word," he said.

Two years later, while preaching in Lady Huntingdon's chapel in London, Charles attended a meeting of the Religious Tract Society. There he shared his vision for Welsh Bibles and told the story of Mary Jones. A Baptist minister, Joseph Hughes, stood up and said, "Surely a Society might be formed for such a purpose, and if for Wales, why not also for the Empire and for the world?" This proposal led

to the founding of the British and Foreign Bible Society two years later. Within a hundred years, the Bible Society had distributed about two hundred million Bibles. Through its work the Bible has been translated into hundreds of languages.

In God's providence, this great work has been accomplished because a teenage girl was hungry for God's

Thomas Charles of Bala

---

1. This Bible is kept at the Cambridge University Library in the British and Foreign Bible Society's Archives.

Word. Thomas Charles would spend the remaining fourteen years of his life getting Bibles to the people of Wales.

The story of Thomas Charles of Bala marks the full flowering of the eighteenth-century Welsh revival through evangelism, church planting, and education.

A Difficult Mission Field

Griffith Jones, the renowned Welsh minister whose preaching was used by the Spirit for the conversion of Daniel Rowland and Howell Harris, was burdened with a longing for the Welsh people to be able to read the Bible in their own language. This led him to start the first general education system in Wales in 1731, through "circulating schools." Classes would be held in one place for three months or so before the school moved on to another. In these early years of the Methodist revival in Wales, hundreds of people were being converted by the preaching of the gospel. But the gospel work led by Griffith Jones, Howell Harris, and Daniel Rowland saw most of its success in South Wales.

The northern area of Wales was another story altogether. Extremely hostile to the gospel, North Wales was a dangerous mission field where there were few conversions and much persecution. When they ventured north to preach the

The Gordon Riots
CHARLES GREEN

gospel, Rowland and Harris were attacked by angry mobs. Harris was often beaten. On one such trip to Hay-on-Wye in 1740, one of Harris's assistants, William Seward, was killed by a violent mob. The next year Harris preached "in a private house in Bala, North Wales." An angry mob disrupted the service and nearly killed Harris. But there was fruit that day: a young woman named Jane Jones was converted under Harris's preaching. Jane and her husband, David, kept a shop in Bala. In 1753 they had a daughter, Sarah, also known as Sally, who was "famous for her personality, her attractiveness, and her zeal for the gospel." Years later she would become the wife of Thomas Charles.[2]

---

2. Erroll Hulse, "Editorial—A Significant Anniversary," *Reformation Today* 202 (November/December 2004): 2. See also "Thomas Charles," Banner of Truth, https://banneroftruth.org/us/about/banner-authors/thomas-charles; Iain H. Murray's "Biographical Introduction" to *Thomas Charles' Spiritual Counsels: Selected from His Letters and Papers by Edward Morgan* (Edinburgh: Banner of Truth, 1993); J. M. Jones, William Morgan, and John Aaron, *The Calvinistic Methodist Fathers of Wales* (Edinburgh: Banner of Truth, 2008), 2:239–342; and John Aaron, "God's

Thomas Charles: Early Life and Conversion

Thomas Charles was born in 1755 in South Wales near St. Clears. A gentle boy by nature, young Thomas was serious and very studious. Although his parents were not religious, his aptitude for learning made them think that he should go into the ministry. They sent him to school in Llanddowror, where Griffith Jones was the rector of the parish church, when Charles was about ten years old.

At school Thomas began reading the Bible and books such as John Bunyan's *The Doctrine of Law and Grace Unfolded*. At first he complained that there were few spiritually minded people to speak with in Llanddowror. But soon he met Rees Hugh, a former student of Griffith Jones, who mentored Thomas and frequently discussed spiritual matters with him. This fellowship caused spiritual stirrings in Thomas's heart, but he did not yet know how to respond to them. Under some spiritual conviction, he began to lead family worship when he returned home.

When Thomas was fourteen, he continued his schooling at Carmarthen and joined a Methodist society there. His grasp of the gospel began to grow. Then on January 20, 1773, eighteen-year-old Thomas heard Daniel Rowland preach a sermon on Hebrews 4:15: "For we have not an high priest which cannot be touched with the feeling of our infirmities; but was in all points tempted like as we are, yet without sin." Thomas ever remembered that day as the time of his conversion, the beginning of his life of faith. He wrote,

Ever since the happy day I have lived in a new heaven and a new earth…. The change a blind man receives when he gets his sight does not exceed the change I at that time experienced in my mind. Then I was first convicted of the sin of unbelief or entertaining narrow, contracted, and hard thoughts of the Almighty. I had such a view of Christ as our High Priest, of His love, compassion, power, and all-sufficiency as filled my soul with astonishment…. Praise the Lord, O my soul, and forget not all His benefits![3]

It is most remarkable and refreshing when a young man or woman begins to live fully for God. Thomas's conversion at eighteen left him with a deep awareness of his sins, an unshakable trust in the redemption that is in Christ, an unquestioning confidence in God's provision for all his needs, and a strong sense of a call to the gospel ministry.

Training for the Ministry

In 1775 twenty-year-old Thomas Charles enrolled in Jesus College at Oxford University to begin his training for the ministry.[4] Two years into his study his trust in God's provision was sorely tested. He had a tuition bill of £20, but his parents were no longer able to pay for his tuition, and he was out of money. Charles hoped that somehow God would resolve the situation, but without knowing how God would do so, he planned to leave school temporarily to work

---

Gift to North Wales: Thomas Charles of Bala (1755–1814)," *Evangelical Times*, October 2005, https://www.evangelical-times.org/27438/gods-gift-to-north-wales-thomas-charles-of-bala-1755-1814.

3. Eifion Evans, *Daniel Rowland and the Great Evangelical Awakening in Wales* (Edinburgh: Banner of Truth, 1985), 331–32.

4. It is noteworthy that Charles was not persecuted at Oxford like other students who identified as Methodists had been.

Jesus College
KRZYSZTOF IŁOWIECKI, CC BY-SA 2.0

and earn the money. A few days later, however, "a gentleman asked him to dinner, gave him the £20 he needed and ensured that he could afford to finish his time at Oxford."[5] This experience taught Charles to rely on God and to wait for His provision.

In the summer of 1777, Charles spent his vacation with former slave trader John Newton, who had been converted and had become both an abolitionist and an Anglican minister at Olney. Charles formed a close friendship with Newton and learned much from his character and relationship with Christ. Most importantly, he learned from Newton the importance of seeking the power of the Holy Spirit when preaching the gospel.

The following summer (1778), Charles went on a walking holiday to Bala with his friend Simon Lloyd. In Bala they met Sally Jones, the daughter of the shopkeeper who had been converted years earlier at the house in Bala where Harris had preached. Sally would eventually become Charles's wife, but for years before that they corresponded through letters. A year after that summer she received her first letter from Charles.

Beginnings in the Church of England

Charles's beginnings in ministry further taught him to trust God's leading. In 1778 he was ordained as deacon at Oxford. He was assigned to be the curate "of Sparkford in Somerset."[6] Before taking up his duties, he spent time with a friend in

Bala, toured North Wales, heard Rowland preach twice, visited Sally Jones, and preached at Llanvihangel. Charles was happy to see his old mentor, Rees Hugh, present at his sermon.[7] Hugh passed away a few weeks later.

After his encouraging tour of Wales, Charles began his discouraging curacy in Somerset, a parish of forty-one homes and 230 people. Charles's superior despised him because he considered him a Methodist, but instead of firing him, he cut his pay to an amount he was barely able to live on. The people in his parish were hostile to the gospel and hardened against godly living.[8] Charles struggled each day to live a godly life under the pressures of persecution. But he held to past lessons learned about waiting on God's provision. He even turned down another curacy that offered a higher salary, convinced that God wanted him to finish his assignment even in so difficult a place as Somerset. Again, waiting on God bore fruit. After Charles was ordained priest at Oxford in May 1780, he moved to another curacy in Somerset, but this time his superior was a gospel-centered man.

For four years he enjoyed his labors there under the Spirit's power, but his desire was to be in Bala so that he could marry Sally. Charles wrote to Sally often. In 1782 he began looking for a position near Bala, where Sally wanted to remain, to be near her family and run her shop. The following year, Charles married Sally, having found a position with a friend at Llangynog, near Bala.

Life as an Anglican priest located in a single parish did not work out as Charles had expected. Because of his

---

5. "Thomas Charles," UK Wells, https://ukwells.org/revivalists/thomas-charles. This page is based on Edward Morgan, "A Brief History of the Life and Labours of the Rev. T. Charles, A. B." (London: Hamilton, Seeley, Hatchard, Jones, Hughes, 1828).

6. "Thomas Charles," UK Wells.

7. "Thomas Charles," UK Wells.

8. He wrote, "Most look upon [religion] as something very bad, though they know not what it is; and they are exceedingly afraid of taking the infection." "Thomas Charles," UK Wells.

gospel-centered focus, he was driven out of three posts in less than a year. He was confused and needed yet again to trust and wait on God. God was moving him from being a settled Church of England priest to his true calling, to labor as an itinerant Methodist preacher.

Around this time, he had a troubling dream about the day of judgment. Charles understood himself to be the idle and slothful servant to whom the Judge said, "Bind him hand and foot, and take him away, and cast him into outer darkness, there shall be weeping and gnashing of teeth" (Matt. 22:13). In the dream, Jesus said to him, "Why standest thou here idle?" In response to this dream, Charles felt he had to do something. So, he began to teach some children from Bala in his house on Sunday evenings. The dream also gave him the courage to do something that he had avoided for some time: openly join the Methodist cause. In 1784 Thomas Charles was the first clergyman in North Wales to embrace Methodism.

A Methodist Preacher and an Educator

Charles began preaching for the Calvinistic Methodists in 1784. Within a year thousands of people were flocking to hear his itinerant preaching, and hundreds were converted. When Daniel Rowland heard him preach in 1785, he said that Charles was "the gift of God to North Wales."

As Charles preached and organized Methodist societies, he also faced persecution. Church authorities threatened him with legal action and imprisonment. A crowd once attacked him with stones, breaking a number of his teeth. But Charles persevered, driven on by his passion to bring the gospel of saving grace to lost souls.

Charles learned the value of trusting God in affliction, whether it is not having enough money for tuition, being in a discouraging job, or being persecuted for the gospel. He wrote,

> God's designs in afflictions are various—but all are gracious, and for our good. He may intend to bring us to repentance for some past sins…. Or, it may be that the affliction is sent to prevent our being overtaken in some dangerous snare…. Or, it may be that the affliction is sent to exercise some grace, that it may thereby gain strength…. These designs may for a long season be concealed from the believer himself, as was the case with Joseph. Yet…God has assured us that He causes all things to work together for our good.[9]

Afflictions and persecution may also be the prelude to gospel fruit. In 1791 a woman in Bala became strongly convinced of her sin and godless state. After a great struggle, the Holy Spirit enabled her to surrender her entire life to the Lord. Shortly after this, when Charles finished an evening service one Lord's Day in October, many in the congregation started to cry out, "What must I do to be saved?" Multitudes of people came under conviction of sin. The revival quickly spread from Bala to the surrounding areas. From this time until around 1815 revivals sprang up in different parts of North Wales.

When the number of children Charles taught on Sunday evenings outgrew his home, the Methodists allowed him use of their chapel. Charles tried teaching the children

____

9. Thomas Charles, *Essays, Letters, and Interesting Papers of the Late Rev. Thomas Charles, A. B.*, ed. Edward Morgan (London: R. B. Seeley & W. Burnside, 1836), 83–84.

the catechism, but he found that most children from poor families could not read. For the sake of their souls, the children of North Wales needed to learn to read in their native language. So Charles started something more basic: he relaunched the same kinds of circulating schools that Griffith Jones had run fifty years earlier.

The first step was to raise money for a teacher. Charles took six to nine months to teach the teacher to read in Welsh. Then, he would set the teacher to work in one town before moving on to the next town and repeating the process. In 1787 Charles started Sunday schools for all ages (as Robert Raikes had done in Gloucester in 1784). When the circulating teachers left a town, they would establish a Sunday school to carry on their work, often taught by their former students. By 1798 there were fifteen teachers rotating around Wales. Because few Welsh books existed to serve the needs of these schools, Charles authored three elementary textbooks and two catechisms. He also started a magazine in 1795 known as *The Spiritual Treasury*, the first magazine of its kind in Welsh, which contained Bible lessons, missionary biographies, and reports on revivals and mission work. In the Sunday schools, whole families learned the catechism together and recited what they learned. Some boys and girls memorized entire books of Scripture, such as Hebrews or Ephesians. One girl learned seventy-two psalms. Another learned ninety-two.

As children who learned to read grew into adults, North Wales gradually became more literate, and more people became willing and able to read English so that, just twenty years later, there were "a hundred times more English books in Wales than there had been when he started the schools."[10]

With the success of the Sunday schools now established, Charles turned to his next major goal: getting Bibles into the hands of the Welsh people.

Distributing Bibles and Publishing Books

Mary Jones's story of poverty, her unquenchable desire for God's Word, and her determination to buy a Bible inspired the founding of the British and Foreign Bible Society in 1804 and continues to inspire people today.

Charles spent the rest of his life raising money for the British and Foreign Bible Society, which distributed over two million Bibles and three million New Testaments within its first twenty-five years at a cost of £1.4 million.[11] A scene in a Welsh town shows how eager the people were to get Bibles. In 1806 a cart carrying the first batch of Bibles produced by the Bible Society rolled into a village in Wales. Villagers came in great crowds to follow the cart of Bibles, which quickly sold out. Laborers brought their Bibles with them to work. Young people passed the night reading them. Within four years over sixty thousand Bibles and forty-five thousand New Testaments were distributed in Wales. Within ten years the Bible Society had supplied Wales with one hundred thousand copies of God's Word.

Charles also kept publishing good books. In 1803 he built a printing press in Bala, first printing his catechism for children, his Welsh magazine, and two books on grammar that he had written. Charles's greatest literary achievement was his four-volume Welsh Bible dictionary, published from 1803 to 1811. The dictionary had a great effect on the quality of theological training in Wales. In time, the three books that

---

10. "Thomas Charles," UK Wells.

11. "Thomas Charles," UK Wells.

GEIRIADUR YSGRYTHYROL:

YN CYNNWYS

ARWYDDOCAD GEIRIAU ANGHYFIAITH

ARFEREDIG YN YR YSGRYTHYRAU:

YNGHYD AG

ENWAU AC HANESION YR AMRYWIOL GENEDLOEDD, TEYRNASOEDD,
A DINASOEDD, Y CRYBWYLLIR AM DANYNT YN Y BEIBL;

HEFYD,

EGLURHAD BYR AR HOLL BRIF BYNCIAU CREFYDD:

GYDA

SYLWADAU BEIRNIADOL AR LAWER O YSGRYTHYRAU;

AC Y MAE YN DANGOS

SEFYLLFA A MAINTIOLI MYNYDDOEDD; NATURIAETHAU CREADURIAID; COEDYDD A
MEINI GWERTHFAWR; ABERTHAU, GWYLIAU A DEFODAU IUDDEWIG,

FEL CYSGODAU O BETHAU YSBRYDOL AC EFENGYLAIDD.

GAN Y DIWEDDAR

BARCH. THOMAS CHARLES, B. A.,

O'R BALA.

CYFROL II.

YL AIL ARGRAFFIAD AMERICANAIDD, GYDAG YCHWANEGIADAU.

UTICA, E. N.:

ARGRAFFWYD GAN EVAN E. ROBERTS,
DROS Y CYHOEDDWR, T. T. EVANS, FLOYD, E. N.

1863.

---

trosodd, yr hyn a fydd tua diwedd Ebrill, bydd parhad o hin hyfryd yn canlyn, heb y cyfnewidiadau hyny yr ydym ni yn ddarostyngedig iddynt. Os golygwn y fan hon, a'r amrywiol ymadroddion yn eu cysylltiad â'u gilydd, yn gyffelybiaethol, arwydda gwanwyn, goruchwyliaeth yr efengyl.

1. Y mae y gauaf yn rhagflaenu y gwanwyn; felly y rhagflaenodd amserau o anwybodaeth, diffrwythdra, a thymhestloedd, oruchwyliaeth ogoneddus a ffrwythlawn yr efengyl. Geilw Paul hwynt, 'amseroedd yr anwybodaeth.' Act. 17. 30.

2. Tymhor ffrwythlawn yw y gwanwyn; felly dan yr efengyl, y mae y cenedloedd a'r eneidiau hyny, y rhai oeddynt o'r blaen yn ddiffrwyth, yn cael eu gwneyd yn ffrwythlawn yn ffrwythau cyfiawnder a sancteiddrwydd. Esa. 61. 11.

3. Tymhor cariad a llawenydd yw y gwanwyn; yr hyn a hysbysir wrth yr adar yn canu, a llais y durtur; felly y mae yr efengyl yn oruchwyliaeth cariad a llawenydd. Eph. 2. 4. Luc 15. 7, 10, 32.

4. Yn y gwanwyn y mae adfywiad a math o adgyfodiad ar wyneb yr holl ddaear; yr oedd pob peth megys yn farw yn y gauaf oer: ond yn y gwanwyn tirion y mae pob peth yn adfywio; felly y mae yr efengyl yn cael pawb yn feirw mewn pechod a chamweddau, ac yn eu bywhau yn nerthol trwy ras, i fyw i'r hwn a fu farw drostynt, ac a gyfodwyd.

PASUR, פשחור [*helaethwr rhyddid*] 1. Mab Immer, yr offeiriad, a phen-llywodraethwr yr Arglwydd. Jer. 20. 1. Gelwir ef hefyd Magor-missabib. Edr. JEREMIAH.—2. Un y dychwelodd 1247 o'i hiliogaeth i Babilon. Ezra 2. 38. Neh. 7. 41.

PATARA, Παταρα [*sathredig*] dinas gyfagos i'r môr, yn Lycia. Act. 21. 1.

PATMOS, Πατμος [*marwol*] ynys yn y Môr Egea, nid pell oddiwrth Melitus, (Malta, neu Molta) yn nghylch dengain milltir o du y gorllewin i Ephesus. Y mae o gylch 25 i 30 o filltiroedd, ac yn ddiffrwyth. Gelwir hi yn bresenol Yatmo, Patmol, neu Patmosa. Yma yr alltudiwyd Ioan, ac y cafodd ei weledigaethau rhyfedd. Dat. 1. 9. Edr. DADGUDDIAD, IOAN.

PATRIARCH-IAID-EIRCH, *Gr.* πατριαρχης; *Llad.* PATRIARCHA; *Ffr.* PATRIARCHE; *Saes.* PATRIARCH: pen-teulu. Priodolir yr enw hwn yn benaf i'r hen dadau cyn Moses, megys Abraham, Isaac, &c. Felly gelwir Dafydd hefyd. Act. 2. 29. a 7. 8, 9. Heb. 7. 4.

Ni anfuddiol fyddai rhoddi yma yn fyr, pa fodd yr oedd rhai o'r patrieirch yn cyd-oesi â'u gilydd:—

		Blynyddoedd.
Adda a gyd-oesodd a	Lamech	56
	Methuselah	243
	Jared	470
	Mahalaleel	535
	Cainan	605
	Enos	695
Noah a gyd-oesodd a	Lamech	565
	Methuselah	600
	Jared	366
	Mahalaleel	234
	Cainan	179
	Enos	84
Sem a gyd-oesodd a	Lamech (*cyn y dilyw*)	93
	Methuselah	98
	Noah	448
	Abraham (*ar ol y dilyw*)	150
	Isaac	50

Wrth y daflen hon canfyddir mor hawdd oedd trosglwyddo hanesion o Adda i Isaac, yspaid o 2158 o flynyddoedd.

PATROBAS, Πατροβας [*tadawl*] dysgybl yn Rhufain a enwir gan Paul yn ei anerchiadau at y duwiolion yno. Rhuf. 16. 14.

PATHROS, פתרוס [*taeniad o wlith*] talaeth a dinas yn yr Aipht, gwlad y Pathrusim, hiliogaeth Mizraim. Esa. 11. 11. Jer. 44. 15. Ezec. 29. 14. a 30. 14.

PAU, פער [*yn llefain*] dinas yn Edom, preswylfod Hadar. Gen. 36. 39.

PAUL, Παυλος [*bychan*] yr oedd o lwyth Benjamin, a'i rieni, o bob tu, yn Hebreaid Ganwyd ef yn Tarsus yn Cicilia, yn freiniawl o holl freintiau perthynol i ddinesydd rhydd Rhufeinaidd. Act. 9. 11. a 21. 39. a 29. 28. Saul oedd yr enw y gelwid ef wrtho, nes dychweliad Sergius Paulus i'r ffydd. Hwyrach, mai Saul oedd ei enw Hebreaidd, a Paul ei enw Rhufeinaidd, yr hwn a arferodd yn mhlith y Cenedloedd. Neu, hwyrach i Sergius ewyllysio ei anrhydeddu â'i gyfenw. Yn ol arfer yr Iuddewon o ddwyn eu plant i fedru rhyw gelfyddyd, dysgodd ei rieni ef yn y gelfyddyd o wneuthur pebyll. Act. 18. 3. Dywed Rabbi Judah, 'Beth a orchymynir i dad tuag at ei fab? *Ateb.* Ei enwaedu, ei adbrynu, dysgu y gyfraith iddo, dysgu celfyddyd iddo, a chwisio gwraig iddo.' Yr un peth, meddent, i rieni beidio dysgu celfyddyd i'w plant, a dysgu iddynt i fod yn lladron. Addysgwyd ef yn forcu, tebygol, yn Tarsus, yn holl ddysgeidiaeth y Groegiaid, ac anfonodd ei rieni ef yn ieuanc i Jerusalem, lle y cafodd ei ddwyn i fynu wrth draed Gamaliel, a'i athrawiaethu yn ol cyfraith fanylaf y tadau. Yr oedd yn ieuanc o blaid y Phariseaid o ran ei grefydd, yn dwyn zel dros Dduw, ac yn ol y ddeddf yn ddiargyhoedd. Act. 22. 2. Phil. 3. 5.

Nid oes un prawf nac arwydd dangosiadol ei fod yn trigo yn Jerusalem yr amser yr oedd Crist yn gweinidogaethu yn y byd. Ond, tebygol, iddo ddychwelyd i Tarsus at ei alwedigaeth fel pebyllwr, wedi gorphen astudio dan Gamaliel, ond byddai, hwyrach, yn ymweled â Jerusalem, yn achlysurol, ar brydiau. Nid ydyw yn cyfeirio at ddim yn ei holl ysgrifeniadau ag sydd yn arwyddo ei adnabyddiaeth bersonol o Grist; felly yr erlidiodd yr eglwys 'yn ddiarwybod,' heb adnabod Crist, 'mewn anghrediniaeth.' Ni ellir meddwl ei fod yn Jerusalem y pasc y croeshoeliwyd Crist, heb grybwylliad ei fod yn bresenol, ac yn weithgar gyda gelynion Crist.

Charles's Bible dictionary, called Geiriadur Ysgrythyrol *in Welsh*

most Welsh families owned were the Bible, John Bunyan's *Pilgrim's Progress*, and Thomas Charles's Bible dictionary.

Death and Legacy

Charles fell sick in 1812 and never fully recovered. The last thing he accomplished was to edit a new edition of the Welsh Bible and a Welsh Bible concordance. He successfully completed the new edition of the Welsh Bible but not the concordance, which he was trying to complete before 1814.

The reason the year 1814 is significant relates to an event fifteen years earlier when Charles almost died. In 1799 Charles became seriously ill while traveling in freezing weather. His left thumb had to be amputated due to frostbite and he developed a deadly infection. Christians in Bala gathered to pray for him. At one prayer meeting an older saint fervently prayed that God would extend Charles's life for fifteen years like Hezekiah: "Fifteen years more, O Lord. We beseech thee to add fifteen years more to the life of thy servant. And wilt thou not, O our God, give fifteen years more for the sake of thy church and thy cause."[12] Charles recovered and, when he learned about this prayer, he was more determined than ever to do as much as he could for God in his remaining time. The year before his death Charles wrote, "I feel ashamed when I think how little I have done, compared with what I ought to have done…. 'O God, be merciful to me a sinner,' is the language of my heart daily."[13]

A statue of Charles in Bala
GRAEME WALKER, CC BY-SA 2.0

---

12. "Thomas Charles," UK Wells.

13. D. E. Jenkins, *The Life of Thomas Charles of Bala* (Denbigh, Wales: Llewelyn Jenkins, 1910), 1:392.

Near the fifteenth year from his illness in 1799, Charles died on October 5, 1814. He was buried at Llanycil parish church. His dear Sally died just nineteen days later.

The part of Charles's character that people noticed most was his love for them. "He often gave away his coat when he came across someone on the road who could not afford one to keep warm. His schools were born out of love and compassion for the people of Wales. His drive to bring thousands of Bibles into Wales was born out of that same love." He wrote, "The only happiness to be obtained in this world consists of doing good to the souls and bodies of our fellow-creatures."[14]

He may not have been as gifted a preacher as Daniel Rowland, but people recognized the presence of God with Charles because of his great humility, which can be rare in people as intellectually gifted as he was, with his Bible dictionary, his Welsh catechisms, his school books, and his editorial work on the Bible. His humility shows in his own memoir, where he leaves out his name as he speaks of the development and growth of the Bible society, which he created.

Thomas Charles is less known among the revivalists because church historians have given less attention to Wales in the story of the revival. Dr. Martyn Lloyd-Jones wrote that Thomas Charles is "definitely one of the most neglected of the spiritual leaders."[15]

____

14. "Thomas Charles," UK Wells.

15. A good way to begin reading Charles's writings is *Thomas Charles' Spiritual Counsels: Selected from His Letters and Papers by Edward Morgan* (Edinburgh: Banner of Truth, 1993). This book is filled with spiritual wisdom from beginning to end, reflecting the Holy Spirit's profound work in the mind, soul, and life of Thomas Charles.

Study Questions

1. What can you learn from Mary Jones's passion for the Bible? Do you treasure the Word of God or do you take its inspired books and pages for granted?

2. When you read about Thomas Charles's conversion under Daniel Rowland's sermon on Hebrews 4:15, how should this impact you about the value of preaching? Why does God use preaching more than any other means of grace to save sinners?

3. Throughout his life, Charles often had to learn to trust God in matters both spiritual and natural. Have you learned that lesson as well? How can we learn to grow in waiting on God as Psalm 27:14 urges us to do?

4. God used Charles mightily as a preacher, as an educator, as a promoter of Sunday schools, and for the spread of God's Word to many. What gifts do you have that God might use to spread His gospel? How can you know what God wants you to do for His cause?

5. Despite all that he accomplished for God and His kingdom, Charles felt he accomplished very little. Why is this a common conviction of those who are passionate for the evangelistic spread of the gospel?

~ 11 ~

Archibald Alexander

1772–1851

In the spring of 1791, nineteen-year-old Archibald Alexander and his mentor, Dr. William Graham, were riding their horses to a presbytery meeting in Augusta County, near Lexington, Virginia. Alexander was on the way to his preaching licensure examination. As his instructor and mentor, Graham sensed Alexander's call to the ministry and was encouraging him to pursue licensure.

Alexander, however, had a different goal in mind. He hoped to persuade the presbytery not to license him too soon. As their horses crossed a creek swollen with snowmelt, Alexander said to Graham, "Maybe the presbytery will decide that it is best to wait a while before licensing me."

"Perhaps," Graham said. "Or they might decide you are ready and license you now."

Alexander's stomach sank at the thought of himself—short and boyish in appearance as he was—being licensed to preach! *If they just waited a few more years*, Alexander thought, *at least I might be taller or healthier or better prepared.*

Dr. Graham, however, saw in the young man what many in Alexander's family, church, and community had already seen. Under Graham's guidance, Alexander excelled in the study of theology, the humanities, psychology, and the sciences. More importantly, Alexander had been brought to assurance of his salvation in Jesus Christ out of a lengthy time of spiritual searching and struggle. Graham had witnessed all of this as Alexander's instructor and mentor since his childhood.

"Don't be anxious, Alexander," Graham said, reading his pupil's inner turmoil. "Do your best and leave the outcome to the Lord." Having Alexander even apply for licensure was an accomplishment. Dr. Graham persuaded him that being licensed would enable him to join Graham on an itinerant preaching tour of the area and that the travel could benefit his health.

Alexander arrived at the presbytery and began his exams. Each part worried him—Latin, Scripture exegesis, and lecture writing—but his training under Dr. Graham paid off, and he passed most of the tests in his first round of exams. The lecture he delivered was on the difference between a living and a dead faith. In his second round of exams, focusing on theology and sermon

Archibald Alexander

delivery, he greatly disliked the text that the presbytery gave him to preach because it brought him face-to-face with his own insecurities and excuses to postpone God's call: "But the LORD said unto me, Say not, I am a child: for thou shalt go to all that I shall send thee, and whatsoever I command thee thou shalt speak" (Jer. 1:7). The presbytery chose this text on purpose to teach Alexander how to put his own insecurities aside when preaching the Word. And that is just what Alexander did. After he delivered the sermon, the presbytery was impressed with his maturity and his focus on the passage's teaching without the slightest personal reference.

"Congratulations, Alexander," Graham said after hearing the presbytery's feedback on the sermon. "The presbytery spoke highly of your sermon. It was a carefully prepared message on a pivotal topic—the call to the ministry!" Graham could not help smiling. Having passed his exams, Alexander was licensed. No one at that time knew that Alexander's licensure would change the history of the Presbyterian church in important ways.

Early Years, Education, and Conversion

Archibald Alexander was born in 1772, the third of nine children. His family descended from Scotch-Irish immigrants who were converted during the eighteenth-century revival called the First Great Awakening, which was inspired by the ministries of William Tennant, Jonathan Edwards, and George Whitefield, among many others. Living in a log house in mountainous Virginia, seven miles east of Lexington, Alexander grew up surrounded by stunning views of valleys and mountain peaks, streams and water-falls. The rugged beauty of God's creation influenced

Home in the Woods
THOMAS COLE

Alexander's understanding of the majesty of God and His powerful ordering of all things to His own glory.

Noticing his son's academic giftedness, Alexander's father sent him to a nearby school, in the Timber Ridge meetinghouse, where William Graham instructed Alexander in classical studies, science, mathematics, theology, and preaching. When Alexander was seventeen, he became a tutor for a few months in the home of Revolutionary War veteran General Thomas Posey. In General Posey's home there lived an elderly Mrs. Tyler, who had an early influence on Alexander's spiritual awakening. A religious revival called the Second Great Awakening was occurring around this time. Mrs. Tyler told Alexander of her conversion experience and often asked him to read Puritan works aloud to her because of her weak eyesight. "On one of these Sabbath evenings," Alexander wrote, "I was requested to read out of [John] Flavel…on Revelation [3:20], 'Behold I stand at the door and knock.'… The truth took effect on my feelings, and every word I read seemed applicable to my own case."[1] During these months Alexander's heart would often fluctuate from the joys of understanding more of the gospel through greater views of Christ to the depression of sensing the greatness of his own sin and the wickedness of his heart. Although his spiritual struggles continued for some time, he made a public profession of faith in Christ at the end of 1789. He later wrote, "I am of opinion, that my regeneration took place while I resided at General Posey's, in the year 1788."[2]

---

1. J. W. Alexander, *The Life of Archibald Alexander* (New York: Charles Scribner, 1854; repr., Harrisonburg, Va.: Sprinkle, 1991), 44–45 (hereafter cited as *LAA*).

2. *LAA*, 72.

Beginnings of Gospel Ministry and a College President

Alexander's plans to continue his studies at the College of New Jersey[3] were halted through a providential illness that lasted several months. Instead, God opened the way for him to study with Dr. Graham at Liberty Academy (now Washington and Lee University), where his hunger for God's Word and interest in gospel ministry deepened. Graham helped Alexander develop an independent style of reasoning that depended on Scripture rather than established works of theology or confessions, which prepared him to be a more able defender of the Reformed orthodoxy of the Presbyterian tradition, embodied in the Westminster Standards.[4]

Alexander once recounted an early preaching experience from an itinerant preaching tour of the area around Lexington, Virginia. "Although I did not know a single word which I was to utter," he wrote, "I began with a rapidity and fluency equal to any I have enjoyed to this day. I was astonished at myself, and as I was young and small, the old people were not less astonished."[5] Alexander developed great skill as an extemporaneous preacher, not relying on the use of notes or manuscripts. This style of preaching was especially useful to him as an itinerant preacher since he could adapt sermons more directly to the needs of different hearers as he went from place to place.

---

3. The foundation of today's Princeton University.

4. Westminster Standards: The doctrinal confessions and catechisms that were produced by a large group of mostly Puritan theologians at Westminster Abbey from 1643 to 1649 and that guide orthodox Presbyterian church to this day.

5. *LAA*, 86.

In 1793 he began to serve churches in Prince Edward County, preaching, visiting homes, and maintaining his personal study of theology, science, and radical Enlightenment[6] thought. Alexander heard one of the speeches of Patrick Henry (1736–1799), an American Founding Father and former governor of Virginia, who lived nearby. Alexander was greatly influenced by Henry's oratory skills, for which he was renowned (the revolutionary battle cry "Give me liberty, or give me death!" was Henry's). In 1798 Alexander reluctantly accepted the position of president of Hampden-Sydney College, a once-thriving but then-failing institution. With the help of other pastor-professors, he combined his pastoral experience and academic skill to resuscitate the institution, beginning with strictly drilling the students in common college subjects of the day. Alexander promoted literature and the sciences as important vehicles for the advancement of God's kingdom. With his health suffering under the pressure of multiple roles, Alexander resigned his position as president in 1801. The college kept the position of president open for him, hoping that he would soon return.

General Assembly in Philadelphia and a New England Journey

In 1801 Alexander went to Philadelphia to serve as a commissioner to the General Assembly of the Presbyterian Church in the USA. On the way, Alexander lodged in the home of Dr. James Waddel, an aged minister once known for his eloquent preaching in that part of Virginia. His eyesight now failing, Dr. Waddel was assisted by his daughter, Janetta; she would help her father around the house and read books to him, some in Latin. Janetta's godliness and selfless care for her father deeply impressed Alexander. Before continuing his journey, Alexander proposed to her and was granted permission for Janetta's hand in marriage. He would marry her upon his return from Philadelphia.

The General Assembly in Philadelphia was establishing links with the Congregational churches of New England in hopes of combining forces in a "Plan of Union" for the westward expansion of their denominations. Alexander was sent as a delegate of the assembly to visit the New England churches. Journeying throughout the region and preaching in various churches and institutions, he came face-to-face with the Arianism, Socinianism, and Unitarianism that were then spreading in New England (Harvard University would appoint a Unitarian, Henry Ware, to be a professor of theology by 1805).[7] Passing through the mountains of New Hampshire exposed him to Quakers, Quietists, the Green Mountain Boys, and whole communities isolated from the influence of religion and preaching.[8] This trip enlarged Alexander's

---

6. The Enlightenment was a movement among the thinkers of Europe in the 1700s that eventually spread to common people and many parts of the world; it emphasized a kind of logical thinking that dismissed the importance of God, the Bible, and the supernatural. Enlightenment thinkers argued that "reason" made monarchies and church power unnecessary and called for political revolutions and revisions of biblical doctrine.

7. Arianism, Socinianism, and Unitarianism are denials of the orthodox doctrine of the Trinity. Arianism is a belief system according to which Christ is God's highest creation, a divine being less than the Father. This was taught by Arius in the early fourth century. In Socinianism and Unitarianism, Christ is said to be a highly exalted man, and the Father alone is God. Faustus Socinus taught this view in sixteenth-century Poland, which led to the movement known as Unitarianism.

8. Quakers are members of the Society of Friends, which teaches

awareness both of the expanding horizons of God's kingdom and the breadth of religious opinion in the country.

Stepping into married life with Janetta Waddel in April 1802, Alexander decided to resume his former position as president of Hampden-Sydney College. Janetta's strong character and experience as a pastor's daughter was a good match for her husband's personality and work. Two of their sons would follow in their father's footsteps, one as a renowned Old Testament scholar and commentator, Joseph Addison Alexander (1809–1860), and the other as a highly regarded preacher and pastor, James Waddel Alexander (1804–1859).

At Hampden-Sydney College, Alexander witnessed what was becoming an increasing problem at many American colleges at that time. Student conduct was marked by defiance, disregard for

that Christians should rely on an "inner light" to guide them through life rather than ministers or the outward means of grace. "Quietist" was often another name for groups related to Quakers in belief or practice. Led by Ethan Allen and his brother Ira, the Green Mountain Boys were a patriot military force of several hundred men who controlled and defended the area west of the Green Mountains in Vermont. The group put up armed resistance to officials who tried to enforce New York land grants in their area.

The building of Third Presbyterian Church, now called Old Pine Street Church
MORRIS LEVIN

authority, and lack of discipline in studies. Exhausted with the students at Hampden-Sydney College, Alexander wrote, "I grew weary of governing them."[9] In 1806 he accepted a call to pastor the Third Presbyterian Church of Philadelphia.[10]

9. *LAA*, 275–76.

10. Also known as Old Pine Street Presbyterian Church, "Church of the Patriots," founded in 1768.

A Pastor-Scholar in Philadelphia

The Alexander family settled in Philadelphia while Alexander engaged himself in many creative ministry endeavors in the city. He began a sermon series on the basic doctrines of Christianity at Third Presbyterian Church. He started an evening evangelistic outreach effort called the Evangelical Society that enlisted pastors from nearby churches to preach the gospel to the children, the poor, and the marginalized communities of the city. Seeing a link between a decline in doctrinal knowledge and the people's taste for low-quality reading material, Alexander got involved in producing and distributing Christian literature, tracts, and newspapers. The many libraries and bookstores in Philadelphia also helped him to upgrade the quality of his personal study of the canon of Scripture; biblical studies; systematic, polemic,[11] and historical theology; and the works of many American, British, and Continental theologians. Alexander's strongest areas of interest were church history and the Latin and Greek church fathers.[12] In his six years as pastor at Third Presbyterian, its membership increased by 50 percent; his extemporaneous, evangelically solid, and experiential preaching was well received; and his scholarly pursuits were recognized when the College of New Jersey conferred on him an honorary doctor of divinity degree in 1810.

A Scholar-Pastor in Princeton

A sermon Alexander preached to the Presbyterian General Assembly in 1808 led to the planning and establishment of Princeton Theological Seminary three years later. In a time when well-known institutions Yale and Harvard were sliding into rationalism and deism, Alexander and the assembly envisioned a school where both academic excellence and the pursuit of godliness were promoted. "Filling the Church with a learned and able ministry, without a corresponding portion of real piety," the seminary's plan read, "would be a curse to the world, and an offence to God and his people," so the seminary must be "a nursery of vital piety, as well as of sound theological learning: and to train up persons for the ministry, who shall be lovers, as well as defenders, of the truth as it is in Jesus; friends of revivals of religion; and a blessing to the Church of God."[13] In 1812 Alexander was unanimously appointed the first professor of didactic and polemic theology at Princeton, an office he would hold until 1840. This was an important milestone in the history of American Presbyterianism, whose confessional standards were defended for generations by able men trained at Princeton in the face of the advance of modernism's secular sway on other denominations.

Alexander immersed himself in his new responsibilities at Princeton, designing a curriculum and preparing lectures for the incoming class while waiting for additional faculty to assist him. Student enrollment doubled between the years 1817 and 1829, increasing from under fifty to over a

---

11. Polemic theology is the area of Christian doctrine dealing with the defense of the faith against errors, unbiblical ideologies, heresy, and world religions.

12. *LAA*, 355.

13. Anonymous, *A Brief History of the Theological Seminary of the Presbyterian Church, at Princeton, New Jersey; Together with Constitution, Bye-laws, etc.* (Princeton: John Bogart, 1838), 8.

Alexander Hall of Princeton Theological Seminary

hundred. In 1820 Charles Hodge, a graduate of the seminary and of the College of New Jersey, was hired as professor of biblical languages. Samuel Miller, also an important founder of the seminary, served alongside Alexander as professor of ecclesiastical history and church government from 1813 until his retirement in 1849.

Preaching and Piety

Even while serving as a seminary professor and administrator, Alexander kept up his usual practice of preaching to nearby congregations, and his experiential sermons became a source of religious renewal in the Princeton community. In his preaching, he demonstrated a gift for "dissecting the heart, unravelling long trains of experience, discovering hidden refuges, holding the mirror up to self-deceiving souls, and flashing rays of gracious hope on the lingering and self-righteous; he was equaled by few."[14] Charles Hodge describes what it was like to sit under Alexander's preaching:

> Those who heard were convinced. Their conscience… bore testimony to the truth of what he said. They were judged, or examined. Their feelings…were analyzed, examined, and their true character discerned and estimated…. All classes of persons felt the power of this searching process. The procrastinating, the skeptical, the hardened, were astonished to find with what accuracy they were depicted, and thoughts and feeling, misgivings and purposes, which they thought hidden from all eyes, were brought to light….

Personal experience, observation, and Scripture, not fancy, were sources whence he drew.[15]

For Alexander, his role as a Christian, father, and husband did not exist in a separate world from his role as a pastor, professor, and seminary administrator. He lived an integrated life, where his piety and professional life were in harmony. By the Spirit's work in his life as he lived before God's Word, he possessed an enriched intellect, combined with the simplicity of a child, so that he "possessed the finest skill in interpreting and in treating with acute precision, the states and frames of all who sought his counsel or listened to his instructions."[16] Alexander loved Christ, His church, and lost sinners. He put his detailed knowledge of the human heart to use in counseling others. His students often pointed out that even his lectures were devotional in character and effect.[17]

Alexander daily made time for his family and would often engage in conversation with them on any topic that interested him from "his newspaper, his book, his class, from visits, church or journey."[18] Unless he was in private devotions, he kept his study open to his children, whose noise, toys, and activities did not distract him from the work at hand. He enjoyed playing with his children, telling them stories, and leading family Bible reading, singing, and prayer.

---

14. *LAA*, 686.

15. Charles Hodge, "Memoir of Dr. Alexander," *The Biblical Repertory and Princeton Review* 27, no. 1 (January 1855): 155–56.

16. Charles Hodge, *Conference Papers: Or Analyses of Discourses, Doctrinal and Practical; Delivered on Sabbath Afternoon to the Students of the Theological Seminary, Princeton, N. J.* (New York: Charles Scribner's Sons, 1879), v.

17. Hodge, "Memoir of Dr. Alexander," 158–59.

18. *LAA*, 405.

Alexander was a reluctant writer, but three of his books were highly influential in the training of ministers worldwide. The first, *Outlines of the Evidences of Christianity*, responded to rationalistic skepticism by providing evidences for the reliability of the Scriptures and the gospel message. Another was *The Canon of the Old and New Testament*. And third was *Thoughts on Religious Experience*, which is a masterpiece of experiential and pastoral divinity of soul exercises.[19] Alexander is also remembered as the chronicler of the history of eighteenth-century revival preacher William Tennent and the "school of the prophets" he founded, called the Log College, to which both Princeton University and Princeton Theological Seminary trace their beginnings.[20]

Divisions and Controversy

In the 1820s and 1830s, the Presbyterian Church found itself embroiled in theological controversy. The Plan of Union of 1801 had introduced the modified Calvinism of New England into the church, and those who favored it came to be known as "New School" Presbyterians. Those who opposed the New England theology were "Old School" Presbyterians. At stake were a host of issues, including the nature and extent of Christ's atonement; original sin and the degree of fallen man's natural light, ability, and freedom of will; the proper conduct of revivals of religion; subscription to the Westminster Standards; and the divine or biblical warrant for Presbyterian church government. In 1837 the Old School Presbyterians acted to excise, or cut off, New School presbyteries and synods from the denomination, and the conflict of many years ended in outright division of the church into two opposing, often competing denominations.

Widespread theological change was impacting the seminary, denomination, and country.[21] In 1837 Alexander wrote a letter expressing dismay at the disunity that marked gatherings of the General Assembly. He had firm opinions on the issues that were being debated but did not make a platform for himself in their defense. His teaching and writing were outlets for promoting awareness of key biblical doctrines that he hoped would bring clarity and promote unity.

In the decades before the Civil War, slavery was also a major source of concern and contention among Presbyterians, and, when hostilities broke out in 1861, would further divide both the Old School and New School bodies. The General Assembly's 1818 "Declaration of Slavery" condemned the practice as inconsistent with the law of God and the "principles of the Gospel of Christ," but this action only added fuel to the fires of conflict in the church. Alexander tended to agree with the General Assembly, thereby supporting the view of Ashbel Green (1762–1848), an American Presbyterian minister and academic who was a contemporary and collaborator of Alexander's.

In the late 1830s, Alexander's junior colleague, Charles Hodge, tried to find a more moderate and middle way by arguing that slavery was neither forbidden nor condemned by Scripture but was to be regulated by the principles of

19. Archibald Alexander, *Thoughts on Religious Experience*, 3rd ed. (Philadelphia: Presbyterian Board of Publication, 1844).

20. Archibald Alexander, *The Log College: Biographical Sketches of William Tennent and His Students, Together with an Account of the Revivals under Their Ministries* (1851; repr., London: Banner of Truth, 1968).

21. For an overview of the changes, see Paul K. Conkin, *The Uneasy Center: Reformed Christianity in Antebellum America* (Chapel Hill: University of North Carolina Press, 1995).

The Battle of Chantilly
AUGUSTUS THOLEY

Christian charity. Hodge did oppose slavery, however, but argued for its abolition by process of gradual attrition as these principles of Christian charity worked their way into the hearts and lives of Christians everywhere. The men of Old Princeton found themselves fighting a war on two fronts, resisting both the false logic of those who defended the South's "peculiar institution" and the intense zeal of some who demanded its immediate and total abolition.[22]

In addition to all this, America's religious landscape was changing. Charles Finney's man-centered "revivalism" was promoting a Pelagian gospel of moral self-improvement and perfectionism that denied core Christian doctrines such as man's total depravity and salvation by grace alone through faith. Finney's methods in procuring and conducting his "revival" meetings were the practical implementation of New England theologian Nathaniel Taylor's denial of the doctrines of original sin, regeneration, and the bondage of the will. Facing a changing religious scene in America, Princeton Seminary was an environment of lively debate, for the students came from different denominations—Baptist, Congregationalist, Episcopalian, and Presbyterian. But the strong campus culture of piety helped to maintain a climate of unity that prevented major divisions among the students. In this debate, however, like every other, Alexander himself stood strong as a faithful Calvinist who defended the truth both objectively and subjectively against the errors and heresies of his day. Consequently, Alexander took the traditional,

Calvinistic side of Asahel Nettleton (1783–1844), a highly influential theologian during the Second Great Awakening, on the question of revivals and how they should be sought and conducted.

Finally, and not surprisingly, engagement in the intellectual and spiritual battlefields of the day moved Alexander to take a strong and bold stand against the radical skepticism and rationalism of philosopher David Hume. Alexander warmly advocated for "Common Sense Philosophy" as propagated by Thomas Reid as a major antidote to Hume's thinking. After expounding basic characteristics of judgment, Reid asserted that certain

Asahel Nettleton
PORTRAIT BY SAMUEL WALDO
AND WILLIAM JEWETT

commonsense principles about how the external and internal worlds function should be taken for granted as true.

Finishing the Race

In 1850, a year before his death, Archibald Alexander attended the annual meeting of the Synod of New Jersey. Alexander was surprised when he was asked to deliver one of the evening sermons. He replied, "I am too old; you must select some other person." But the minister who asked him

---

22. See David B. Calhoun, *Princeton Seminary* (Edinburgh: Banner of Truth, 1994, 1996), 1:325–26. Calhoun's entire chapter, "The Church and the Country," from which much of this material is drawn, is an informative picture of Princeton Theological Seminary's engagement with the cultural issues of antebellum America during the 1830s and 1840s.

replied, "You see, sir, that a large proportion of the ministers of the Synod have been your pupils, and this may be the last time that they will ever have the privilege of listening to your voice." These words struck Alexander. He consented to preach, and as he spoke, it seemed to many who heard "that he stood on the very verge of heaven, and was fully ready to say, I have fought a good fight, I have finished my course, I have kept the faith; henceforth there is laid up for me a crown of righteousness, which the Lord, the righteous Judge, shall give me at that day" (cf. 2 Tim. 4:7–8).[23] For most who were present, this was the last time they saw him. Alexander's public ministry would conclude in September 1851. He died a month later.

Alexander's Significance

Archibald Alexander's life holds forth valuable lessons for us. First, when Christians and ministers become lifelong learners of a wide variety of subject areas, as Alexander was, they can often be of great service to the work of God's kingdom.

Second, Alexander lived the belief that academic skill is useless without a sincere, deep love for Christ expressed in a lifelong pursuit of godliness that bears fruit in the home and in the church. He knew that if biblical orthodoxy and piety were not maintained as equal priorities, then rationalism would eventually render any seminary useless to the needs of the church. Very few schools maintained this double focus on academic expertise and personal piety. Princeton taught that theology must lead to love for Christ, love for His people, and childlike humility. Alexander teaches us that what we say and teach has to be rooted in the power of the character of our lives, not just in great scholarship.

Third, as worldly ideologies constantly assert themselves against the doctrines of the gospel (like the rationalism of Alexander's day, or the identity politics and postmodernism of our day, or the next new idea to come along in the future), Alexander teaches us that there is always a need for Christians in each generation to resist the subtle or direct assaults against Reformed orthodoxy, defend biblical doctrine, and bring "into captivity every thought to the obedience of Christ" (2 Cor. 10:5). Alexander was a transitional figure, standing between an old world and a new world. He promoted a more academically focused Presbyterianism that could stand up to modern rationalism and, through Princeton Seminary, ensured for generations the availability of ministers who maintained the right balance between academic rigor and personal godliness. Princeton's graduates were committed not just to Princeton but to sound biblical doctrine and genuine biblical godliness. In response to the rise of theological liberalism at Princeton in the 1920s, J. Gresham Machen and other theologians left the school to establish Westminster Theological Seminary, where the spirit of the Princeton tradition of academic skill and piety was carried on.

---

23. *LAA*, 587–90.

1. Why was Alexander hesitant to be licensed to preach at the time of the presbytery meeting in 1791?

2. What can some aspects of Alexander's licensing teach us about a proper attitude in response to God's gifting and call on our lives?

3. What truths do Alexander's spiritual struggles demonstrate about how God brings different people to faith in Jesus Christ?

4. What were some of Alexander's skills academically and pastorally? What were some of his character traits personally and in the home? How are each of these important to the other in the life of a pastor?

5. What can the divisions and controversies that occurred in the Presbyterian Church during Alexander's midlife teach us about our human limits, God's faithfulness, and the need for us to be faithful, diligent students of Scripture as well?

~ 12 ~

Mary Winslow

1774–1854

Mary Forbes Winslow grew up in a wealthy family surrounded by every comfort she desired. She was born in Bermuda in 1774, the only child of Dr. and Mrs. George Forbes. In 1791, at age seventeen, she married Lieutenant Thomas Winslow, a British soldier of the Forty-Seventh Regiment, who was temporarily based on the island. After her wedding, Mary attended a ball at which she was the center of attention as the young bride. For most of the evening, all eyes seemed to be fixed on her. She felt that she had it all.

But later that night, the emptiness of a life that lacks nothing filled her heart. As she remembered the evening, it seemed she had everything she wanted. She sighed and whispered to herself, "Is this all?" She knew that there had to be more to life than the transient pleasures she had just experienced.[1]

In Thomas's hometown of Romford, England,[2] where the new couple made their home, God began to bring Mary under conviction of sin, despite the outward comforts of her lifestyle. She began reading the Bible. She had known virtually nothing about the gospel except that a sinner could be saved. At first, she tried to seek salvation through her good works, which made her sink deeper into misery. Her husband wanted to relieve her distress, but not knowing the cause, he guessed it was loneliness. So, he rented a house in Pentonville, in North London, where he thought Mary would be cheered by the company and busier atmosphere of the city. Thomas did not know that in this relocation God was setting a plan in motion to save Mary's soul.

Mary began attending services at the Chapel of St. James ("Pentonville Chapel") in North London, but there was nothing in the preaching to satisfy her soul. In God's providence, however, a new minister was soon appointed. Rev. Thomas Sheppard vividly communicated the experience of the Christian life through his own character and through his doctrinally sound gospel preaching. God worked through Sheppard's ministry to direct Mary away from a works-righteousness mentality. She began searching the Scriptures to

---

1. Kenneth D. Macleod, "The Throne of Grace—A Blessing," *Banner of Truth*, March 19, 2014, http://banneroftruth.org/us/resources/articles/2014/throne-grace-blessing/.

2. A town northeast of London, in Essex.

Mary Winslow

see whether it was true that God justified sinners by grace alone through faith in Christ.

One evening when anxiously searching her Bible, Mary was brought to meditate on Jesus's promise, "Ask, and it shall be given you" (Matt. 7:7). She fell on her knees and asked Jesus how such a wretched sinner as she could be saved. She received no answer, so she returned to her Bible, still searching for the answer. Her mind still left in darkness and confusion, she went again to prayer a second time. As she prayed a third time, "In an instant light broke in upon my soul," wrote Mary. "Jesus stood before me and spoke these blessed words—I am thy salvation!"[3] She immediately knew Jesus was with her and had spoken to her. She knew that her soul was saved, and her burden of sin removed. She arose from prayer in praise and wonder. She had not seen Christ with her eyes, but she was sure that the Lord had communed with her soul. Mary later wrote that from that evening when she met Jesus, through the rest of her life, Jesus "blessed me, chastened, upheld, and comforted me; and even down to old age has He carried me."[4]

That next morning Mary told her husband what had happened. Thomas could neither understand nor believe what had occurred. From then on Mary began a pilgrimage with God that her husband would not share for most of their life together.

---

3. Octavius Winslow, *Life in Jesus: A Memoir of Mrs. Mary Winslow* (New York: Robert Carter & Brothers, 1860), 27.

4. Winslow, *Life in Jesus*, 203.

A Young Bride, Newly Wedded to Christ

Mary and Thomas were nonetheless a happily married couple. In 1795 Mary and Thomas had their first child. They went on to have twelve more (three of whom died before their first birthday). Three of her sons became ministers. Octavius Winslow was born in 1808 in Pentonville, England, the eighth surviving child. He became a well-known minister of the gospel. Octavius wrote Mary's biography, which included many of the letters and diary entries she had written.

Mary's husband did not share her faith in Christ until he neared the end of his life. In 1813, when he fell ill, Mary was instrumental in helping him seek the Lord and pray for the first time in his life. But his spiritual concern weakened as soon as his health strengthened. His prayers were prompted by "a fear of death" and not "by sin committed against a holy, good, and righteous God."[5] Some good did result from the illness, however. Thomas's heart would never again be hardened against the church, her ministers, or the truth of God's Word. The tension between Mary's faith and Thomas's lack thereof, which had hung over their marriage like a dark cloud, was somewhat relaxed.[6]

Love for God's Word Written and Preached

Mary's early instinct to search the Bible as an unconverted woman blossomed into a lifelong commitment to studying Scripture. Not a single word of God had fallen to the ground for Mary. With Scripture as the foundation of her faith and conduct, Mary bowed to the authority of God's revealed Word with her entire soul. Submission to Scripture was one of the

5. Winslow, *Life in Jesus*, 49.
6. Winslow, *Life in Jesus*, 50.

Octavius Winslow

clearest features of her Christian walk.[7] Before an open Bible she kept an open heart, heeding Christ's call to observe "all things whatsoever I have commanded you" (Matt. 28:20).

Now that she lived in North London, she often attended gospel services at Tottenham Court Road and the Moorfields Tabernacle, where George Whitefield (1714–1770) used to preach. These services greatly helped her in seasons of spiritual dejection. She also heard William Wilberforce (1759–1833) speak at a London missionary meeting.[8]

Mary had a lifelong gift of discerning the biblical depth and fidelity of the preaching she heard. She longed to hear Christ richly and fully preached in every sermon. To her son Octavius she wrote, "The more your sermons are filled with Christ, from first to last, the more Christ will honour your ministry.… The whole Bible points to Christ and you must make it all bear upon the subject—Christ, the sum and substance of the whole. In him, God and the sinner meet, and they can meet nowhere else. All the promises are in Christ Jesus, and we must get into Christ before we can get at the promises; and then they are all *yea and amen* to us."[9]

As a student of the Bible, Mary also loved the theology and spirituality she discerned in Puritan writings. References to authors such as John Owen, Stephen Charnock, John Bunyan, and Samuel Rutherford are scattered throughout her diaries and letters. She advises, "Keep to the old divines. Modern divinity is very shallow—has very little of Christ and experience."[10]

---

7. Winslow, *Life in Jesus*, 73.

8. Winslow, *Life in Jesus*, 52.

9. Winslow, *Life in Jesus*, 115.

10. "She was wont to remark that there was more of Christ, more of the marrow of the gospel, and more of Christian experience in a

---

LIFE IN JESUS:

A MEMOIR

OF

MRS. MARY WINSLOW,

ARRANGED FROM HER

Correspondence, Diary, and Thoughts.

BY HER SON

OCTAVIUS WINSLOW, D. D.,

AUTHOR OF

"MIDNIGHT HARMONIES," "PERSONAL DECLENSION AND REVIVAL," "THE PRECIOUS THINGS OF GOD," ETC.

"In her had Nature bounteously combined
The tenderest bosom with the strongest mind ;
I view the Mother and the Saint in one,
And pay beyond the homage of a Son."—*Knight.*

"Her children arise up, and call her blessed."—*Prov. xxxi. 28.*

NEW YORK:
ROBERT CARTER & BROTHERS,
No. 530 BROADWAY.
1860.

Mary Winslow's memoir

The US Ship Franklin, with a View of the Bay of New York
THOMAS THOMPSON

Trials and Tribulations

Mary's new life in Christ was just the beginning of a lifetime of walking with God through severe trials, such as frequent illness and the loss of those closest to her. But the effect of the trials on Mary's life resulted in one of the closest walks with Jesus recorded by pen and paper in modern times. Mary learned to cast all her cares on the one who has overcome.

single page of such authors as Owen and Charnock, Leighton, Bates, and Newton, than in entire volumes of some modern theological writers." Winslow, *Life in Jesus*, 338.

After Thomas retired from the army, his health declined. Worse, he lost most of his wealth nearly overnight in bad investments and in financial disasters of the day.[11] Now with tightened finances, the family had to relocate, and America seemed to be a fitting place for new opportunities and a lower cost of living. In the face of adversity, Mary proved

11. After his retirement, he began having lung troubles. "Now, with too much time on his hands, he occupied himself with dabbling in the stock market, and rapidly lost nearly every penny he had." Douglas Kenelm Winslow, *Mayflower Heritage: A Family Record of the Growth of Anglo-American Partnership* (London: George G. Harrap, 1957), 154.

to be a strong wife and mother, determined to help her husband and family in any way she could. The Winslow family planned for Mary to embark for New York with her ten children months ahead of Thomas.

Mary's determination to follow God fully can be seen on board the ship making its way to New York. She faithfully led family devotions, just as she did at home, but the captain and other passengers soon asked to join in. She loved to say, "Walk in the precept, and God will fulfil the promise."[12] She also ministered to a sickly mother on the ship who had an infant daughter; the mother died as they reached New York, but not without hearing the gospel from Mary.

Mary was inspired by America and saw it as a land of possibilities for the flourishing of the church. But she grieved over slavery as the dark spot in its history, praying often for its removal.[13]

Soon after arriving in New York, however, multiple trials accumulated like dark storm clouds. One of Mary's infant daughters became ill and died. This was now the fourth child she had lost. To make matters worse, before she could bury her daughter, she was informed that her husband had died as well. At forty years old, she was now widowed and responsible for nine children, not yet fully settled in a new land, and in financial circumstances much humbler than she was used to. Mary's entire life was turned upside down, and she was overwhelmed by spiritual darkness and despondency for some months.

Writing to one of her sons in 1816, she said, "My dear suffering infant lies a corpse: and the letter containing the intelligence of your dear father's and my beloved husband's death, was this day put into my hands. I am humbled under the mighty hand of God. My soul is bowed down. The death of my child was almost overwhelming; but the death of my dear, my precious, my ever-to-be-lamented husband, is the heaviest affliction I have ever met with."[14] One comfort was that her husband gave evidence before his death that he had sought and found salvation in Jesus Christ.

Have you suffered the loss of someone dear to you, dear believer? Jesus, the man of sorrows, understands your grief. The all-wise God is drawing you nearer to Himself. He chastens you, not because you are not His child but because you *are* His child. Never let the clouds of sad providence eclipse the fact that God loves you and has good intentions for your soul.

Life in Jesus, the Living One

"In the world ye shall have tribulation," said Jesus. "But be of good cheer; I have overcome the world" (John 16:33). After some time, the Lord delivered Mary from her darkness. Later, she confessed that the affliction was for her welfare: "I think I have learned more of my dreadfully wicked heart

---

12. Winslow, *Life in Jesus*, 58.

13. When God shines the light of the new creation in our souls, we are compelled to make a positive impact on the world around us. With a new heart regenerated by the Spirit's grace, Mary sought to do good in any way she could. In 1813, Mary asked her mother to free the slaves her family owned, which Mary would have inherited upon her parents' death. She was grieved that through inheritance she involuntarily owned slaves and that she was an unwitting participant "in an evil which now appeared in a light so sinful, and in a character so abhorrent." Winslow, *Life in Jesus*, 45.

14. Winslow, *Life in Jesus*, 60.

Gravøl (Funeral)
ADOLPH TIDEMAND, NASJONALMUSEET, CC BY 4.0

and the preciousness of Jesus during this trial than I have ever learnt before."[15]

Her situation was unique. She was a widow responsible for a large family, mostly of sons, who depended on her to train them and help them settle in life. She cast her cares, emotional burdens, and practical needs on the God of the covenant, who strengthened her for the many duties that lay ahead. By gracious and seasoned experience, she learned how to exemplify a spirit of unwavering faith in suffering. Moreover, God graciously granted her remarkable joys to balance her sorrows. He converted all of her children, fulfilling His promise to her that she should have an "undivided family" in heaven. She faithfully led her family in worship and saw three of her sons become orthodox and able ministers of the gospel. Octavius became a well-known preacher and prolific writer.

In the days immediately following her husband's death, Mary had to teach her young children the necessity of hard work. No family member was exempt from helping the family pull through difficult times. She would send her sons "out on the streets of New York selling matches and newspapers as soon as they were old enough for such tasks. She set them to any job they could tackle, gathering them around her at night for scripture reading…and prayers."[16]

Mary's Christianity was practical. One chief principle guided her dealings with money: "Owe no man anything." She never incurred debt and never purchased anything that was not absolutely necessary.[17] "The Lord direct," was always Mary's calm, submissive response to every situation that caused doubt and perplexity.[18]

Mary's strength was rooted in the doctrine of Christ's resurrection. The Holy Spirit impressed this truth thoroughly on her life and thought. She considered Christ's resurrection the single truth grounding all Christianity and biblical doctrine. Her whole Christian life was in interaction with the life of Jesus, which was her source of strength, consolation, and sanctifying grace. A living Christ indwelt her, upheld her, interceded for her, and gave her the purpose and strength for moving forward each day.

Mary knew that a Christian's grasp of theology is shallow without genuine Christian experience to fill out, enliven, and animate the doctrines we hold to. "I believe," she wrote, "that every doctrine, as well as every word of God, is only effectually profitable as it is worked out by the trying providence of God in the soul's deep experience.… A thousand times have I thanked the Lord for all my trials and afflictions," she wrote.[19] "How often has an unkind look or word proved a blessing to my soul! It has made me flee to Christ; and there I have found no unkindness. He has appeared, at such times, more than to make up for the want of all creature-love and created good."[20]

Life of Faith and Prayer

It was easy for people to see Mary's determination and practical efforts to sustain her family. What was unseen was how God sustained her through a remarkably consistent prayer

---

15. Winslow, *Life in Jesus*, 65.
16. Winslow, *Mayflower Heritage*, 155.
17. Winslow, *Life in Jesus*, 151.

18. Winslow, *Life in Jesus*, 423.
19. Winslow, *Life in Jesus*, 236.
20. Winslow, *Life in Jesus*, 105.

life. Prayer was perhaps the gift in which the Holy Spirit enabled Mary to excel the most. She wrestled much at the throne of grace, pleading the promises of God in prayer. Like her Savior, there were times she spent the whole night in prayer. "Oh, the mighty power of prayer!" she exclaimed. "Even the best of Christians know but little what it really is."[21]

She wrote to her children about a priority and lifestyle of prayer: "Oh, commune with Him of all that is in your heart. If you are wounded, go and tell Christ. If you are in need, go and tell Christ—the silver and the gold are His. If you are in trouble, go and tell Christ, and He will deliver you out of it, and you shall glorify Him. Live upon Him as little children would live upon a dear, kind, and tender father. Oh, how happily will you then pass on your way!"[22] Mary's attention to prayer was not only for the benefit of herself and her family. In New York, Mary joined a circle of praying mothers who offered to God petitions for the advance of the gospel work in the city. This prayer group was privileged to witness revivals in their part of the city. And they were privileged to support and further those revivals with their prayers.[23]

---

21. Winslow, *Life in Jesus*, 87.

22. Mary also wrote, "Never neglect private prayer; and plead hard with Jesus for a constant and abiding spirit of prayer, so that you can lift up your heart to Him wherever you are, or in whatever you may be engaged." She counseled her children to plead much for the filling of the Spirit and to be cautious of grieving "this most blessed Guest of your souls." She taught them to keep short accounts with Christ, immediately confessing any and all sinful thoughts, attitudes, and actions, "and He will wash it all away." Winslow, *Life in Jesus*, 116–17.

23. She prayed for the Spirit's blessing on the gospel work in other areas as well, such as Philadelphia and Boston. About Boston she wrote, "Unitarianism, like a pernicious weed, is spreading in Boston; but lately

Woman Praying
VINCENT VAN GOGH

How can we devote more attention to prayer? Why don't we pray as much as we ought? We do not pray because we do not believe. Prayer and faith are closely connected. Mary's prayer life was fueled by faith. She believed that God honors the prayers of faith and that He works mightily through them. "There are two buckets," Mary wrote. "The life of sense, and the life of faith: when one goes up, the other goes down…. I am persuaded, the more we live by faith the holier and happier we are."[24] Mary's faith was childlike: she took God at His Word. She believed Him because He is God. Her simple, unquestioning faith purified her heart, strengthened her under trials, helped her to triumph over things seen, and brought eternal realities solidly and constantly before her mind. Her faith honored God by believing, and God honored her faith by bestowing. It is easy to say that Mary lost much in life, but Mary would reply that God withheld nothing from her and let none of His promises fail her.[25]

Sometimes we ask the Lord to increase our faith but we grow impatient at our slow progress. We doubt that God is answering our prayers. As Mary reflected on the many trials and circumstances God brought her through, she wrote, "Wait on the Lord. The Lord exercises faith, and this is needful to conform us to His own lovely likeness. We want to be like Christ, but we do not like the way He takes to make us so. What a mercy it is that He takes His own way, and not ours!… If He is ours, and we are His, will He withhold anything that is really good for us? No, not even the rod;

for that is often for our good."[26] God always disciplines His children in love. As we strengthen the body through exercise, God lovingly exercises our faith by ordering and guiding us through trials.

Grief over Shallow Christianity

Mary's hope was not in her faith, of course, but in her living Redeemer. She walked closely with Him. She enjoyed an intimate, daily life of communion with Christ. "My first prayer in the morning when I awake," Mary wrote, "is addressed to the Holy Spirit, that He would take possession of my thoughts, my imagination, my heart, my words, throughout the day, directing, controlling, and sanctifying them all."[27] Like the seed sown among weeds, our faith is often choked by the concerns of our hearts, the pressures of life, and the allurements of the world. "Keep close to Jesus," Mary says, "and you have nothing to fear from within or without." To Mary, the Christian's whole duty was to remain near to Christ and keep His commandments.

As a mighty woman of faith and prayer, Mary seemed to live in the heart of God. Mary's consistent walk with God was startling to people whose dealings with God were "distant, cold, and infrequent."[28] "I cannot understand some Christians," Mary wrote, "and they do not understand me…. When I read, *Come out from among them, and be ye separate; Love not the world, nor the things that are in the world…*I am satisfied of the way a believer in Christ should walk, and

<hr>

they have had a more extensive revival than we have had here." Winslow, *Life in Jesus*, 85.

24. Winslow, *Life in Jesus*, 340–41.

25. Winslow, *Life in Jesus*, 422.

26. Winslow, *Life in Jesus*, 347.

27. Winslow, *Life in Jesus*, 418.

28. Winslow, *Life in Jesus*, 423.

have only to regret I so often wander from it myself."[29] "I think many Christians dishonor Christ by refusing to obey Him."[30]

Mary's grief at the lack of serious Christianity in her time is not a reflection of self-righteousness. In fact, she was continually disappointed with herself, almost to a fault, but refused to be disappointed with her God. Grief over her remaining sins was a common refrain in her thought and life: "Oh, the hidden evil of the heart, unknown and unfelt, until the Spirit of Christ sees fit to reveal the depths of iniquity that are there. It is a sickening view; and were it not that Christ Jesus came into the world to save sinners, I should lie down in utter despair.... Oh, if there were a thought of my heart for which Jesus did not atone, I should never enter heaven!"[31] Mary's humility was genuine because it always flowed from the overwhelming love of God; it was not a self-referenced pity: "I cannot trace a single thing I ever did in my whole life that affords me any real pleasure to look back upon," she wrote. But "when I have a glimpse of God as He is in Himself, as well as what He is to my soul, I sink in all my nothingness, melted into love, at His feet."[32] As humiliating as her view of herself was, she never lost the sight of her completeness in Christ. "Her *self-denial* never betrayed her into *grace-denial*."[33]

Lifelong Letter-Writing Ministry

Mary occasionally made trips from America to England to visit family and friends until she permanently returned there in 1834. Whether she was in America or in England, Mary would write letters to family, friends, and officials, and even members of the Royal family—encouraging them to make God's dealings with their soul the priority of their life.

Mary was a constant source of encouragement to her family and friends through letter writing and holy conversation. Her son Octavius wrote, "[God] had given her the 'pen of a ready writer' [cf. Ps. 45:1]. This gift—a rare and a powerful one—she wholly consecrated to God. It is believed she seldom wrote a note, however brief, in which there was not something to lead the thoughts to eternity."[34] Mary Winslow's letters are a treasure of experiential and practical divinity. Throughout her life, she was committed to writing letters to her children that would lead them into a deeper experience of Christ and a practical obedience to God's will.

Living, vital Christianity is set forth in her words in undeniable reality, flowing out of the resurrected Christ. We learn, in her words and by her example, how to

---

29. Winslow, *Life in Jesus*, 98–99.

30. Mary had tasted and seen that the Lord is good, and she was grieved over this lack of experience she saw in other Christians and in herself. "Slumbering saints and dead sinners compose most of the congregations," she complained. "If the religion of Christ is not the business of our whole life," Mary observed, "it is nothing, and we are nothing, and shall be found as nothing, or worse than nothing, when He comes to judge the world." "How little is this understood!" Mary exclaimed. "A cold, formal, heartless prayer often.... No interchange of love, no confession of sin, no adoring gratitude, no emptying of the burdened heart into the loving heart of God." Winslow, *Life in Jesus*, 413, 139, 164.

31. Winslow, *Life in Jesus*, 101, 419.

32. Winslow, *Life in Jesus*, 137.

33. Winslow, *Life in Jesus*, 424.

34. Winslow, *Life in Jesus*, 107.

"deal unceasingly with God, and God deals unweariedly with us."[35]

Mary's letters often displayed her gift for consoling distressed believers. She considered it an honor that God often used her to comfort the distressed with the consolation she received in her own times of trial. Whether it was her sons who lost children, her pastors who were afflicted by illness or the death of spouses, or anxious souls under spiritual darkness, she had a gift for speaking or writing a word in season to the tired and heavy-laden. For instance, when Mary's son Henry died, she wrote to his bereaved spouse words of comfort even as her own heart grieved: "We must not look at second causes. Every circumstance connected with God's children, living or dying, is ordered by Himself. He has not gone a moment sooner or a moment later than God had appointed…. Go to Jesus for all you need. Take Him as your true, your best, your only Friend. There is not another like Him. Take Him as your brother born for adversity."[36]

Why does God allow us to pass through trials? One reason is that God is molding us to depend on Him more. Another reason for trials is to equip us to help others who are suffering by sharing with them the comfort God has given us in our trials.

Heart for Evangelism

From the beginning of her Christian life to her last breath, Mary had a burning desire to see the gospel preached to lost souls. She pledged any means she had available to evangelizing sinners. As her family in Bermuda was wealthy, she asked her mother in 1813 to have a chapel built in St. George and a "gospel minister" be provided so that the people of that area could be evangelized. "How I do love old-fashioned conversions," she wrote, "where sinners are brought to feel they are sinners, crying out under the conviction…and are then led by the self-same Spirit to look to Jesus, and are at once enabled to believe and rejoice."[37]

The business of her Savior was her agenda. Her pen and paper were always ready in the service of encouraging anxious souls to seek the Savior:

> Oh, I could stand upon the housetop, and cry aloud, Come to Jesus—come now—come at once. He is all-sufficient to save, and is as willing as He is able. In a little while, and whether rich or poor, high or low, learned or unlearned, one thing will be of infinite moment—your calling and election made sure to you. Lose no time in this great, this greatest of all great transactions—the salvation of your soul. Delay not, lest the enemy take possession of you, and you are lost forever. "Why will ye die?"[38]

Illnesses, Death, and Significance

In January 1854, while visiting her son in London, Mary became very sick; her family found a skilled doctor to help her. In God's providence, while the doctor brought her back

---

35. Winslow, *Life in Jesus*, 222.
36. Winslow, *Life in Jesus*, 193.
37. Winslow, *Life in Jesus*, 141.
38. Winslow, *Life in Jesus*, 410.

to health, God used her greatly to encourage him in his walk with God.[39]

During this later period in Mary's life, her advanced age and weaker condition made it difficult for her sometimes even to walk from the carriage into the church sanctuary. In spite of this, Mary began attending St. John's Chapel, Bedford Row, in Bloomsbury to hear the preaching of a Reverend Jarman, whose ministry had a blessed impact on her. God had powerfully used his preaching to convert several members of Mary's family. Mary knew that loneliness, depression, and ill health afflicted the minister, so she often visited him to encourage and pray for him.[40] This incident reveals her heart for effective preaching and for encouraging ministers who faithfully executed their calling.

Mary's health began to decline in 1854, and she attended her last Sunday service on July 30. Even when confined to her home, she still delighted to join "the family circle, unite in its devotions, and listen to some of her favourite hymns upon the piano, often affected to tears while they were sung."[41] When she was confined to her bed, her daughter nursed her, and she wrote many reflections in her journal: "Heaven is a reality," she wrote. "We mystify heaven; it is a place. I am going to my family."[42] As her health weakened, she sensed that the very gates of heaven were within her reach. Her heart was stirred at the prospect of seeing her husband in Christ, her children who had gone before her,

St. John's Chapel, Bedford Row

and most of all, her Savior, the one who stood by her so many times in her life and comforted her. She would see Him face-to-face. Mary finally passed away on October 3, 1854, at eighty-one years old.

Mary Winslow's significance lay in her intimate spiritual walk with God. In a time when most people went to church out of custom or habit, she stood out as a woman who kept a close, personal walk with Jesus Christ—not as a pastime or because of her upbringing. Rather, through God's dealings with her, and by His gracious work in her heart, she learned the reality of God behind all things seen.

We often hear people saying that, because of some suffering that entered their lives, they no longer believe in God. But Mary's life shows us how God can use many afflictions in a believer's life to draw her to a nearer, deeper experience of God's grace and all-sufficiency. As a result of her Christian experience, Mary Winslow became a grace-filled

---

39. Winslow, *Life in Jesus*, 369.

40. Mary kept up the correspondence with Reverend Jarman until her final illness brought her near to her final rest in Christ. Winslow, *Life in Jesus*, 381.

41. Winslow, *Life in Jesus*, 410.

42. Winslow, *Life in Jesus*, 413.

example of true spirituality. Not only that, she also worked hard for the conversion of her family and friends and the comfort and encouragement of distressed believers through an unceasing writing ministry. God truly raised Mary up as "a mother in Israel." Godly people speak long after their death, and her story deserves to be heard today. What we can learn from her is what she spent her life saying and writing to others: "Keep close intimacies with Jesus. We must live upon Christ, and we must die upon Christ."[43] The Bible teaches us that all of us can access the grace of such a close walk with Christ: "Ask, and it shall be given you."

Study Questions

1. Compare the comforts of Mary's early years with the painful losses of her later years. In which years was she the happiest? What accounts for the difference?

2. When God was bringing Mary's heart to conviction of sin shortly before her conversion, where did she go for answers? What are some other places people usually try, but fail, to find answers to their conscience accusing them of being an unredeemed sinner in the eyes of God?

3. What were some of the most severe trials Mary met with after her arrival in America? How was she able finally to recover from the profound spiritual depression into which she was brought?

4. What seemed to be Mary's driving purpose in life? How did her trials and experience of God's provision, faithfulness, and love in Jesus help her in this lifelong work?

5. What was Mary's frustration about the Christianity of her day? How is Christianity similar in our day? How can we cultivate a genuine walk with God in an era of spiritual dullness and deadness?

6. What most resonates with you from Mary's story, thoughts, or writings? What do you want especially to pray for after reading about her life?

---

43. Winslow, *Life in Jesus*, 417.

Thomas Chalmers

1780–1847

"All the world is wild about Dr. Chalmers," wrote abolitionist William Wilberforce. Many readers will have heard of most people featured in this volume. Some readers, however, will know very little or nothing at all about Thomas Chalmers. Chalmers is included in this book in part to correct that historical forgetfulness.

Renowned Scottish geologist Hugh Miller wrote of his contemporary Thomas Chalmers that he "may be said to have *created* than to have *belonged* to an era." British prime minister William Gladstone extolled Chalmers as "a man greatly lifted out of the region of mere flesh and blood."[1] So loved and revered was Chalmers that at his death in 1847, life in the city of Edinburgh came to a standstill in his honor.

Thomas Chalmers
PORTRAIT BY JOHN FAED

---

1. John Piper, "'The Expulsive Power of a New Affection': The Life-Changing Insight of Thomas Chalmers," Desiring God, October 23, 2019, https://www.desiringgod.org/articles/the-expulsive-power-of-a-new-affection.

Early Life, Conversion, and Ministry

Born March 17, 1780, in Anstruther, Scotland, in the shire of Fife, Thomas Chalmers attended the local grammar school until age eleven. He then became the second-youngest student to be accepted at the University of St. Andrews, where he studied mathematics and imbibed the intellectual atmosphere of the times. Academic life "was at this time over-run with Moderatism," he later wrote, "under the chilling influences of which we inhaled not a distaste only but a positive contempt for all that is properly and peculiarly gospel."[2]

2. William Hannah, *Memoirs of the Life and Writings of Thomas Chalmers* (New York: Harper and Brothers, 1851), 1:11.

Chalmers's birthplace in Anstruther
KIM TRAYNOR, NASJONALMUSEET, CC BY 4.0

Moderatism was a term coined to describe the stance of many ministers in the Scottish national church who had made peace with the powers that be in church and state, subscribed to formal confessional orthodoxy, and deplored all extremism in religion, such as the "enthusiasm" of evangelical Christianity or the "radicalism" of the Reformed Presbyterians. For the Moderates, Christianity had more to do with morals than with doctrines, and for authority they looked to reason more than to Scripture.

In 1802, upon completion of his undergraduate studies, Chalmers accepted a ministerial call to the farming town of Kilmany, a community of eight hundred souls under the patronage of the nearby University of St. Andrews. As the minister of Kilmany, he was confident in his own righteousness and a good moralist who urged his flock to be moral and upright in their dealings. But by his own later confession, he was a hireling, an unbelieving minister, and cared far more about intellectual pursuits and academic life than the spiritual or temporal needs of his flock. For him, the ministry was a paycheck with as few responsibilities as possible. In 1805 he wrote that a minister should get his public duties done as quickly as possible, after which "a minister may enjoy five days in the week of uninterrupted leisure." He later admitted, "I thought not of the littleness of time—I recklessly thought not of the greatness of eternity."[3]

Chalmers went on this way until sickness and death descended on his family and life. In 1808, while preparing for a pleasant visit to the literary circles of London, his plans were abruptly interrupted. His sister suddenly became gravely ill. At her bedside, he watched her life ebb away. Shortly after her death, an uncle fell sick, and he also died. Hard on the heels came Chalmers's own health crisis.

He fell gravely ill and was bedridden for four months. Chalmers was forced to feel the full weight of the shortness of time and the greatness of eternity. During those months of uncertainty, what he had heartlessly read in the Bible became vividly real. He realized his total inability to keep the law of a holy God. "On the system of 'Do this and live,'" he wrote, "no peace, and even no true and worthy obedience, can ever be attained."[4] As he read the Scriptures, he came across the text, "Believe on the Lord Jesus Christ, and thou shalt be saved" (Acts 16:31). By God's amazing grace, Chalmers truly repented before God and believed in Christ alone for salvation. He was truly converted! Everything had become new; eternity had eclipsed time and the temporal. "With the magnificence of eternity before us," he wrote, "let time, with all its fluctuations, dwindle into its own littleness."[5] Thereafter, his life and ministry dramatically changed.

The first and most profound change was in Chalmers's view of Holy Scripture. Previously, a neighbor in his parish had commented to the still-unbelieving minister, "I find you busy, sir, with one thing or another, but come when I may, I never find you at your studies for the Sabbath." To which Chalmers had carelessly replied, "Oh, an hour or two on the Saturday evening is quite enough for that." In the ensuing weeks after Chalmers's conversion, the neighbor noticed the profound change in his pastor. "I never come in now, sir,

---

3. Iain Murray, *A Scottish Christian Heritage* (Edinburgh: Banner of Truth, 2006), 83.

4. Thomas Chalmers, letter to Alexander Chalmers, February 14, 1820, in Hannah, *Memoirs of the Life and Writings of Thomas Chalmers*, 1:193.

5. Thomas Chalmers, *Political Economy* (Glasgow: William Collins, 1832), 584.

but I find you aye [always] at your Bible!" Tearing himself away from the pages in front of him, Chalmers replied, "All too little, John, all too little."[6]

Immersed as he now was in the Word of God, Chalmers became intensely concerned for the souls of his congregation, and he became equally concerned for the lost in foreign lands. And the more he looked around him in Scotland, the more compassion he felt for the masses of people living in abject poverty—both spiritual and temporal poverty. His pastor's heart overflowed with a new affection for the downtrodden lost. And this new affection permeated his preaching. Meanwhile, another new affection came upon Chalmers. In 1812 he met, fell in love with, and married Grace Platt. Together they had six daughters.

As Chalmers's hearers were brought to faith in Christ, they told others about their minister's sermons. His reputation as one of the most eloquent and passionate preachers of the Word of God spread throughout Scotland, and calls to other pulpits came his way. On July 21, 1815, Chalmers was installed by the town council as minister of the Tron Church, one of the most influential pulpits in Glasgow, a city well on the way to becoming the greatest city in the British Empire, despite degradation ravaging the working poor. The Tron Church seated 1,400 people, but under Chalmers's faithful preaching, there was standing room only. His gospel eloquence and Christ-centered passion in the pulpit soon brought him to national attention. At the same time, Chalmers was appalled by the condition of the poorer classes, the masses that had flocked to Glasgow to find employment in the city's burgeoning mercantile and industrial economy.

---

6. Hannah, *Memoirs of the Life and Writings of Thomas Chalmers*, 1:268.

The Tron Church today
FINLAY MCWALTER, CC BY-SA 3.0

Reaching Every Door

A scholar of moral philosophy, Chalmers cared deeply for the poor and yearned for a more just society. Full of heartfelt compassion, Chalmers posed one of the most important questions to himself: "What is the most effectual method of making Christianity so to bear upon a population, as that it shall reach every door and be brought into contact with all families?"[7] The care of the poor by long-established custom had been lodged with the authorities of each church and parish in the city, assisted by a host of benevolent societies. Parish authorities were overwhelmed by the population boom, and so were societies. The churches of Glasgow had the obligation, and certainly the opportunity, but no one had organized them for work on the scale required.

Chalmers believed he had a solution. It never occurred to him to call on the resources of the state or the nation at large. "I am not one of those who underrate the value of civil and political liberty," he wrote, "but I am well assured that it is only the principles of Christianity which can impart true security, prosperity, and happiness either to individuals or to nations."[8] For Chalmers, the government could never be the ultimate solution to poverty and social disfunction. It had to be the local church. He wanted the church to become the nerve center and network of spiritual and temporal care for the poor living in a localized community—a parish. He believed the church of Jesus Christ ought to be the hub and center of ministry with both hands—the hand of the gospel but also the hand of benevolence and care for the neediest in the local community, offering a cup of cold water in Christ's name. At first, the Church of Scotland leadership agreed to let Chalmers implement his new plan.

Ten thousand souls were living in a single parish, St. John's Parish in Glasgow, which was but one parish of the many filled with squalor, poverty, sickness, and high mortality rates visible in every gutter. Undaunted, Chalmers set to work. He divided up the parish and assigned elders and deacons to smaller, more manageable districts and much smaller numbers of people. His plan also required him to plant new churches—over two hundred of them! Now, elders and deacons could know their flock personally, could visit the poor and sick, bear their burdens, and meet their needs. Chalmers equipped his leaders so they in turn could provide training and resources to their people so that the downtrodden could be lifted up and begin to meet their own needs and the needs of their less fortunate neighbors.

Giant of learning that he was, Chalmers also cared deeply for children, establishing Sabbath schools for the poor, with twelve hundred children regularly attending each week. For many children, Dr. Chalmers's Sabbath schools were all the formal education they would have. He set his prodigious pen to use by writing textbook curriculum for the Sabbath schools. All his efforts were focused on the vigorous and faithful preaching of the Word of God. Under Chalmers's direction and care, gradually many working families were converted to Christ and began to rise above poverty and to flourish.

Effective as Chalmers's commonsense plan was, self-interested politicians and economists, careless of the poor, began first to resist and then to oppose his plan openly. "There is nothing more uncommon than common sense!"

---

7. Thomas Chalmers, *On Church and College Establishments* (Glasgow: William Collins; London: Hamilton, Adams, & Co., n.d.), vi.

8. Hannah, *Memoirs of the Life and Writings of Thomas Chalmers*, 3:269.

Poor living conditions in Glasgow
THOMAS ANNAN

said Chalmers. Still more maddening was the opposition from other leaders in the Church of Scotland. Discouraged and frustrated, in 1823 Chalmers accepted a position as professor of moral philosophy at the University of St. Andrews, his alma mater. He believed that moral philosophy, or the systematic study of ethics, ought to be a gateway to Christian theology and the gospel. Perhaps he could have an influence on young scholars not yet hardened by the soul-killing priorities of "Enlightenment" rationalism and a rapidly secularizing society and state church.

Worldwide Missions

In his new professorship, Chalmers encountered dozens of young, earnest scholars who at first were impressed merely by his eloquence and the vastness of his knowledge. They began gathering around him, wanting to learn more. For Chalmers, his eloquence was merely an instrument to be employed to infuse his passion for the Word of God and the spread of the gospel into the minds and hearts of his students. For him, troubled Scotland and the warring world at large needed the good news of Jesus Christ. The more he taught and preached, the more he was looked to as the inspiring champion of worldwide gospel missions.

The St. Andrews Seven by John Roxborogh and Stuart Piggin, tells the riveting story of Chalmers's profound effect on seven of his students during his professorship at St. Andrews University in the 1820s. Chalmers used his zealous influence to instill in them a new and higher affection. For these young men, "only one thing seemed to matter: to discover God's will and do it."[9] Doing it—leaving the comfort

---

9. Stuart Piggin and John Roxborogh, *The Saint Andrews Seven: The*

and sophistication of academic life in Scotland and crossing oceans to take the gospel to unreached people—cost most of them their lives.

Blood-Earnest Preacher

What gave such force to Chalmers's pervasive influence across so many fields? It was in part the spellbinding vigor of his words. One listener declared that Chalmers's oratorial skills "bordered on wizardry." Apparently, this was a listener unaware of how contradictory such a metaphor was; Chalmers was wholly committed to the power of the Spirit of God to give his words effect in sinners' hearts. Christian Parliamentarian and abolitionist William Wilberforce first heard Chalmers preach in 1817; feeling the penetrating strength of the man's words on his own heart and the hearts of the crowds clamoring to hear him, Wilberforce recorded that evening in his diary, "All the world [is] wild about Dr. Chalmers!"[10]

No doubt Chalmers preached thousands of sermons in his years of ministry. But many agree that his best-known and perhaps most important sermon was preached from 1 John 2:15, "Love not the world, neither the things that are in the world. If any man love the world, the love of the Father is not in him." In this famous sermon, titled "The Expulsive Power of a New Affection," Chalmers explored the ways we sometimes attempt not to love the things of the world. But he argued that this negative approach is wholly ineffective as a way of altering our affection for sin. So, how is it

Thomas Chalmers
PHOTO BY DAVID OCTAVIUS HILL
AND ROBERT ADAMSON

that Christians are to stop loving the world, to stop thinking that sinful ways are more pleasant ways, and to start developing right affections for God the Father and His will and His way? Is it by creating a deeper sense of legal obligation to put off sin and the world's ways, or something else? Chalmers answered by taking his listeners back to the foundations of the gospel:

Salvation by grace—salvation by free grace—salvation not of works, but according to the mercy of God—salvation on such a footing is not more indispensable to the deliverance of our persons from the hand of justice, than it is to the deliverance of our hearts from the chill and the weight of ungodliness. Retain a single shred or fragment of legality with the Gospel, and we raise a topic of distrust between man and God.[11]

Finest Flowering of Missionary Zeal in Scottish History (Edinburgh: Banner of Truth, 1985), 77.

10. Hanna, *Memoirs of the Life and Writings of Thomas Chalmers*, 1:425.

11. Thomas Chalmers, "The Expulsive Power of a New Affection," in *Discourses on the Application of Christianity to the Commercial and Ordinary Affairs of Life* (Edinburgh: Sutherland and Knox; London: Hamilton, Adams, and Co., 1801), 231.

Hence, the solution to wrong affections is not merely layering on more legal obligation, more external command, more willpower, more teeth-clenching resolve: I'm just going to stop loving the world! Chalmers argued that doing so simply will not work. It is not in the "constitution of our nature" merely to stop loving the world.[12] Arguments demonstrating the negative outcome of loving the world don't work either: "The love of the world cannot be expunged by a mere demonstration of the world's worthlessness."[13] Though laboring to show the consequences of loving the world might produce good moralists, it will not cause true growth in grace and love for Christ and His ways.

Chalmers demonstrated the contrast: "A practical moralist may attempt to displace from the human heart its love for the world…by a demonstration of the world's vanity, so as that the heart shall be prevailed upon simply to withdraw its regards from an object that is not worthy of it."[14] That would merely leave a void in the heart. After showing how ineffectual the practical moralist's method is for expelling the unworthy affection, he made the case that there is only one way that works:

> By setting forth another object, even God, as more worthy of its attachment, so as that the heart shall be prevailed upon not to resign an old affection, which shall have nothing to succeed it, but to exchange an old affection for a new one…. From the constitution

of our nature, the former method is altogether incompetent and ineffectual…the latter method will alone suffice for the rescue and recovery of the heart from the wrong affection that domineers over it.[15]

The solution to shedding love for the world is the expulsive power of a new affection, a new love. And what does that new love look like? "Love may be regarded in two different conditions," Chalmers said. "The first is, when its object is at a distance, and then it becomes love in a state of desire. The second is, when its object is in possession, and then it becomes love in a state of indulgence."[16] This sounds right and biblical to most Christians' ears—until we land on the last word. When we hear the word *indulgence*, we may think of the error of Roman Catholicism selling an indulgence so the sinner can feel at liberty to indulge himself in more sinning. Or, in our self-indulgent world, we tend to think of self-gratification, the central modern-day activity of indulging one's self. After all, popular psychology and our self-referential culture have made a virtue of doing what feels good at the moment. But the word as Chalmers used it here means quite the contrary. For Chalmers, indulgence was the sense of pouring one's self into, loving, and serving (indulging and gratifying) *not* one's self but another—ultimately, Christ Himself.

"Such is the grasping tendency of the human heart," Chalmers continued, "that it must have a something to lay hold of—and which, if wrested away without the

---

12. Chalmers, "The Expulsive Power of a New Affection," in *Discourses*, 209.

13. Chalmers, "The Expulsive Power of a New Affection," in *Discourses*, 219.

14. Chalmers, "The Expulsive Power of a New Affection," in *Discourses*, 209.

15. Chalmers, "The Expulsive Power of a New Affection," in *Discourses*, 209.

16. Chalmers, "The Expulsive Power of a New Affection," in *Discourses*, 209.

substitution of another something in its place, would leave a void and a vacancy as painful to the mind, as hunger is to the natural system."[17] Hence, for Chalmers, the only way to "love not the world" is to fill the mind and heart with a new affection. The Christian filled to overflowing with love for Christ Himself will have no room left in his heart for loving the world.

First Preacher of Scotland

While minister at the Tron Church in Glasgow, Chalmers began a series of sermons delivered during working hours every Thursday. At first a handful gathered to listen to the midweek sermons. By the Spirit's gracious power, his oratorial skills, always a servant to the substance of the biblical text he was expounding, made for electrifying messages. Chalmers held his listeners spellbound. Word spread throughout the city. Soon businessmen and bankers shuttered their places of business or employment and clamored to listen to the first preacher of the realm at the Tron. In 1817 Chalmers's series of Thursday sermons appeared in published book form. They created a publishing sensation and went into reprinting in short order.

From academic volumes on moral philosophy, geology, and natural theology, Chalmers moved to his favorite topics: theology, apologetics, and biblical exposition, including volumes on Paul's epistle to the Romans—204 published works in all. His complete works run to nine large volumes today.

Chalmers's learning and oratory were unmatched throughout the realm. On October 31, 1827, he was

unanimously awarded the chair of the divinity school at the University of Edinburgh, placing him in the most influential city in Scotland. At 11:00 a.m., November 10, 1828, Chalmers was scheduled to deliver his first lecture. It was a foul Scottish winter day as snow and hailstones pummeled the cobbled streets of the city and the people flocking into those streets. Undaunted by the weather, a crowd began gathering well before the lecture was to begin. As still more people pressed in to hear the famous orator, the university authorities, fearing a riot, called in the city police to keep order.

Chalmers's reputation spread throughout Europe. In 1834 he was made a member of the Royal Institute of France. In 1835 he was awarded the degree of doctor of law by Oxford University and later the degree of doctor of divinity by the University of Glasgow.

As the state-controlled Church of Scotland became increasingly more liberal in its theology, Chalmers's commitment to confessional Reformed orthodoxy placed him in the center of a debate on the power of the state over the church. At issue was the long-contested practice of patronage—the civil appointment of patrons, usually men of wealth and prestige, who had power to appoint the ministers of parish churches without consulting the will of the people. Such a practice was in conflict with the ancient Scottish Presbyterian ideal of a free church in a free state. For ten years the evangelical party in the church contended against patronage in the assemblies of the national church and the courts of the state but could not prevail.

As the unrivaled leader of the evangelical party, Chalmers was forced to rise at the 1843 General Assembly of the Church of Scotland and lead other ministers to take their stand for doctrinal purity, zeal for Christ's gospel, and a

---

17. Chalmers, "The Expulsive Power of a New Affection," in *Discourses*, 214.

church under the headship of Christ alone. In what came to be called the "Great Disruption"—after much prayer and prodigious labors for reformation—Chalmers led over 450 faithful gospel ministers out the door of the assembly.

Chalmers was the principal founder of the Free Church of Scotland—free from the doctrinal corruptions and civil entanglements of the national church. All eyes were on Chalmers. It was clear to all that God had uniquely gifted him to be the voice of the nation. He was unanimously elected moderator of the new denomination's first General Assembly. His *Addresses Delivered at the Commencement and Conclusion of the First General Assembly of the Free Church of Scotland* were gathered together and published in book form shortly after the Great Disruption and the formation of the Free Church.

Final Days and Death

Chalmers was not only the leading preacher of the day but also a man of inexhaustible energy, even in his later years. He was constantly lecturing at the Free Church divinity school as he started writing two new books simultaneously, a practical book built around daily Bible readings and another on systematic theology.

Disruption Forming Free Kirk
DAVID OCTAVIUS HILL

After delivering an address on national education in London, May 28, 1847, Chalmers returned to his wife and family at their home on Church Hill in the Morningside district of Edinburgh. Next morning, he got up and began drafting a report to the forthcoming General Assembly of the Free Church. But on Sunday morning, May 30, he didn't come down to breakfast. His family found him lying peacefully in his bed. He had died without struggle in his sleep.

June 4, 1847, a great crowd accompanied his casket to burial in the Grange Cemetery. Chalmers's remains were the first interred in the new cemetery.

Chalmers's wife, Grace, died January 16, 1850, and was buried with her husband. His eldest daughter, Anne, married William Hanna, who went on to memorialize his father-in-law in a comprehensive biography. Alongside William Wallace, Robert the Bruce, John Knox, David Livingstone,

The grave of Thomas and Grace Chalmers
STEPHEN C. DICKSON,
CC BY-SA 4.0

and other luminaries of Scottish history, Chalmers is fittingly memorialized with a bust in the Hall of Heroes at the Wallace Monument near Stirling, Scotland.

One observer of Chalmers's life and influence described him as "the holy wrestler, gentle to his own and to his enemies terrible."[18] What made all the world wild about Thomas Chalmers? Was it his prodigious intellect? His eloquence and oratory skills? His vast influence over an entire era? Chalmers would likely put it far more simply: he bent every fiber of his being to bring to bear on the hearts and minds of his listeners and readers the truth and power of the gospel of Jesus Christ. That, by God's grace, is what makes a genuine, evangelical hero in any century past or future.

Study Questions

1. It was said of Thomas Chalmers that he created an era rather than just belonged to a moment in history. List several ways Chalmers created the era in which he lived.

2. In his early adult life, Chalmers thought little about eternity and the matters of his soul. What great event happened in his life that forced him to reckon with eternity? List several changes that came over him as a result.

3. But Chalmers did have a plan to help the poor in Scotland. Describe his plan. How did the Church of Scotland respond both at first and as time passed on?

4. Chalmers believed that the only way to overcome an unworthy affection was by replacing it with an infinitely more worthy affection. Give examples of how he demonstrated this in his preaching, in his pastoral ministry, and in his work of education and social reform.

5. How was Chalmers remembered after his death? How is he an example to us today?

---

18. "Thomas Chalmers: Unrelenting Advocate for the Poor," *Christianity Today*.

~ 14 ~

Charles Hodge

1797–1878

One spring morning in 1819, Charles Hodge walked into the home of Archibald Alexander on the campus of Princeton Theological Seminary. Hodge, then twenty-two, was four months away from completing the seminary's course of studies. After Dr. Alexander had taken care of other matters, he abruptly asked Hodge, "How would you like to be a professor in the seminary?"

Hodge didn't know what to say. The question overwhelmed him with equal measures of surprise and confusion. No such thought had ever crossed his mind. *Why me?* he thought. *I'm not even the best student. My best friend, John Johns, would clearly be a better choice.*

Seeing that Hodge was left speechless, Alexander continued, "Of course, I have no power to determine such a result. It will depend on the judgment of the General Assembly. Say nothing now, but think upon it. My plan for you, at present, is simply that you spend the next winter in Philadelphia learning to read Hebrew with some competent instructor."

Hodge left the house, turning the offer over and over in his head. He worried that being a professor might take away from his preaching opportunities. *I believe that preaching the gospel is a privilege superior to any other entrusted to men*, he thought. But this was a needless worry, for his teachers, Dr. Alexander and Dr. Samuel Miller, preached nearly as much as full-time pastors.

Another worry entered his mind: *The weight of responsibility I would have for the souls of my students would be tremendous, and I would constantly be influencing students by the quality of my character and Christian walk.* Without godliness, the work of a seminary professor is ineffective and uninspiring, but an able professor with real personal piety can do incalculable good. The heart, even more than the head, of an instructor in a Christian seminary qualifies or disqualifies him for this high calling.

Yet another matter concerned him. *If I were to choose a subject to teach*, he thought, *it would not be Hebrew. If I am to be successful, I'll have to prepare more diligently and work harder than I ever have, for I am not naturally talented in languages, and I have many things to do other than study Hebrew. Yes*, he told himself, *the seminary is taking a huge risk in asking me to teach this subject.*

Charles Hodge

Hodge resolved to do the language study Dr. Alexander suggested that winter while waiting for the seminary's decision on the position. He felt that this was the way God would make His will clear—either by opening the door or closing it.

As Hodge awaited the decision on his hiring, God was guiding him to take the first step toward becoming one of the ablest and strongest defenders of the Reformed faith in the United States, one whose legacy would impact many generations.

Family and Background

In 1743 a group of members at First Presbyterian Church in Philadelphia withdrew and formed their own congregation, calling it the Second Presbyterian Church. These worshipers, led by Rev. Gilbert Tennent, had been converted under George Whitefield's revival preaching, but most of the members at First Presbyterian, called "Old Lights," did not support the revival or welcome the zeal of its supporters, who were called "New Lights." One founding member of Second Presbyterian Church was an immigrant from Ireland named Andrew Hodge, Charles's grandfather. He and his two brothers settled in Philadelphia, where he became a successful merchant.[1] One of Andrew's eight children, Hugh Hodge, served as a surgeon in the Continental Army in the Revolutionary War and afterward as a doctor in Philadelphia. He died of yellow fever in 1798, leaving behind his wife, Mary, and their two young sons, Hugh Jr., who was two years old, and six-month-old Charles. Mary was diligent and

---

1. S. Donald Fortson III, *Charles Hodge* (Darlington, England: Evangelical Press, 2013), ATLA e-book, chap. 1.

industrious in raising her sons. She provided for their needs and education through income from boarding guests in her home, and she gave them doctrinal and practical instruction through the Westminster Shorter Catechism. Charles and Hugh were close in brotherly affection, and both treasured their mother and felt they owed her everything: "To us she devoted her life. For us she prayed, labored and suffered."[2]

Education

In 1810 the brothers moved to Somerville, New Jersey, where they studied Latin at a classical academy. They moved to Princeton to continue their education in 1812; Hugh attended the College of New Jersey (later renamed Princeton University), and Charles would enroll soon afterward. Ashbel Green, who was a copastor at Second Presbyterian Church in Philadelphia and had a great influence on the boys' early years, was at this time appointed president of the College of New Jersey. This was the same year that Princeton Theological Seminary was established, where Dr. Archibald Alexander was appointed its first professor.[3] Through Dr. Alexander's influence, Princeton Seminary became a school where personal piety was just as important as a well-schooled intellect—and where both were developed to high standards. Dr. Alexander met Charles Hodge during this time, and they forged a father-and-son relationship that lasted the rest of their lives.

When Hodge was seventeen, a revival swept through the college. Students became more serious about seeking personal salvation. Hodge was converted, made a public profession of faith, and, in 1815, was received as a communicant member of the Presbyterian Church. Upon graduating from the college, Hodge entered Princeton Seminary, where he diligently applied himself to his studies in theology and the biblical languages and attended Princeton's weekly meetings ("conferences") on practical Christian life and character development.

In September 1819, Hodge graduated from Princeton Seminary. The next month he was licensed to preach by New Brunswick Presbytery, writing, "May the Lord Jesus work within me all the good pleasure of His will, making me such a minister as He would have me to be." Preaching his first sermons, he became aware of how easily fear of the people or desire for applause could corrupt his heart as a preacher: "I feel myself entirely dependent on His sovereign grace for the continuance and increase of this great mercy. Were He to let me alone, I should indeed become dreadfully corrupt in practice as well as in

Ashbel Green

---

2. A. A. Hodge, *The Life of Charles Hodge* (London: T. Nelson and Sons, 1881), 10.

3. Hodge, *Life of Charles Hodge*, 18.

heart. Bless the Lord, O my soul."[4] On the Lord's Days, he was sent to preach and do mission work at various locations in the Philadelphia area.

Months before Hodge's graduation, Dr. Alexander had asked him to consider teaching the biblical languages at the seminary. In preparation for this possibility, Hodge went to Philadelphia in the winter of 1820 to study Hebrew under the guidance of Dr. John Banks, minister of the Associate Presbyterian Church and one of the most eminent Hebrew scholars at that time in America. That winter Hodge wrote Dr. Alexander, "Dr. Banks is very much what you said he was. He will talk all day on anything connected with Hebrew. It is quite amusing to see his zeal on the subject, especially for the points and accents…which he thinks does everything, regulating the rhetorical and grammatical construction, pointing out the ellipsis, indicating the emotions, etc."[5]

Hodge's time was not spent in vain. In the spring of 1820, the General Assembly approved Hodge's appointment as instructor in the "original languages" (Hebrew and Greek) at Princeton. In May 1822, Hodge was promoted to professor of Oriental and biblical literature. In his inaugural address he illustrated "the importance of piety in the interpretation of Scripture."[6] He busied himself with lecturing, seminary administration, preaching, editorial work, student interaction, and his ongoing personal study of Hebrew, Aramaic, and Arabic. Aware that he had only begun to master

Charles Hodge
PORTRAIT BY REMBRANDT PEALE

---

4. Hodge, *Life of Charles Hodge*, 73.

5. Hodge, *Life of Charles Hodge*, 70.

6. Hodge, *Life of Charles Hodge*, 94.

the field, he wrote, "I look forward to a pretty severe term, for I must keep before [ahead of] my students or they will find it out."[7]

Marriage and Children

Hodge was not too busy, however, to court the woman he loved. When Sarah Bache's father passed away a decade earlier in 1813, the Bache family was forced to board as guests in the Hodge home. Thus, teenagers Sarah and Charles came to know each other and developed a strong friendship. She had dark auburn hair and large blue-grey eyes, was musically and artistically inclined, and was full of enthusiasm, imagination, and self-sacrifice—qualities that became increasingly consecrated by the love for Christ that she displayed throughout her life.[8] The relationship blossomed, and Charles and Sarah married in the summer of 1822. Their first son, Archibald Alexander Hodge, was born the next year, and in 1825, their daughter, Mary Elizabeth. By the 1830s the Hodges had eight children.

Charles and Sarah cultivated a joyful, Christ-centered family atmosphere. Hodge led family devotions and always allowed his wife and children access to him in his study: "While some of his children remained too small to unfasten the latch themselves, he had left it unfastened, so that even the least of us might come and go as we pleased." Hodge made his children his priority: "If they were sick, he nursed them. If they were well, he played with them. If he were busy, they played about him." At a later time, he took the

latches off the doors and put spring hinges on them so that the youngest children, and later the grandchildren, could go in and out at will.[9] Hodge's attitude toward his children reflects God the Father's attitude toward the least of us— whoever comes to Him He will in no wise cast out.

Two Years' Study in Europe

The more Hodge's responsibilities increased, the more strongly he felt that he was inadequately trained for his duties and needed to spend time in Europe for further study. His senior colleague, Dr. Samuel Miller, thought Hodge underestimated his abilities, but he respected the desire for further study. At that time, Europe had more advanced biblical scholarship and better equipped libraries for language study than were available in the United States. Plus, learning French and German would give Hodge access to a larger body of scholarly literature. The seminary approved Hodge's plans and appointed a senior student at the seminary to teach Hodge's courses until he returned. With arrangements made for Sarah Hodge and the children to live in Philadelphia with Hodge's mother, Hodge set sail for Europe in 1826.

In Paris he studied Aramaic, Arabic, and French, and later, in the German universities at Halle and Berlin, he studied theology. He worked under some of Europe's most renowned scholars.[10] Most importantly, Hodge struck a life-

---

7. Hodge, *Life of Charles Hodge*, 99.

8. Hodge, *Life of Charles Hodge*, 95.

9. Hodge, *Life of Charles Hodge*, 96, 227.

10. He was personally tutored in Hebrew for a semester by Hebrew scholar Wilhelm Gesenius. His German tutor was George Müller, who later became famous for establishing a faith-based orphanage in England. He made acquaintance with church historian August Neander and

La Place Louis XVI (Paris, 1829)
GUISEPPE CANELLA

long friendship with August Tholuck, theology professor at Halle, whose learning, personal piety, and preaching deeply impressed him.[11] Hodge also heard the preaching of famed theologian Friedrich Schleiermacher, who wanted German rationalists to see their need for faith in Christ. Hodge had serious disagreements with Schleiermacher's "speculative" theology, however, as it made "religious feeling," rather than Scripture, the basis of Christian faith. Hodge wrote, "Even the Biblical theologians of Germany are so led away by the speculative spirit…, that it seems impossible they should be restrained within the bounds of sober and important truth, except by the influence of religion on their hearts."[12] Hodge's ability to maintain a charitable spirit toward people with whom he had serious disagreements (such as Schleiermacher) is a skill increasingly rare today, an example that we need to follow and cultivate.

Hodge was joyfully reunited with his family in September 1828. He returned to his post at Princeton, which now had more than one hundred students. In his address to the class of 1828–1829, he said of the state of religion in Germany, "The leading parties are the Orthodox, the Rationalists, and the Pantheists.… Wherever you find vital piety—that is, penitence and a devotional spirit—there you find the doctrines of the fall, of depravity, of regeneration, of atonement, and of the deity of Jesus Christ.… Holiness is essential to the correct knowledge of divine things and the great security from error.… When men lose the life of religion, they can believe the most monstrous doctrines."[13] Seeing firsthand in Europe what can happen when personal piety and purity of doctrine are not held together, Hodge was more convinced than ever that Princeton Seminary must always emphasize both.

Professor of Theology

In 1834 Rutgers College in New Brunswick, New Jersey, conferred on Hodge the degree of doctor of divinity. He continued editing the journal he had established in 1825, the *Biblical Repertory*, "one of the oldest quarterly journals in the United States," and later renamed the *Princeton Review*.[14] He contributed thirty-six articles between 1829 and 1840 and another thirty-five between 1858 and 1868, when he finally retired from editing it. He shaped the journal into a conservative voice for biblical truth, with "no interest in originality, but [only in] defending the doctrines of our [Westminster] standards."[15]

Oriental languages professor and Bible commentator Wilhelm Hengstenberg.

11. Tholuck was influenced by German Pietism, which reacted against the dead orthodoxy of the state Lutheran church and emphasized heartfelt religion, missions, and holy living. Among German theologians there was a widespread rationalism that rejected the inspiration of Scripture and the supernatural. Hodge was astonished at the coldness and deadness of religion in Germany. Many theological students boasted of not having a trace of "fanaticism" among them. In a letter to Hodge (October 1827), Dr. Alexander wrote, "I rejoice to learn that you live in an infected atmosphere, without being yourself infected. May God preserve you." Tholuck, by holding a personal commitment to biblical truth, was somewhat unique among theology professors at the time.

12. Hodge, *Life of Charles Hodge*, 119.

13. Hodge, *Life of Charles Hodge*, 204.

14. Fortson, *Charles Hodge*, chap. 2.

15. Fortson, *Charles Hodge*, chap. 7.

In 1833 what had been occasional discomfort in Hodge's right thigh became severe pain, which confined him to his bed that summer. Hodge tried multiple treatments over the next several years and eventually was able to walk again with difficulty, though not without a cane. Hodge's condition meant that he now spent most of his time in his study at home, where colleagues, students, friends, and family would gather and where his classes (from 1833 to 1836) and seminary faculty meetings were held. A central piece of furniture in his study was a couch his brother, Hugh, had given him, from which he lectured, studied, prepared sermons, edited the *Biblical Repertory*, debated colleagues, met with students, and entertained visitors.

Around this time, Dr. Hodge began publishing his first books, most notably his commentary on Romans. He wrote this work "during the darkest days of his confinement, the winter of 1834 and 1835, while stretched horizontally on a couch, and his right [leg] often bound in a steel-splint."[16]

In 1840 Hodge was elected as professor of didactic and exegetical theology at Princeton Seminary, the former post of Dr. Alexander, who was moved to the role of professor of pastoral and polemic theology.[17] The change was very beneficial to Hodge, but his acceptance of it was more submission to the will of Dr. Alexander and the church than his own plan.[18] Remarkably, all of his effort in mastering the biblical languages and doing biblical exegesis equipped him to be a solid systematic theologian whose lectures had both clarity and depth.[19] Princeton continued its tradition of Sabbath afternoon "conferences" or gatherings of professors and students to discuss practical Christian living. A. A. Hodge counted these conferences as among his most memorable activities at Princeton.

In the following three decades of his career, Hodge published his *Systematic Theology*, several biblical commentaries, various devotional studies, and, notably, a summary of basic Christian doctrine titled *The Way of Life*.[20]

Division in the Presbyterian Church

In the years 1828–1837, debates within the Presbyterian Church led to division into Old and New School branches. New School Presbyterians were in favor of a reinterpretation of Presbyterian doctrine as set forth in the Westminster

---

16. Hodge, *Life of Charles Hodge*, 271.

17. Systematic theology is the organization of biblical teaching into topics such as God, man and sin, redemption, the Holy Spirit, the church, the last things, and so on. Polemic theology is the system of defending the Christian faith against "Christian" heresies, non-Christian religions, and the atheistic and relativistic philosophies of the world. Didactic theology focuses on the methods of teaching systematic theology through the lens of a confessional tradition (e.g., the Westminster Standards). Exegetical theology is the science of applying knowledge about the biblical languages to understanding, translating, and interpreting the Bible.

18. Hodge, *Life of Charles Hodge*, 322.

19. He delivered his systematic theology lectures in a question-and-answer format designed to push students to think for themselves. When his *Systematic Theology* was published in 1872, this became the primary text not only for his courses but "for conservative Presbyterian and Reformed churches in the United States and abroad for the next century." Fortson, *Charles Hodge*, chap. 7.

20. He wrote *The Way of Life* to equip young people with a firm foundation for key Bible doctrines, such as the divine origin of Scripture, original sin, and salvation by grace through faith in Christ. In the preface, he asks, "Are the Scriptures really a revelation from God? If they are, what doctrines do they teach? And what influence should those doctrines exert on our heart and life?" Laypeople, ministers, and scholars alike received this book with acclaim.

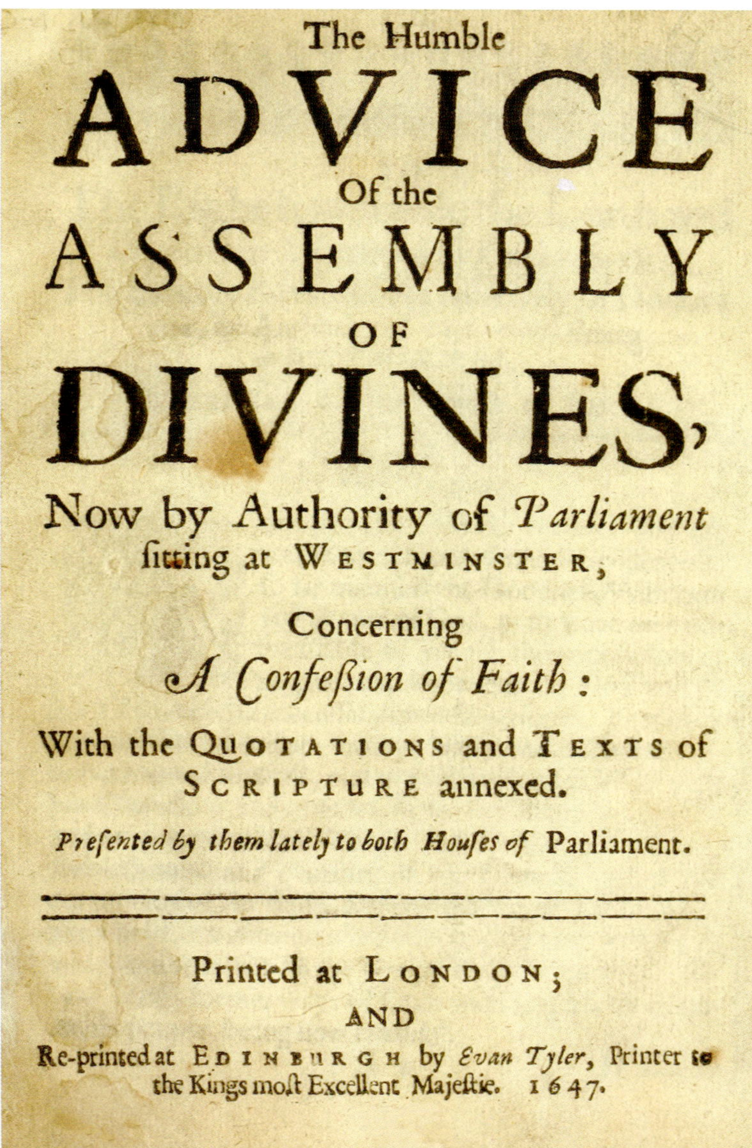

The first edition of the Westminster Confession of Faith

Confession of Faith. Under the influence of Nathaniel Taylor's "New Haven theology," they called for modifying core Calvinist doctrines such as original sin and regeneration. The Old School branch resisted, wanting to maintain historic Calvinism in their church. Hodge argued that ministers should hold at least to the core doctrines of Calvinism as expressed in the Westminster Confession but were not bound to think identically on everything else in such a large statement of faith. The rest of the faculty of Princeton Seminary, agreeing with Hodge, supported a peacemaking, middle position, refusing to take sides, and Dr. Alexander urged Presbyterians to stop quarreling with one another.

Presbyterians also debated each other on accepting or rejecting the new revivalism of the day. Popular revivalist Charles Finney adopted innovative revival methods that targeted the emotions of his hearers and emphasized the power of personal decision. Hodge wrote a *Repertory* article against the methods of Finney, who preached that while God influenced a person's heart to turn to Him, man was the real author of his own change of heart. Hodge charged Finney and his followers with denying, in practice, if not on principle, the doctrines of original sin and the need for the Holy Spirit to convert one's heart. New School Presbyterians were in favor of Finney's revivalism, but the Old School branch rejected it.

Decades after the 1818 General Assembly's antislavery statement, the issue of American slavery had roused fresh debate among Presbyterians. In an 1835 article in the *Repertory*, Hodge argued that slavery is not condemned in the Bible as sinful in itself. He also rebuked abolitionists who would bar from church membership anyone holding slaves. In pursuit of unity and peace in his church, Hodge tried to

Charles Grandison Finney
PORTRAIT BY H. ALONZO PEASE

find a middle ground between what he viewed as extremes. It is clear that he himself was personally opposed to slavery as practiced in the American South as well as all the dreadful evils connected with it: an institution rooted in the crimes of manstealing and human trafficking and maintained from generation to generation by savage oppression, inhumane treatment, and keeping a subject people in ignorance and squalor.[21]

---

21. When Hodge wrote an article against card playing and dancing, he used a similar logic (that the Bible does not condemn these as sinful in themselves), but he added that there may be a *kind* of card playing and dancing that is evil, because of the association with "frivolity and world-

By 1836 it was all but certain that the Presbyterian Church would divide. Old School Presbyterians complained that the General Assembly was hostile to the doctrines of the Westminster Confession and tolerated the errors of Nathaniel Taylor and Charles Finney. In addition, the Old School branch accused the New School branch of abolitionism. In 1837, despite great efforts to promote unity by Hodge and the Princeton faculty, the Presbyterian church split into two denominations.[22] When the break came, however, the men of Princeton cast in their lot with the Old School Presbyterian Church.

In the Valley of Affliction

In the fall of 1849, Sarah Hodge fell ill, and on Christmas morning, at age fifty-one, "she softly and sweetly fell asleep in Jesus." Great sorrow clouded Hodge for many months. On what would have been his and Sarah's twenty-eighth

---

liness," which professing Christians have no business indulging in. Why did Hodge not apply the same logic to slavery—that even if it were not evil in itself, there may be a "kind" of slavery "associated" with manstealing and brutality, such that no professing Christian can indulge in it "without injuring his influence and the cause of religion"? Hodge, *Life of Charles Hodge*, 397. Hodge seemed to be stricter in prohibiting Christians from card playing than from slaveholding. This is an unfortunate way in which Hodge reflected the thinking of his times. Hodge was "a product of his age, caught in the web of this all-consuming social dilemma, and like so many nineteenth-century Christians he could not differentiate plainly between race-based black American slavery and color-blind biblical slavery." Fortson, *Charles Hodge*, chap. 4.

22. In 1839–1840 Hodge published his *Constitutional History of the Presbyterian Church in the United States* to help the public understand the present controversies in the Presbyterian church and to "increase the respect and affection of Presbyterians for the church of their fathers." Hodge, *Life of Charles Hodge*, 317.

wedding anniversary, he wrote to his brother, "No human being can tell, prior to experience, what it is to lose out of a family its head and heart, the source at once of its light and love."[23] Shortly after Sarah death, Charles's nephew, Hugh's seventeen-year-old son, also died. Out of Hodge's own experience with sorrow, he was able to empathize with and help Hugh through his sorrow.

During this dark season, his two senior colleagues at Princeton—Samuel Miller and Archibald Alexander—also died. Samuel Miller had been one of Hodge's early professors and was an esteemed colleague for three decades, a man of thorough Christian character and greatly admired by all. Dr. Alexander had been the closest person Hodge had to a father for decades. Hodge had been Alexander's assistant, practically a member of his family, a colleague, and then his successor. When Hodge visited Alexander on his deathbed, Dr. Alexander extended his hand to his former pupil and longtime friend and called him his son. He presented to Hodge a white bone walking stick that he said served as a kind of symbol of orthodoxy, to be passed down to Hodge's successors at the seminary. He said, "Now, my dear son, farewell." When Hodge returned to his office from this encounter, he was in an agony of weeping, exclaiming, "It is all past; the glory of our seminary has departed." At Alexander's funeral, Hodge took his seat among Alexander's sons. The loss of these two men plunged Hodge and the seminary into a season of sadness. Hodge was now the

senior faculty member at Princeton Seminary, responsible for carrying forward its work and witness.

A glimmer of light broke into this dark period in 1852 when Hodge married Mary Hunter Stockton, a widow who had been a friend of Sarah's and was well known by the children. She fit in perfectly with the family, being of tremendous service to Hodge in the nurture of his younger children.[24]

Due to Hodge's health problems and the emotional turmoil resulting from these losses, the period from 1848 to 1855 was a less productive time in his career. Yet history reveals to us that these dark providences of God were preparing Hodge in an unseen way for even more productive days. By faith, we know that God uses His dark providences to purify, protect, and prepare our souls for His kingdom and for the work ahead. And Hodge's work was not finished.

The American Civil War

The election of Abraham Lincoln to the presidency in 1860 put the nation into crisis. Since 1850, Southerners had promoted the idea of secession from the Union as the solution to the slavery question. Since they mistakenly regarded Lincoln as a radical on the issue of slavery, they seized on the election of Lincoln as a pretext to secede. As the country was dividing, many American denominations broke into northern and southern branches, including the Old School Presbyterians.

During the Civil War, Hodge supported the Union and Lincoln's policies. When slavery was abolished, Hodge wrote, "This is one of the most momentous events in the

---

23. Two years after Sarah's death, he wrote that he "shed tears to her memory" daily and visited her grave twice a week. Adding to this emotional pain was a sharp decline in his own health due to a choking accident. Hodge, *Life of Charles Hodge*, 373.

24. Hodge, *Life of Charles Hodge*, 392.

The Last Hours of Lincoln
ALONZO CHAPPEL

history of the world. That it was the design of God to bring about this event cannot be doubted."[25] When Abraham Lincoln was assassinated, the shock sent Hodge into a period of depression. Princeton students recalled how he sobbed while leading a campus prayer meeting after Lincoln's murder. Hodge wrote a heartfelt eulogy for Lincoln in the *Princeton Review.* As Southern states were being readmitted into the Union during Reconstruction, many American denominations that had split apart during the war years reunited. During the war, Old and New School Presbyterians in the South reunited and continued after the war as the Presbyterian Church in the United States, or Southern Presbyterian Church. By 1870 the two branches of Presbyterians in the North had reconciled, something Hodge opposed. He continued to serve as a member and minister of the reunited church but warned that unless Presbyterians pursued "real inward unity," union on the surface would not last.

Last Days and Legacy

In 1872 the seminary celebrated Hodge's fiftieth year as professor and a career that had reached three thousand students in the classroom. Hundreds of alumni, trustees of the seminary, family, and friends gathered to mark this milestone. After many had spoken words of love for Hodge, he stood up and told those gathered that he, too, was a Princeton alumnus and loved his school. In a spirit of humility, he said, "Princeton Seminary is what it is, and what I trust it will ever continue to be, because Archibald Alexander and Samuel Miller were what they were."[26] Nevertheless, the

Archibald Alexander Hodge

alumni gave honor to whom honor was due and raised a generous financial gift for Hodge, who described this day as the high point of his life.

As an elder professor, Hodge enjoyed visits from alumni, extended family, and grandchildren. "Long gone were the controversies; all that remained were his relationships with people."[27] His son, A. A. Hodge, was appointed to follow his father as Princeton's professor of didactic theology in 1877. In the spring of 1878, the elder Hodge taught his final classes. That summer, his health declined until one day he

---

25. Fortson, *Charles Hodge*, chap. 6.

26. Hodge, *Life of Charles Hodge*, 519.

27. Fortson, *Charles Hodge*, chap. 7.

became too weak to leave his bed. Two days later, on June 19, 1878, at the age of eighty-one, he passed away.

Hodge's legacy can be summed up in these core values: the supremacy of Scripture, the necessity of sound doctrine, the priority of Christian unity, and the importance of true piety. Charles Hodge's life motto was "Thy word is truth" (John 17:17). Scripture was his supreme standard of faith and conduct. From the *Repertory* articles he penned, to the books he wrote, to the classes he taught, his legacy was the conviction that Scripture must have a supreme place in our private lives, in the church, and in the academy.

Hodge displayed a passion for Christian unity that withstood the storms of controversy within his own denomination. He also showed a charitable attitude toward Roman Catholics, seeing them as brothers in trinitarian faith despite the gross errors and corruptions of their tradition. He refused to require former Roman Catholics to be rebaptized when received into membership in a Presbyterian church. "It was said that the next best thing to being his friend was being his adversary, because he diligently tried, though imperfectly, to critique others with fairness."[28]

Moreover, Hodge's personal piety became a model his students tried to emulate. "The professor's public life exhibited the same genuine character that his family personally experienced at home."[29] Many seminaries today still follow the example that resonates from the Princeton tradition—that faculty and students must pursue not only an informed intellect but a God-filled heart leading to personal godliness.

---

28. Fortson, *Charles Hodge*, chap. 8.
29. Fortson, *Charles Hodge*, chap. 8.

Study Questions

1. What were some of the difficult circumstances of Hodge's childhood? What people did God put in Charles's life in light of his background? What does this teach us about God's provision for those who have had such backgrounds?

2. What worried Hodge about his heart as a preacher? How could such a problem ruin the usefulness of any preacher?

3. How did Hodge respond to Dr. Alexander's offer to teach Hebrew at Princeton? What should this teach us about seeking to discern the will of God for our lives?

4. What were some of the darkest moments of Hodge's life? How do you think these trials prepared him for his later work? What can we learn about the purpose of trials in our own lives?

5. Why is it important in the study of theology to have not only an informed intellect but also a character and soul that are submitted to Christ, gentle toward others, and eager for usefulness in the kingdom?

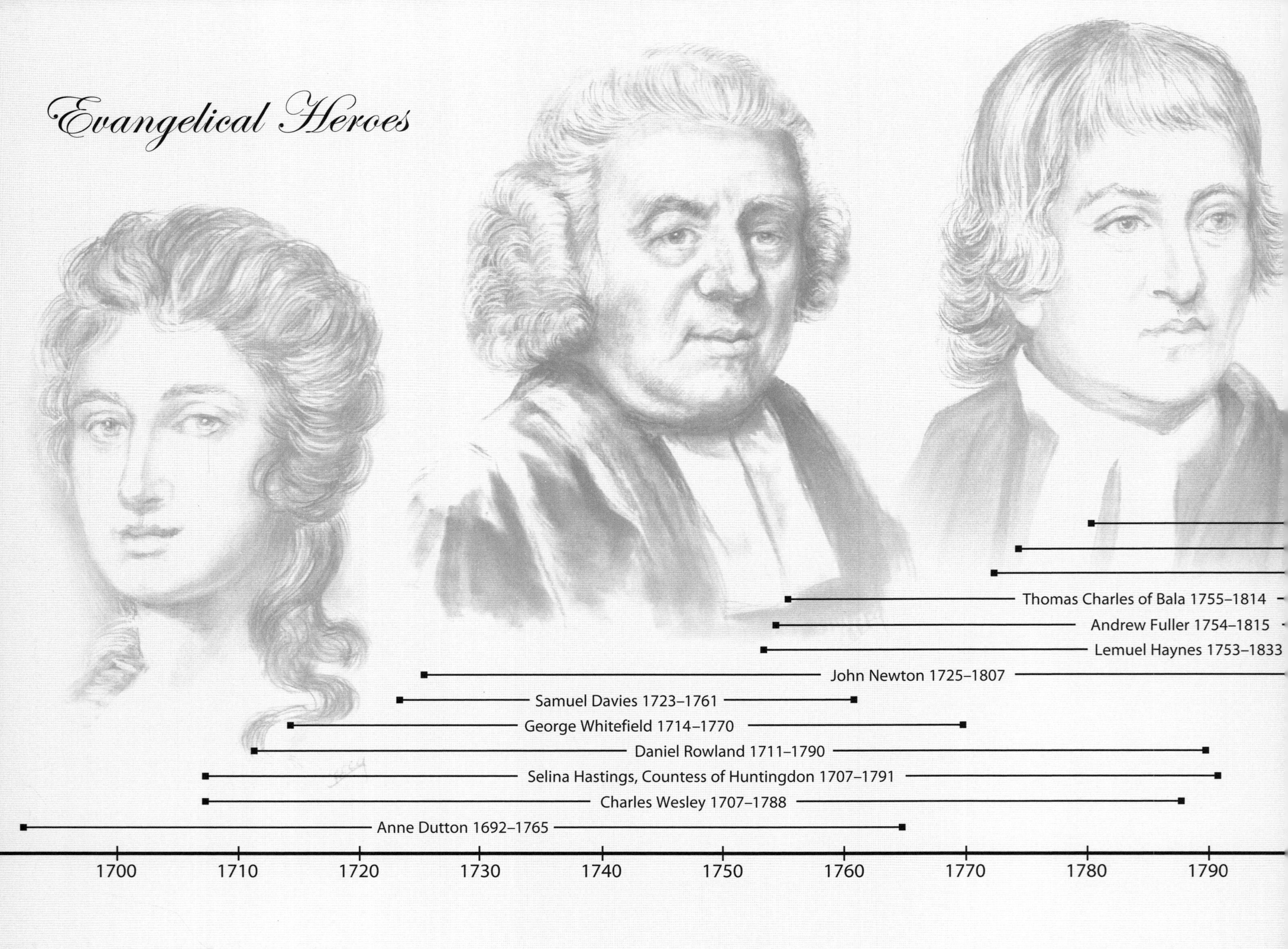

Evangelical Heroes

Thomas Charles of Bala 1755–1814
Andrew Fuller 1754–1815
Lemuel Haynes 1753–1833
John Newton 1725–1807
Samuel Davies 1723–1761
George Whitefield 1714–1770
Daniel Rowland 1711–1790
Selina Hastings, Countess of Huntingdon 1707–1791
Charles Wesley 1707–1788
Anne Dutton 1692–1765

1700   1710   1720   1730   1740   1750   1760   1770   1780   1790